Wizards vs. Muggles

Also Edited by Christopher E. Bell and from McFarland

From Here to Hogwarts: Essays on Harry Potter Fandom and Fiction (2016)

Hermione Granger Saves the World: Essays on the Feminist Heroine of Hogwarts (2012)

American Idolatry: Celebrity, Commodity and Reality Television (2010)

Wizards vs. Muggles

Essays on Identity and the Harry Potter Universe

Edited by Christopher E. Bell

McFarland & Company, Inc., Publishers
Jefferson, North Carolina

LIBRARY OF CONGRESS CATALOGUING-IN-PUBLICATION DATA

Names: Bell, Christopher E., 1974– editor.
Title: Wizards vs. Muggles : essays on identity and the Harry Potter universe / edited by Christopher E. Bell.
Other titles: Wizards versus Muggles
Description: Jefferson, North Carolina : McFarland & Company, Inc., Publishers, 2016. | Includes bibliographical references and index.
Identifiers: LCCN 2015050049 | ISBN 9780786499304 (softcover : acid free paper) ∞
Subjects: LCSH: Rowling, J. K.—Criticism and interpretation. | Rowling, J. K.—Characters. | Children's stories, English—History and criticism. | Identity (Psychology) in literature.
Classification: LCC PR6068.O93 Z958 2016 | DDC 823/.914—dc23
LC record available at http://lccn.loc.gov/2015050049

BRITISH LIBRARY CATALOGUING DATA ARE AVAILABLE

ISBN (print) 978-0-7864-9930-4
ISBN (ebook) 978-1-4766-2329-0

Printed in the United States of America

McFarland & Company, Inc., Publishers
Box 611, Jefferson, North Carolina 28640
www.mcfarlandpub.com

For M & O & H & K & S

Acknowledgments

As I normally do, I am going to use this page to thank people who, probably, are not you. Skip to the Introduction, if you like. I don't mind.

My first thank you will always go to my Megan and my Olivia and my H & K & S. I love you and love you and love you. Three and four and five.

My research assistant, Jayne Simpson, worked incredibly hard, reading and annotating, to help me prepare this manuscript. It has been very worth it to continue to forgive (most of) her sass.

Thank you friends and family, near and far, for your love and support.

Thanks to the Southwest Popular/American Culture Association, for believing in our community of scholars and providing us time and space to gather. We continue to flourish in the soil you've provided.

Finally, as always, thank you to J.K. Rowling, for giving us a platform to discuss the human condition.

Table of Contents

Naming Conventions

For ease of reading and the sake of consistency, in this volume, the titles of the books/films will be abbreviated as follows:

Harry Potter and the Sorcerer's/Philosopher's Stone	*SS* or *PS*
Harry Potter and the Chamber of Secrets	*CoS*
Harry Potter and the Prisoner of Azkaban	*PoA*
Harry Potter and the Goblet of Fire	*GoF*
Harry Potter and the Order of the Phoenix	*OotP*
Harry Potter and the Half-Blood Prince	*HBP*
Harry Potter and the Deathly Hallows	*DH* or *DH1/DH2*

Introduction

CHRISTOPHER E. BELL

The book you are currently reading is a reflection of the continuing relevance and growth of *Potter* Studies as a legitimate field of inquiry within the field of popular culture. This is the fourth volume of *Potter* scholarship I have had the honor of editing since 2012, fueled, in large part, by my tenure as chair of the *Harry Potter* Studies division of the Southwest Popular/American Culture Association. Every year since 2012, scholars have gathered to discuss the *Potter* works in a level of detail that would boggle the mind of the casual reader/fan. Yet, despite the eclectic, interdisciplinary, and often esoteric nature of our colloquium, membership in the division continues to expand. More and more people attend our sessions every year, and are coming from a wider variety of places. In the past few years, we have had scholars travel from Canada, India, Great Britain, Mexico and Brazil to present research and engage in our discussions, which has brought a new, lively, international perspective to the proceedings.

This internationality is reflected in the authors for this collected volume of essays, as scholars from as disparate countries as Spain, Israel, and Serbia join our U.S. authors in presenting their work in these pages. Their essays reveal the true gift that *Harry Potter* has given the study of popular culture: a remarkable platform for discussing the nuances of human identity across cultures and around the world.

People have been studying identity issues using popular culture for a long, long time. Matters related to sexuality (Burgess, 2000; Evans & Dyson, 2015; McLelland, 2000; Williams & Harper, 2014), race (Adams-Bass, Stevenson & Kotzin, 2014; Ng, 2015; Sealey-Ruiz & Greene, 2014), gender (Gannon, Byers & Gonick, 2014; Happel-Parkins & Esposito, 2015; Hinton, 2014; Miltner, 2014) and class (Bettie, 2014; España-Maram, 2013; Graham, 2012) have all been interrogated and made easier to conceptualize and understand through the use of popular culture artifacts. Particularly for those of us who teach about identity development and/or identity representation in media, "using popular culture to demonstrate the ways in which societies are taught the constituent ideologies that construct those world views can oftentimes soften the blow and open students up to a new way of thinking about the issues without so much 'skin in the game'" (Bell, 2015, p. 269).

Even then, identity discussions can get incredibly heated, although discussing not one's personal identity, but that of fictional characters. One almost always sees the incredibly thin border between the conception of a character in a fictional story and that of the reader, who imbues the character with some small measure of him/herself. For example, for the past three years or so, I have found myself carrying around the mantle of the Great Defender of Emma Watson. Within our *Potter* Studies enclave, there is a small but vocal contingent who believe in the "Emma Watson is too pretty to play Hermione" argument. I spent a good deal of time in the introduction to *Hermione Granger Saves the World: Essays on the Feminist Heroine of Hogwarts* (McFarland, 2012) explaining why that categorization is a projection of the reader without actual foundation in the text. Rowling mentions Hermione's appearance in the text only a handful of times, and always in terms that are vague rather than specific. The argument for "Hermione as plain or even ugly" draws from three places: first, Rowling uses the term "bushy" to categorize Hermione's hair and describes Hermione's front teeth as "large." Second, in *GoF*, there is a three-line passage in which Pansy Parkinson (a Slytherin) remarks, "*Stunningly pretty? Her?*... What was she judging against—a chipmunk?" (*GoF*, p. 316), and Rita Skeeter refers to her as "a plain but ambitious girl" (*GoF*, p. 512). Third, and, for me, most importantly, is our cultural predilection for immediately equating intelligence with unattractiveness, particularly when it comes to women.

Each of these arguments can be dismissed fairly easily: Nearly every child's front teeth are "large"—much too large for their faces—because by age 11, those front teeth are almost certainly adult teeth residing in a child-sized mouth. That Rowling makes it a point to draw attention to it, as a character description, is of negligible import; by *GoF* (when Hermione is 14 years old), Hermione has magically "normalized" the size and shape of her teeth (*GoF*, p. 405), making them no longer an issue.

The term "bushy" can mean a lot of things when describing hair; everything from a perm to an afro can be termed "bushy" without being viewed as a negative term denoting "unattractiveness." In fact, the latter example is fuel for a different engine that has roared to life recently in *Potter* Studies—the description of Hermione Granger, strictly speaking, without taking the films into account, can clearly be read as a description of Hermione not as a white girl, but as a black girl. When I read Rowling's description of Hermione strictly and literally—"She had a bossy sort of voice, lots of bushy brown hair, and rather large front teeth" (*SS*, p. 105)—it takes me no work at all to use that description to picture Quvenzhané Wallis in the 2014 revival of *Annie* (Gluck, 2014). Interestingly, Wallis' Annie has lots of bushy brown hair, a bossy sort of voice, and rather large front teeth—yet she is far from an unattractive or plain child. She is 12 years old, as of this writing (just one year older than Watson when she began playing Hermione); give her another 13 years, and she may well match Emma Watson's supermodel-level beauty.

Also, the two sources of outside appraisal of Hermione's looks are dubious at best. Rita Skeeter is an unethical gossip columnist with a vested interest in distorting the truth—during the whole of *GoF*, the reader is given clues at every turn that Skeeter's words are never to be trusted. Any girl connected to Harry Potter would have received Skeeter's thinly-veiled insults. On the other side, given that Pansy Parkinson is a Slytherin that regularly pals around with known bullies and generally terrible people like Draco Malfoy, Vincent Crabbe and Gregory Goyle, I am not sure anything she says can be taken at face value. Her statement is clearly meant as an insult, and while children sometimes are insightful in their choice of slurs, a dig at the physical attractiveness of a teenage girl (regardless of how she actually looks) is sure to score a hit the vast majority of the time. I hesitate to put too much stock in her assessment of Hermione's looks, given that, in that same story, Hermione is the one girl in the whole of Hogwarts that attracts the attention of Viktor Krum. Sure, Hermione has tons more to offer than just her looks, but it is telling that Krum, who has no way of knowing a single thing about Hermione, singles her out amongst all of the other girls at Hogwarts.

In truth, Emma Watson's Hermione is the victim of "skill capping"; that is, she has had an arbitrary limit of the number of positive traits she may possess placed upon her by some readers. It is almost as though Hermione couldn't possibly be smart *and* funny *and* thoughtful *and* hard-working *and* well-liked *and* beautiful, primarily because in Western popular culture, being beautiful normally requires a woman to trade one or all of their other positive attributes—particularly intelligence (Magoulick, 2006; Stern, 2004; O'Reilly, 2005). We are enculturated to believe a woman cannot "have it all," and are taught to resent and dismiss her if she does. What *right* does Hermione have to be all of the wonderful things she is and still look like Emma Watson? And, thus, I find myself defending Emma and her version of Hermione Granger, on the basis that a woman really can exist without the artificial constraints imposed upon her by the socialization of her readers. It *is* possible for a woman to be intelligent, kind, funny, *and* beautiful, all at the same time. I should know. I married one, and I'm raising another.

This is just a single instance of the way in which the *Potter* texts can help us unpack issues of social identity. Within this tiny discussion—fewer than 900 words—representations of both race and gender were raised, the history of the relationship between beauty and power was invoked, and an argument was laid out and counter-argued, using two disparate popular culture texts. Imagine the richness of thought, argumentation and deconstruction that can be found in the other 99,000 words of this collection.

Wizards vs. Muggles is, appropriately, broken into two parts. The first, "Transfiguration: Wizard Identity," is focused on constructions of identity within the *Potter* texts themselves. Raymond I. Shuck leads off the discussion with a consideration of Harry as a representative of white privilege. This leads into Lauren R. Camacci's contemplation on the nature of masculinity in the series. Brendan G.A. Hughes uses the series to make parallels between Remus Lupin's lycanthropy and the real-world HIV epidemic. My own essay is a musing on the Horcrux, and the symbolism of which person leads to each Horcrux's destruction. Hillary A. Jones uses classical rhetorical theories, chiefly Burkean identification and Bourdieu's conception of *habitus*, to explore the wizarding world. Finally, closing out this part, Shira Wolosky skillfully recategorizes Harry's story as a gendered heroic narrative, placing some of the locus of power where it rightfully belongs—in *Potter*'s female characters. Transfiguration is the class in *Potter* where students learn to turn one thing into another; in this first part, the authors turn wizarding society into an examination of our own world.

The second part is, fittingly, titled "Muggle Studies: Muggle Identity." In this part, like the *Potter* course that serves as its namesake, the authors focus on real-world readers. The authors push consumption and uses of the *Potter* texts into areas rarely, if ever, dealt with before. Jelena Borojević kicks things off with a fascinating look at the creative work of fans and the online communities that spring up around fan-based *Potter* art, such as fanfiction. Kristen L. Cole uses the *Potter* series to unravel the tangled web of bullying and aggression present in our own real-world schools. In what has to be one of the more enthralling applications of *Potter* I have read, Levi Cooper demonstrates how he uses various instances from the series—Voldemort's murder of Lily and James, Bertie Botts Every Flavor Beans—to teach law students how to argue cases. A trio of scholars from Spain, Pilar Lacasa, Sara Cortés and Rut Martínez-Borda, explicate their project of measuring the connection between players of the *OotP* video game by Electronic Arts and the characters they are actively portraying in the game. Finally, rounding out the volume, Ryan S. Rigda takes on real-world collegiate players of Quidditch and the blogs they create.

In all, once again, the scholars of *Harry Potter* Studies have pulled together to present a captivating collection of interdisciplinary scholarship, from law to medicine, women's and ethnic studies to rhetoric. Do not feel obligated to read these essays in order; skip around within the parts, or float back and forth between our world and Harry's. As always, scratch notes in the margins, underline with highlighters and sticky notes—use our work to inspire your own. If something is burning a hole in your brain, jot it down and send it to me at dr.christopher.bell@gmail.com. I won't be able to respond to everything, but I will try to pass your queries on to the authors or use them as the foundation for discussion at our next conference. Speaking of which, you should consider joining us yourself—whether you are an undergraduate student, graduate student, junior faculty, senior faculty, or independent scholar, you are welcome. Details can be found at http://southwestpca.org.

Thank you for connecting with us once again, or for entering our conversational space for the first time. In either case, we are happy to have you here, *Potter* scholar. Now, "let us step out into the night and pursue that flighty temptress, adventure" (*HBP*, p. 56).

References

Adams-Bass, V. N., Stevenson, H. C., & Kotzin, D. S. (2014). Measuring the meaning of Black media stereotypes and their relationship to the racial identity, Black history knowledge, and racial socialization of African American youth. *Journal of Black Studies*, *45*(5), 367–395.

Bell, C. (2015). Princess pedagogy: Race, gender, and the Disney construct. In Jennifer L. Martin (Ed.), *Racial battle fatigue: Insights from the front lines of social justice advocacy*. Santa Barbara: ABC-CLIO. 269–283.

Bettie, J. (2014). *Women without class: Girls, race, and identity*. Berkeley: University of California Press.

Burgess, C. (2000). Internal and external stress factors associated with the identity development of transgendered youth. *Journal of Gay & Lesbian Social Services*, *10*(3–4), 35–47.

España-Maram, L. (2013). *Creating masculinity in Los Angeles's Little Manila: Working-class Filipinos and popular culture in the United States*. New York: Columbia University Press.

Evans, E., & Dyson, D. (2015). From princess to queen: A Black feminist approach to positive sexual identity development. *Journal of Black Sexuality and Relationships*, *1*(3), 25–56.

Gannon, S., Byers, M., & Gonick, M. (2014). Girls, sexuality, and popular culture. *Becoming girl: Collective biography and the production of girlhood*. Toronto: Women's Press.

Gluck, W. (2014). *Annie*.[Motion picture]. Sony Pictures Entertainment.

Graham, H. (2012). Smoking, stigma and social class. *Journal of Social Policy*, *41*(01), 83–99.

Happel-Parkins, A., & Esposito, J. (2015). Using popular culture texts in the classroom to interrogate issues of gender transgression related bullying. *Educational Studies*, *51*(1), 3–16.

Hinton, P. (2014). Representation or misrepresentation? British media and Japanese popular culture. *NECSUS: European Journal of Media Studies*, *3*(1), 89–108.

Magoulick, M. (2006). Frustrating female heroism: Mixed messages in Xena, Nikita, and Buffy. *The Journal of Popular Culture*, *39*(5), 729–755.

McLelland, M. J. (2000). Male homosexuality and popular culture in modern Japan. *Intersections* (3), 1–15.

Miltner, K. M. (2014). "There's no place for lulz on LOLCats": The role of genre, gender, and group identity in the interpretation and enjoyment of an Internet meme. *First Monday*, *19*(8).
Ng, K. (2015). What race does online: "Gangnam Style" and Asian/American identity in the digital age. *Verge: Studies in Global Asias*, *1*(1), 109–113.
O'Reilly, J. D. (2005). The Wonder Woman precedent: Female (super) heroism on trial. *The Journal of American Culture*, *28*(3), 273–283.
Rowling, J. K. (2000). *Harry Potter and the goblet of fire*. New York: Scholastic.
Rowling, J. K. (2005). *Harry Potter and the half-blood prince*. New York: Scholastic.
Sealey-Ruiz, Y., & Greene, P. (2015). Popular visual images and the (mis) reading of Black male youth: S case for racial literacy in urban preservice teacher education. *Teaching Education*, *26*(1), 55–76.
Stern, S. (2004). All I really needed to know (about beauty) I learned in kindergarten: A cultivation analysis. In Rebecca Ann Lind (Ed.), *Race/Gender/Media: Considering Diversity Across Audiences, Content and Producers*. Boston: Pearson Education Press, 22–28.
Williams, C. D., & Harper, S. (2014). Toward complex and inclusive studies of sex scripts, college students' sexual behaviors, and hookup cultures on US campuses. *Masculinities & Social Change*, *3*(3), 271–298.

Transfiguration: Wizard Identity

"The anti-racist-white-hero premise": Whiteness and the *Harry Potter* Series

RAYMOND I. SCHUCK

> "I have a dream that my four little children will one day live in a nation where they will not be judged by the color of their skin but by the content of their character"
>
> —Rev. Martin Luther King, Jr. (King, 1963)

> "It is our choices, Harry, that show what we truly are, far more than our abilities"
>
> —Albus Dumbledore to Harry Potter (*CoS*, p. 333)

The Harry Potter novels have been one of the most successful book series in history. As United States Harry Potter publisher Scholastic reports, each of the seven books has topped both the *New York Times* and *USA Today* bestseller lists, the books have altogether amassed more than $450 million in sales, and the series has been published in 74 languages ("Online press kits," n.d.). Additionally, the final book of the series set a record by selling 8.3 million copies within the first 24 hours after its release—a record previously held by the sixth book, which sold 6.9 million in the same time frame (Rich, 2007).

The books center around the adventures of an English boy, Harry Potter, who begins to attend Hogwarts School of Witchcraft and Wizardry upon discovering at the age of 11 that he is a wizard. Each new book depicts a new year of school, while all of the books revolve around an ongoing and increasingly urgent clash between "bad" wizards, led by former Hogwarts student Voldemort, and "good" wizards, in large part led by Albus Dumbledore, the headmaster of Hogwarts. The books portend and then culminate with a clash between Voldemort and Potter as the climax of the series. In the process, the books set up two sides in a feud that centers on who should receive access to the world of wizardry. On the side of Voldemort are "pure" wizards who can trace their genealogies through families of wizards. In their alignment with Voldemort, these wizards declare the intention that the world of wizards should be open only to those of "pure" status. The other side calls for greater inclusion that includes acceptance of individuals who have been born to non-wizard parents. This group includes "pure" wizards who are sympathetic to such inclusion as well as wizards who have been born with one or more parents who are Muggles, which is the name given to humans who do not have the powers of wizardry.

The stories have garnered much praise. Each of the books was named an American Language Association (ALA) Notable Book or Best Book, and the books have won multiple additional awards ranging from the National Book Award in the United Kingdom ("*SS*," "*Cos*," and "*OotP*") to the Whitbread Award for Children's Literature ("*PoA*") to the Hugo Award for Best Novel ("*GoF*"), among many others. Additionally, critics and readers alike have applauded the books for the lessons they teach. For example, *Washington Post* culture writer Alyssa Rosenberg (2011), writing for *The Atlantic*, argues that "if Harry Potter endures down the years, it will be because J.K. Rowling found sly ways to use fantasy to create a timeless statement about human rights and dignity" (para. 1). Rosenberg suggests that the world Rowling created aligns with leftist politics, though she also suggests that it does so in subtle ways that do not alienate conservative readers. Additionally, Emily Griesinger (2002), writing for a Christian audience, argues that "despite potential problems associated with magic, witchcraft, and the occult, Harry Potter can be interpreted as a creative narrative fantasy grounded in Christian ethics and a Christian theology of hope" (pp. 477–478). Like Rosenberg, Griesinger finds appeal in the lessons the Potter series teaches, particularly as Griesinger (2002) suggests that that the Harry Potter books speak to right and wrong through a sense of deep magic, which she describes as C. S. Lewis's concept of "the moral law, the law of fair play, human decency, some deep-seated conviction of right and wrong" (p. 476).

Given the books' popularity and the praise they have received for the lessons they provide, the Harry Potter series merits critical examination of the ramifications of its lessons that examines not only what these lessons explicitly provide, but also what they implicitly produce and reproduce. Such an examination involves what Henry Giroux (1994), writing about popular culture, defines as an approach that "illuminates the relationship among knowledge, authority, and power[,] … draws attention to questions concerning who has control over the conditions for the production of knowledge …

[and] delineates the ways in which knowledge, identities, and authority are constructed within particular sets of social relations" (p. 30). From such an approach, the stories can be critically examined for their treatment of issues of race, including examination of how the series reproduces white power and white privilege. In this work, I examine how whiteness is embedded in the Harry Potter stories in the very basis for the stories. I argue that the representations of race relations in the fictional struggle between "pure" and "Muggle-born" wizards within the Harry Potter stories offer a version of what Kelly J. Madison (1999) has called "the anti-racist-white-hero premise." Demonstrating how these stories build upon a fictional representation that reenacts this premise can show how the lessons taught by the Harry Potter series, while potentially progressive, also present a version of inclusion that reinforces white privilege and white power.

Harry Potter and the Study of Whiteness

Over the past couple of decades, studies of constructions of race have turned to what Dyer (1997) calls "the matter of whiteness" (p. 1). According to Dyer (1997), the examination of racial imagery has aided understanding of "the organization of the modern world," but "as long as race is something only applied to non-white peoples, as long as white people are not racially seen and named, they/we function as a human norm" (p. 1). Dyer suggests that white identity, at least in the United States, has been defined in terms of images of Christianity, race, and imperialism. Furthermore, Dyer suggests the importance of examining popular culture to see how whiteness has been constructed without being named.

Similarly, Nakayama and Krizek (1995) suggest that among possible spaces of analysis, "'white' is a relatively uncharted territory that has remained invisible as it continues to influence the identity of those both within and without its domain" (p. 291). Nakayama and Krizek suggest that "whiteness" constitutes a strategic rhetoric exhibited in popular and everyday texts and practices. In making such an argument, Nayakama and Krizek (1995) rely on Michel de Certeau's concept of strategy, which they describe as actions taken by "'a subject with will and power'" (p. 295) to manipulate power relationships. Strategy stands in opposition to tactics, in which subjects take actions for which they must "play on and with a terrain imposed on [them] and organized by the law of a foreign power" (Nakayama & Krizek, 1995, p. 295). The difference between these two concepts rests on understanding strategies as things that can groups in power employ, while tactics involve the practices of people who must work within a situation in which others maintain power over them. Whiteness involves strategy in this conceptualization because white identity carries with it empowerment, while non-white identities require individuals to act within a world in which others have more power. Nakayama and Krizek (1995) suggest that "what is required are more sophisticated maps of the discursive field of whiteness" (p. 305), and they consider their essay an invitation to contribute to such a map.

In the wake of this invitation, the project of mapping whiteness has proceeded. Crenshaw (1997), for instance, suggests that rhetorical scholars engage in "ideological rhetorical criticism designed to reveal white privilege" (p. 258), thus seeing the rhetoric of whiteness as ideological in its construction, produced and reproduced in practice. Taking up Crenshaw's call, Jackson (1999) examines white privilege by "having Whites analyze what White culture means to them, though written through the 'lenses' of an African American researcher" (p. 39). In the study, Jackson recognizes a diversity of ways in which whites self-define being white and, from this diversity, he concludes that "if we view whiteness as a collection of self-definitions that potentially balance and imbalance relationships with others, then we enable ourselves to move toward progress" (p. 52). In other words, in order to map the territory of whiteness effectively, rhetorical scholarship on whiteness must recognize the diversity of ways in which whites themselves come to define being white.

Moon and Flores (2000) concur, suggesting that "whiteness projects ... need to avoid the tendency to fall into monolithic and/or essentialist discourses" (p. 111). This essentialism can occur in the definition of whiteness; it can occur in the definition of other racial categories such as blackness; or it can occur in the definition of other parts of identity—such as when studies of race essentialize gender. Regardless of its form, the essentialism of which Moon and Flores write provides the basis for an uncritical view of whiteness that reproduces white privilege and runs counter to the critical impetus for studying it. Among studies that have sought to show how essentializing whiteness reproduces white privilege, Brooks and Rada (2002) examine media coverage of support for President Clinton during the 1998 Monica Lewinsky scandal to show that media depictions positioned the diversity of reasons African Americans gave for supporting the president against an uncritically generalized representation of white opinion as not supporting the president. This generalized representation of white opinion was normalized by the lack of diversity and critique it depicted.

Meanwhile, Willis-Rivera's and Meeker's (2002) examination of multicultural children's books shows the reproduction of white privilege through the essentializing of non-white groups in discourse. According to Willis-Rivera and Meeker (2002),

> these books, as well as the research about multicultural children's literature in general, casts a white gaze which is nearly impossible to see beyond. Through the white gaze, a reader experiences the pleasures of multiculturalism, as it is

> covertly defined in these texts, without the threat of white guilt *or* the threat of losing white privilege. If a reader of color attempts to engage these texts, s/he is frequently positioned as both the other—other than the assumed reader—and as the object of culture rather than the gatherer of (other) cultures. Both these are different than how white people are portrayed. S/he is also often acted upon by the white actor rather than able to control his or her own actions [p. 277].

In other words, not only does this multicultural discourse essentialize non-white groups; it also subjects them to white power in the very ways that narratives of children's literature depict multiculturalism.

Harry Potter and the Politics of Inclusion

While the Potter books have received praise for the inclusionary messages that they offer, the politics of these inclusions warrant interrogation—a process that academic researchers and critics examining the series have begun. Weiss (2013), for instance, points out the strong female figures who serve in maternal roles within the Harry Potter series. Additionally, Doughty (2002) suggests that the Harry Potter series offers a balance on the "boys' book market" by offering a less violent and more compassionate version of masculinity than other options, though Doughty also recognizes that "we *would* read the Potter books differently if they were about Harriet Potter" (p. 257). Meanwhile, Schoefer (2000) suggests that the Harry Potter series maintains heavy gender stereotypes with girl characters who, "when they are not downright silly or unlikable, are helpers, enablers, and instruments" (para. 2). Lavoie (2003) also critiques gender positioning in the Harry Potter series by noting how, among the four houses that make up Hogwarts School of Witchcraft and Wizardry, men established the two more significant houses for the stories while women established the two less significant houses. Meanwhile, Dresang (2002) suggests that women occupy a marginalized position of "otherness" in the Harry Potter books but also claims that this position "is enabling rather than entrapping because it allows for change and difference" (p. 241). Gallardo-C. and Smith (2003) agree that Schoefer "has a point" (p. 191), but argue that the series feminizes its main character, Harry, in ways that "challenge standard constructions of gender and gender roles" (p. 191) and "allow female readers to identify strongly with a male protagonist" (p. 191). Smith (2010) also recognizes some of the conflicting aspects of gender representation in the Harry Potter series but claims that "Rowling's world resonates with the values of radical feminism" (p. 80). Still, no matter how much female readers might be able to identify with him, the protagonist, Harry, remains male.

At the same time, as Park (2003) contends, the Harry Potter series inevitably offers a middle-class worldview that caricatures—and, thus, to at least a degree, excludes the full participation of—working class characters such as Hagrid the groundskeeper and the enslaved house-elves. Along related lines, Harmon (2013) argues that the Forbidden Forest serves as "a space possessing multiple identities—identities that inevitably lead to the marginalization and Othering of the centaur community" (pp. 33–34). Meanwhile, Bell (2013) examines how the forms of marginalization that Tom Riddle faced as a boy led to him becoming Voldemort, arguing that

> Voldemort is wholly a creation of environmental circumstance; he is the logical conclusion of the Wizarding world itself. The systematic Othering of Tom Riddle, wherein he is continually pushed to a weaponized society's margins from the moment of his birth, provides a fertile environment for the cultivation of moral disengagement [p. 44].

Additionally, Clifton (2013) specifically examines the social stratification of the wizarding world as social class aligns with wizarding ability to show how "bloodlines are a clear distinction of power and are stressed throughout the series" (p. 69). Similarly, Westman (2002) argues that in the Harry Potter series "the tensions among 'Mudbloods,' pure bloods, and Muggles, among werewolves, house-elves, giants, and wizards echo the fervent tensions between race and class in the 'real' contemporary British body politic … of British readers' own experiences" (p. 307). Westman suggests that the books reflect a heritage of Margaret Thatcher's policies as British prime minister in the 1980s. According to Westman, "Thatcher's rejection of multiculturalism, her isolationist nationalism, her dislike of [labor] unions, and her endorsement of strong-arm police tactics would warm Voldemort's heart" (p. 307). Westman notes that the books do involve a multicultural and more class-inclusive agenda than Thatcherism but argues that this agenda "harbors social inequities and injustices that masquerade behind the draperies of democracy, much as they do in the time of John Major and Tony Blair" (p. 307). Westman's analysis of the social vision embodied in Harry Potter suggests a more hegemonic kind of exclusiveness—one that allows for inclusion of subordinate or marginalized groups on a limited basis and casts this inclusion as a true democracy while hiding exclusions that exist. A potentially progressive and inclusive story reinforces the privilege of the included group by only offering inclusion of the minority class or race on a limited basis.

In a similar vein, other work has examined how the Harry Potter series involves racial or ethnic exclusion. Carey (2003), for instance, suggests that the books offer a story revolving around the inclusion of Muggles while simultaneously offering a depiction of slavery that exists among those who fight against the exclusion of Muggles as wizards enslave house-elves. Carey (2003) suggests that because of the framing of the house-elves slavery, "young people are implicitly invited to follow Hermione's lead [in trying to free the house-elves], unpopular though it might initially seem to be, and take political action against prejudice" (p. 114). Anatol (2003) suggests that the books express a form of multiculturalism that condemns bigotry against wizards by Muggles, against Muggles by wizards, and against house-elves and other non-magical groups by magical groups. This multiculturalism also promotes inclusion to the degree that Hogwarts admits students of color and the books depict interracial couples. Yet, according to Anatol (2003), "the novels portray not integration and acceptance, but the complete assimilation of ... [non-white students] into the all-white landscape of Hogwarts students and teachers" (p. 174). Similarly, Ostrey (2003) suggests that the message of ethnic and racial inclusion promoted by the books "seems somewhat contradictory" (p. 93). According to Ostrey, even those characters who defend Muggle-born wizards tend to look down on Muggles, at best seeing them as charming yet beneath wizards, as in the case of Mr. Weasley, Harry's best friend Ron's father. Ostrey (2003) also notes that "minorities are mentioned, but they are not heroes; all the major players are Anglo-Saxon" (p. 93). In other words, non-white characters are important to the story because their inclusion remains a significant part of the story, but their inclusion remains limited to a supporting role for the white characters who help them and who reproduce white privilege by doing so.

In this essay, I build from these arguments about representation of race to demonstrate how the struggle for Muggle inclusion that forms the basis for the feud among wizards that drives the stories also takes place within a backdrop of limited exclusion and inclusion. Ultimately, the fight for Muggle-born wizards' rights takes place through a character of privilege—Harry Potter—identified with "pure" wizard lineage. In this regard, the stories represent a limited inclusion at the very basis of the stories, with "pure" wizards as the included group and characters who are not "pure" wizards as the marginalized groups. Using the anti-racist-white-hero premise as a lens demonstrates how the structure of the stories reproduces white power.

Harry Potter and the Reproduction of White Privilege

Kelly J. Madison (1999) suggests that many texts that recount histories of racism utilize the "the anti-racist-white-hero premise." According to Madison (1999),

> the mass dissemination of historical "anti-racist" narratives that marginalize African and African American agency, thereby highlighting "white" heroism, mark whiteness in crisis, resolve the crisis through a paternalistic white supremacist co-optation of anti-racist struggle, and provide a re-legitimating historical fiction supportive of the white backlash against equality [p. 400].

Madison applies this premise to films that depict historical events, suggesting how films such as *Amistad*, *Cry Freedom*, and *Mississippi Burning* depict racial discrimination and persecution yet do so from the perspective of a white protagonist. In the process, these films reproduce white privilege and white power.

Madison (1999) suggests a general narrative structure that anti-racist-white-hero films utilize. This structure includes the following:

> 1) white hero experiences some extreme form of racism vicariously through some black contact, 2) white hero develops a relatively radical anti-racist consciousness, 3) white hero sacrifices a great deal at the hands of white racists to further the cause of black people's struggle (usually in some type of leadership capacity) and 4) white hero suffers terrible for his or her efforts but manages to somehow prevail in the end [Madison, 1999, p. 405].

Madison notes that this is a generalized pattern, so it may hold true to more or less of a degree in a specific film. Madison's concept articulates three features that work together to reproduce white power whether or not a film completely follows this pattern. These features include: (1) a racially stratified society in which the hero of the narrative opposes clearly visible forms of racism, (2) a main character who comes from the privileged group and whose perspective is privileged within the narrative as he or she takes up the cause of the underprivileged group, and (3) an ending to the narrative in which, in at least some form, the hero triumphs against those who perpetuate the blatant forms of racism. The Harry Potter stories exhibit all three of these features.

Harry Potter and the Hierarchy of Race

The Harry Potter series occurs within a society that has been stratified by birthright, as the stories take place within the backdrop of the feud between "pure" wizards who wish to close the wizard world to all others and, basically, everyone else, though particularly those wizards not identified as "pure." The very language used within the stories conveys social stratification along lines analogous to race. The term "pure" as a descriptor for those wizards who come from non-Muggle families connects to notions of purity associated with and utilized by white supremacist groups who condemn racial integration and miscegenation on the grounds of maintaining the purity of white "blood" (Hasian, 1996). The Harry Potter series even uses the term "blood" itself, most notably as "pure" wizards sometimes use the term "Mudblood" to refer to Muggle-born wizards.

The stratification of society into "pure" and "impure" is further reproduced by the sorting of students into the four houses that make up Hogwarts School of Witchcraft and Wizardry—Gryffindor, Hufflepuff, Ravenclaw, and Slytherin. Slytherin, the house that produced Voldemort as well as all of the other characters who wish to exclude Muggle-born wizards, has no recognizable Muggle-born characters within it. On the other hand, Gryffindor, which is the house of Harry Potter and other "pure" wizards who defend Muggle-born characters, contains the most notable Muggle-born characters. Most prominent is Hermione Granger, one of Harry's two closest friends and one of the most significant characters in the stories. Hermione was born of parents who are Muggles, yet she developed wizarding skills. Additionally, in *SS*, Gryffindor resident Seamus Finnigan also clearly identifies himself as not "pure" wizard by mentioning that his mother is a witch, but his dad is a Muggle. While Hermione represents a wizard born with no known wizarding heritage, Seamus represents the product of miscegenation since one of his parents was a wizard and the other was not.

Issues of wizard heritage coincide with issues of class and other marginalizing characteristics when considering some of the other identities of Slytherin and Gryffindor members alongside the dichotomy of "pure" versus Muggle-born. Ron Weasley, Harry's best friend, resides in Gryffindor, as have all of his brothers who entered the school before him, and as does his younger sister, who enters Hogwarts the year after Ron. The Weasleys are both implicitly and explicitly identified as poorer in socioeconomic status to other wizards. For instance, the clothing Ron wears, the books he uses, his broomstick, and even his pet rat Scabbers are either hand-me-downs from his older brothers or cheaper alternatives to what other wizards purchase. Other characters acknowledge this class status. Some do so through efforts to assist the Weasleys, such as when Harry buys Ron candy with some of the money left him by his parents and when Harry gives Ron's twin brothers—Fred and George—money to start a joke shop. Others acknowledge the Weasleys' class status through efforts to devalue their worth. For instance, in SS when Harry and Ron first encounter Draco Malfoy, who becomes Harry's chief antagonist among students at Hogwarts, Draco notes with a disparaging tone Ron's red hair, freckles, and number of siblings and states that he knows Ron is a Weasley. Here, Draco directly mocks Ron and the Weasley family for their lack of money.

Though it does not appear to be related to socioeconomic class, the marginalization of Gryffindor resident Neville Longbottom also converges with the marginalization of non-"pure" wizards. Neville is marginalized by his identity as an inept figure who consistently forgets things. For instance, readers first witness Neville in the first book upon the condition of having lost his toad on the train that takes the students from London to Hogwarts. Neville is also marginalized by his heritage. He lives with his grandmother because his parents went crazy and, though later books reveal the conditions of his parents' insanity as the work of Voldemort, Neville is chastised and marginalized by some wizards for his parents' conditions.

Furthermore, Harry himself, in what provides a potential means by which to identify Harry as not "pure," is not the product of a heritage of only wizards. Harry's mother and father were both wizards, but while his father comes from a long line of wizards, his mother comes from a family of Muggles. As Grigoryan (2013) suggests, this creates a dual "othering" of Harry, in which he is an "other" to Muggles because of his wizard heritage, while he feels like an "other" among wizards because he grew up around Muggles. One place the reader sees Harry's othering most prominently is Harry's mother's sister, Petunia, who has looked after Harry after his parents' deaths and who, along with Harry's uncle and cousin, is not only not magical, but explicitly anti-magical. Harry's aunt, uncle, and cousin set up an anti-world of sorts to the wizarding world in which humans without magic, who often do not even recognize the term "Muggle," marginalize wizards within non-magical society, though ultimately the wizards maintain a level of control since the books offer countless examples of the ability of wizards to intrude and wreak havoc on non-magical society while Muggle cannot do the same to wizards.

The "impure" heritage of Harry's mother, though, does not disqualify Harry as a "pure" wizard. From the beginning, wizards treat Harry as someone who would be acceptable to those who would exclude all who are not "pure" wizards. The reader witnesses this ability to be accepted early in Harry's experience in the wizarding world when Harry meets Draco Malfoy for the very first time. In this first encounter, Malfoy readily introduces himself and his compatriots, Crabbe and Goyle, to Harry and states, "You'll soon find out some wizarding families are much better than other, Potter. You don't want to go making friends with the wrong sort" (*SS*, p. 108). Draco continues by using the term "riffraff" to refer to the Weasley family and Hagrid, the Hogwarts groundskeeper who is not a wizard but a Giant. Draco suggests that Harry, like his parents, can choose whether or not to align himself with such individuals.

The notion of "choice" becomes particularly significant for Harry Potter—something Bassham (2010) examines in fuller detail as a philosophical concept embedded within the series. In perhaps his first defining choice within the wizarding world, Harry rejects Malfoy in favor of Ron Weasley, Hermione, Neville Longbottom, and others with whom he would later ally. In the very next chapter after he meets Draco, Harry faces another choice, though he does not appear to recognize it fully as a choice at the time. When the first-year students enter the dining hall for the first time, they are asked to put a "Sorting Hat" on their heads one by one. The Sorting Hat tells each student, as well as all others who are present, the house with which the student will be aligned for her or his stay at Hogwarts. When Harry takes his turn, he has already developed a dislike for the house of Slytherin because he has developed unfavorable feelings toward Draco, Crabbe, and Goyle, and the

Sorting Hat has already placed each of them in Slytherin. As the Sorting Hat deliberates when trying to determine the house into which it should sort Harry, it hears Harry requesting not to be Slytherin, and though it offers reasons why Harry would fit well into Slytherin, it concedes to Harry's wishes and names him a Gryffindor. In the second book, when Harry wonders whether or not the Sorting Hat made a mistake and should have put him into Slytherin, Hogwarts Headmaster Albus Dumbledore emphasizes that Harry had a choice in the matter. Here, again, the books show Harry as having the opportunity to side with those who would exclude Muggle-born wizards but choosing to side with those who would include such wizards.

At the very end of the series, in the final chapter of *DH*, Harry reconfirms to his son, Albus, that the Sorting Hat accounts for choice, but in practice the Sorting Hat does not appear to give other students such a choice. In no other case does the Sorting Hat appear to deliberate, with the possible exception of Neville, though two possibilities might explain this deliberation: (1) Neville is so scatter-brained that the hat has a hard time finding its way through his mind to place him and/or (2) as readers learn in the fifth book, Neville and Harry share a number of commonalities that potentially might have made Neville the archenemy of Voldemort instead of Harry. For all other students, though, it is as if one's position in the hierarchy was predetermined. In one particular case, the Sorting Hat does not even hesitate in its choice of house for the student. When Draco Malfoy sits down to be sorted in *SS*, the hat definitively declares him as Slytherin as soon as it reaches his head. The hat also seems to have no trouble with Ron. Ron's sorting is rather uneventful, except for his own sickness that he won't make it into Gryffindor. He ends up there, though, without incident, and as it is for Draco, for Ron the sorting is apparently obvious.

Additionally, Muggle-born wizards do not get full choice; they are instantly ineligible for Slytherin. Also largely ineligible for Slytherin, it appears, are wizards marginalized by any means other than gender, such as the forgetful Neville. In terms of race, few non-white populate Slytherin, though the house is not devoid of non-white members, as Blaise Zabini, who is black, sorts into Slytherin. At the same time, Malfoy's sidekicks, Crabbe and Goyle, do not seem to be able to choose either. Their uneventful experiences with the Sorting Hat suggest that they were destined to be placed in Slytherin, to occupy the top of the hierarchy, and to exclude others. The books only depict Harry with the choice that defines his identity.

Harry's position as the sole choice-maker among the students emphasizes two things that reveal his role as the anti-racist-white hero and the power he has within that role. First, his ability to choose comes as a consequence of his position within the dominant racial class. If he was not identified as a "pure" wizard, he would not have the opportunity to choose to take an inclusive approach to the wizarding world. Second, his ability to choose stands in contrast to the apparent inability to choose on the parts of Malfoy and others who take up the more exclusionary perspective. As Madison (1999) argues, anti-racist-white-hero films define white supremacy "in a particularly distant, extreme, blatant, and therefore, superficial way" (p. 406). When films present racism like this, the depiction suggests that racism takes only blatant and extreme forms and that the perpetrators, who act without deliberation, see no viable alternative to exclusion. Harry does see an alternative to the complete exclusion of those who are not "pure" wizards; however, his position as a member of the empowered group allows him the opportunity to see alternatives.

One other character shown to have made a similar choice is Severus Snape, the head of Slytherin house at Hogwarts. The books reveal that Snape was once a Death Eater, which is the name for Voldemort's special army of wizards who do his bidding. However, Snape, apparently of his own choosing (though one could argue that his love for Harry's mom did not give him a choice), has reformed and now works with Albus Dumbledore. In fact, though Harry consistently questions Snape's loyalties, Snape consistently acts in ways to protect Harry and other characters who oppose Voldemort. For example, in the first book, when Professor Quirrell, who is under the influence of Voldemort, attempts to injure Harry by casting a spell on Harry's broom, Snape attempts to counter Quirrell with a spell to protect Harry. In another example, in the fifth book, Snape attempts to assist Potter in his struggle against Voldemort by teaching him Occlumency, which can help Harry close his mind to Voldemort's ability to see within it and potentially influence it. Finally, as Snape lay dying in the seventh book, he gives Harry some memories that Harry can take to Dumbledore's memory-viewing device called a pensieve to help Harry in his struggle against Voldemort. Again, though, Snape's choice to turn from ally of Voldemort to ally of Dumbledore comes as a result of his membership in the privileged racial group, and it also stands in direct comparison to the blatant actions of others who outwardly express exclusionary perspectives. As Deavel and Deavel (2010) suggest, Snape's choice does offer the chance at redemption—a choice he makes because of his love for Harry's mother, in whose eyes, both figuratively and nearly literally, he wants to be redeemed. More broadly, though, Snape's redemption offers a path of redemption for the blatant racists, and it complicates the dichotomy between those who accept Muggles and those who don't.

Late in the series other wizards also face choices that complicate that dichotomy and offer redemption. For instance, Narcissa Malfoy, the mother of antagonist Draco Malfoy, makes the choice in the seventh book to tell Voldemort that Harry has died even though Harry has not. Narcissa does this because Harry has revealed to her that her son Draco remains safe in the

Battle of Hogwarts. In the process of doing this, she gains a measure of redemption for both her and her son—a measure the reader witnesses when, at the very end of the series, Harry and Draco, while not exactly warm to one another, do not appear to engage with one another with the same level of instant antagonism they did as boys, and Hermione tells Ron not to turn Weasley children against Malfoy children unnecessarily. Meanwhile, in *HBP* potions instructor Horace Slughorn feels guilt about having provided Voldemort with the advice that led to Voldemort's creation of the horcruxes that have extended his life and powers. Reluctantly, though in the end willingly and with a sense of recognizing the importance of doing so, Slughorn provides Harry with key information that assures Harry and Dumbledore that Voldemort has created horcruxes. Much like Snape would do in the next book, Slughorn gives Harry a memory to view in the pensieve, and through his action, Slughorn receives a measure of redemption.

Still, Slughorn, like Snape, engages in choices presented within the context of two dichotomies. The first dichotomy exists between those wizards who only accept "pure" wizards and those who accept others. Though both Snape's and Slughorn's choices do offer some blurring of the borders, in the end they have clearly taken a side in this dichotomy, which reaffirms a difference between blatant racism and more subtle forms of racial hierarchy. Narcissa Malfoy's choice complicates this even further, since she has not clearly moved from rejection to acceptance of "non-pure" wizards. Yet, Narcissa does maintain a second dichotomy that exists between "pure" wizards and anyone not a "pure" wizard. She, Snape, and Slughorn—like Harry—are clearly "pure" wizards, and their abilities to choose to be more or less exclusionary rests on the privilege of being "pure" wizards. Wizards who are not defined as "pure" do not have the same opportunities.

Harry Potter and the Privilege of Perspective

The choices of Potter, Snape, and others as well as the Hogwarts sorting process and others' lack of choices represent the racial hierarchy embedded in the very structure of the wizarding world. Within that structure, the books focus the reader's attention on Harry Potter as the protagonist of the novels. The books do not always read from Harry's perspective. For instance, in the beginning of the fourth book, the reader witnesses a murder at the hands of Voldemort that Potter does not witness. Yet, instances like this are exceptions since readers are asked to identify with Harry's perspective for most of the series. As such, the stories reproduce another feature of the "anti-racist-white-hero" premise, which involves "systematically privileging 'white' experiences of these struggles for African people's equality over African and African American experiences" (Madison, 1999, p. 406). Anti-racist-white-hero films ask readers to identify through white protagonists, while they include marginalized characters only as subordinates to white perspectives. Because nearly all parts of the Harry Potter books filter through Harry's perspective, the series presents a social structure that includes the marginalized—in this case those who are not "pure" wizards—only as subordinates to those who, like Harry, are identified as "pure" wizards.

Additionally, the narrative structure of the anti-racist-white-hero premise involves the hero suffering at the hands of the blatant racists who have already perpetrated suffering to characters of the subordinate group. While this feature asks viewers to sympathize with the underprivileged group, these sympathies appear vicariously through acknowledgement of these characters' suffering by the protagonist. In the meantime, this feature asks viewers to sympathize directly with the white protagonist, whose experiences the film actually portrays. In the process, the anti-racist-white-hero film privileges experiences of the white protagonist over experiences of non-white characters, whose experiences appear relevant only in terms of how they bear on those of the protagonist. With white experience privileged, the narrative structure reproduces the dominant social position of white characters. The structure itself reinforces white privilege by "constructing a paternalistic form of white supremacy as the ideological framework within which to understand the critical historical moments in struggles for equality here and abroad" (Madison, 1999, p. 406).

The Harry Potter stories enact this process because they convey the sufferings of others almost exclusively through the experiences of Harry. Even when the books do not depict these sufferings through Harry's experiences, such as when Voldemort murders Muggle Frank Bryce at the beginning of the fourth book, the sufferings of other characters only acquire significance when connected to Harry's experiences. This includes how a major aspect of the books' premise involves the murder of Harry's parents at the hands of Voldemort, though readers only witness the suffering of his parents—and, in particular, his mother, as a Muggle-born wizard—vicariously as understood through Harry's experiences. Meanwhile, readers directly witness Harry enduring a significant amount of suffering in defense of others. For instance, Draco Malfoy consistently teases Harry for Harry's defense of individuals who are not "pure" wizards. Harry also ends up in the infirmary at various points after engaging in struggles with Voldemort, such as at the end of the first book when he must face Voldemort alone to retrieve the sorcerer's stone that would provide Voldemort with more power. He vanquishes Voldemort but in the process passes out and ends up in an infirmary bed. Meanwhile, in the final book, though he actually does not die, Harry allows Voldemort to kill him in order to save the many people fighting for and with him against Voldemort in the Battle of Hogwarts. Yet, even as Harry suffers, the prominent direct accounts of Harry's own suffering, alongside the vicariousness of the suffering of others, reinforce Harry's privileged position. In essence, the books ask readers to care about the suffering of others only in so far as that suffering relates to the suffering of the protagonist who identifies with the dominant group. Even in that moment of ultimate suffering, giving his life for others in the final book, the "pure" wizard Harry's suffering, not the suffering of the less "pure"—and thus less privileged—groups, remains the focus.

Harry Potter and the Triumph Over Blatant Racism

According to Madison (1999), the final part of the narrative structure of anti-racist-white-hero films involves the hero prevailing in some way at the end of the story, which means the hero triumphs in some way over those who have perpetrated blatant forms of racism and, through this triumph, he or she positively affects race relations with some kind of social victory as the result. However, though some kind of social victory may occur, because the anti-racist-white hero, and not the non-white individuals who have experienced racism, triumphs, these narratives reproduce the power of whiteness. The victory supposedly serves the underprivileged, but ultimately someone from the privileged racial group attains the victory.

In the Harry Potter series, each story ends with some sort of triumph, with varying degrees of significance and effect. All of these triumphs involve the success of Harry Potter in thwarting the plans of Voldemort—again, to varying degrees of effect. These triumphs culminate in the seventh book with Harry's final defeat of Voldemort, killing Voldemort after the destruction of all of the horcruxes. The final defeat of Voldemort means that the wizarding world remains safe for residents who are not "pure" wizards. However, their safety hinges on the power of a member who is identified with the "pure" wizard group. So, while the victories at the end of the books contain elements of triumph for subordinated members of the wizarding society, these triumphs reaffirm their subordinated place within that society because a member of the "pure" wizard group—namely, Harry—has accomplished the triumphs. In the process, Harry Potter and other "pure" wizards include others who do not fit that identity but only in so far as those others do not ultimately challenge the authority of those who are "pure" wizard.

Harry Potter and the Implications of White Privilege

Ultimately, within the fictional arena of "pure" vs. "mudblood," the Harry Potter series offers a potentially progressive vision against exclusion and discrimination on a metaphorically racial basis. These novels depict a battle that pits a group that believes in a fictional form of racial purity that rests on natural ability against a group that stands for the acceptance of differently abled and differently birthed. Yet, the Potter series remains couched within practices that reproduce the privilege and power of those identified as pure. To view these stories in terms of the lessons they offer means recognizing the real world application of these lessons for what they are—potentially progressive, inclusionary in ways, but not devoid of racial hierarchy. Characters (and, thus, races) are accepted within a hierarchy, and the ways characters relate to one another in the book reproduce that hierarchy. The prominence of the anti-racist-white-hero premise in these stories reveals this.

In the end, the rhetoric of Albus Dumbledore in the quotation at the beginning of this essay sounds very similar to that of Martin Luther King, Jr., in the excerpt from his "I Have a Dream" speech that I also quote. Both suggest hope for a world in which the judgment of individuals does not occur on the basis of social position offered by birthright—to King "the color of their skin" in reference to blackness or whiteness while to Dumbledore "our abilities" in reference to the wizarding powers of one's self and one's ancestors. In this regard, the Harry Potter series mirrors the Civil Rights movement in the United States. At the same time, though, as analysis of the use of the anti-racist-white-hero premise in the Harry Potter series shows, the stories' depiction of a type of struggle comparable to the Civil Rights movement maintains white privilege even as the stories garner praise for their progressiveness. Like *Mississippi Burning* and *Cry Freedom*, the Harry Potter stories offer the lesson that society should include others and the lesson that the rights of individuals who are oppressed should be defended. Still, just like those films, the Harry Potter books contain the lesson that individuals who are not in the oppressed group should lead that defense and the lesson that the rights of the oppressed are only significant in so far as they relate to the rights of those who are not oppressed.

When such lessons appear within the Harry Potter series, they occur within a set of fictional accounts applauded for the lessons that they teach. If lessons of acceptance can be conveyed through fiction—and, in fact, perhaps done more effectively through fiction since fiction does not involve the kinds of historical accuracy questions that surround historical dramas of the sort Madison examines—then lessons reproducing white privilege can be taught through fiction as well. The Harry Potter series offers a highly successful, highly praised example of fictional literature that reproduces white privilege even as it appears to seek to advance a rhetoric of inclusion. As the series does that, we might return to Dumbledore's edict to Harry Potter and ask what the stories were able to do as well as what they chose to do.

References

Anatol, G. L. (2003). The fallen empire: Exploring ethnic otherness in the world of Harry Potter. In G. L. Anatol (Ed.), *Reading Harry Potter: Critical essays* (pp. 163–178). Westport, CT: Praeger.

Bassham, G. (2010). Choices vs. abilities: Dumbledore on self-understanding. In G. Bassham (Ed.), *The ultimate Harry Potter and philosophy: Hogwarts for Muggles* (pp. 157–171). Hoboken, NJ: Wiley.

Bell, C. (2013). Riddle me this: The moral disengagement of Lord Voldemort. In C. E. Bell (Ed.), *Legilimens! Perspectives in Harry Potter studies* (pp. 43–66). Newcastle upon Tyne: Cambridge Scholars.

Brooks, D. E., & Rada, J. A. (2002). Constructing race in black and whiteness: Media coverage of public support for President Clinton. *Journalism Communication Monographs, 4,* 114–156. Doi: 10.1177/152263790200400301.

Carey, B. (2003). Hermione and the house-elves: The literary and historical contexts of J. K. Rowling's antislavery campaign. In G. L. Anatol (Ed.), *Reading Harry Potter: Critical essays* (pp. 103–115). Westport, CT: Praeger.

Clifton, L. (2013). Work in a magical world: Revisiting the stratification of castes in *Harry Potter*. In C. E. Bell (Ed.), *Legilimens! Perspectives in Harry Potter studies* (pp. 67–74). Newcastle upon Tyne: Cambridge Scholars.

Crenshaw, C. (1997). Resisting whiteness' rhetorical silence. *Western Journal of Communication, 61,* 253–278. Doi: 10.1080/10570319709374577.

Deavel, C. J., & Deavel, D. P. (2010). Choosing love: The redemption of Severus Snape. In G. Bassham (Ed.), *The ultimate Harry Potter and philosophy: Hogwarts for Muggles* (pp. 53–65). Hoboken, NJ: Wiley.

Doughty, T. (2002). Locating Harry Potter in the "boys' book" market. In L.A. Whited (Ed.), *The ivory tower and Harry Potter* (pp. 243–257). Columbia: University of Missouri Press.

Dresang, E. T. (2002). Hermione Granger and the heritage of gender. In L.A. Whited (Ed.), *The ivory tower and Harry Potter* (pp. 211–242). Columbia: University of Missouri Press.

Dyer, R. (1997). *White.* New York: Routledge.

Gallardo-C., X., & Smith, C. J. (2003). Cinderfella: J. K. Rowling's wily web of gender. In G. L. Anatol (Ed.), *Reading Harry Potter: Critical essays* (pp. 191–205). Westport, CT: Praeger.

Giroux, H. A. (1994). *Disturbing Pleasures: Learning Popular Culture.* New York: Routledge.

Griesinger, E. (2002). Harry Potter and the "deeper magic": Narrating hope in children's literature. *Christianity and Literature, 51,* 455–480.

Grigoryan, M. (2013). Wand-ering between worlds: "Other" identities in *Harry Potter.* In C. E. Bell (Ed.), *Legilimens! Perspectives in Harry Potter studies* (pp. 7–18). Newcastle upon Tyne: Cambridge Scholars.

Harmon, J. M. J. (2013). Forbidden forests and forbidden spaces: Reevaluating "the other" in *Harry Potter.* In C. E. Bell (Ed.), *Legilimens! Perspectives in Harry Potter studies* (pp. 33–42). Newcastle upon Tyne: Cambridge Scholars.

Hasian, M. A., Jr. (1996). *The rhetoric of eugenics in Anglo-American thought.* Athens: University of Georgia Press.

Jackson, R. L., II. (1999). White space, white privilege: Mapping discursive inquiry into the self. *Quarterly Journal of Speech, 85,* 38–54. Doi: 10.1080/00335639909384240.

King, M. L., Jr. (1963). I have a dream … *The U.S. National Archives and Records Administration*. Retrieved from http://www.archives.gov/.

Lavoie, C. (2003). Safe as houses: Sorting and school house at Hogwarts. In G. L. Anatol (Ed.)., *Reading Harry Potter: Critical essays* (pp. 35–49). Westport, CT: Praeger.

Madison, K. J. (1999). Legitimation crisis and containment: The "anti-racist white hero" film. *Critical Studies in Mass Communication, 16*, 399–416. Doi: 10.1080/15295039909367108.

Moon, D., & Flores, L. A. (2000). Antiracism and the abolition of whiteness: Rhetorical strategies of domination among "race traitors." *Communication Studies, 51*, 97–115. Doi: 10.1080/10510970009388512.

Nakayama, T. K., & Krizek, R. L. (1995). Whiteness: A strategic rhetoric. *Quarterly Journal of Speech, 81*, 291–309. Doi: 10.1080/00335639509384117.

Online press kits: Harry Potter. (n.d.). Retrieved from http://mediaroom.scholastic.com/HarryPotter.

Ostrey, E. (2003). Accepting Mudbloods: The ambivalent social vision of J. K. Rowling's fairy tales In G. L. Anatol (Ed.), *Reading Harry Potter: Critical essays* (pp. 89–101). Westport, CT: Praeger.

Park, J. (2003). Class and socioeconomic identity in Harry Potter's England. In G. L. Anatol (Ed.), *Reading Harry Potter: Critical essays* (pp. 179–189). Westport, CT: Praeger.

Rich, M. (2007, July 22). Record first-day sales for last "Harry Potter" book. *The New York Times*. Retrieved from http://www.nytimes.com/2007/07/22/books/22cnd-potter.html.

Rosenberg, A. (2011, July 14). The political parable of "Harry Potter." *The Atlantic*. Retrieved from http://www.theatlantic.com/entertainment/archive/2011/07/the-political-parable-of-harry-potter/241946/.

Rowling, J. K. (1998). *Harry Potter and the sorcerer's stone*. New York: Scholastic.

Rowling, J. K. (1999a). *Harry Potter and the chamber of secrets*. New York: Scholastic.

Rowling, J. K. (1999b). *Harry Potter and the prisoner of Azkaban*. New York: Scholastic.

Rowling, J. K. (2000). *Harry Potter and the goblet of fire*. New York: Scholastic.

Rowling, J. K. (2003). *Harry Potter and the Order of the Phoenix*. New York: Scholastic.

Rowling, J. K. (2005). *Harry Potter and the Half-Blood Prince*. New York: Scholastic.

Rowling, J. K. (2007). *Harry Potter and the deathly hallows*. New York: Scholastic.

Schoefer, C. (2000, January 13). Harry Potter's girl trouble. *Salon*. Retrieved from http://dir.salon.com/books/feature/2000/01/13/potter/index.html.

Smith, A. C. (2010). Harry Potter, radical feminism, and the power of love. In G. Bassham (Ed.), *The ultimate Harry Potter and philosophy: Hogwarts for Muggles* (pp. 80–93). Hoboken, NJ: Wiley.

Weiss, M. (2013). The role of maternal females in Harry Potter's journey. In C. E. Bell (Ed.), *Legilimens! Perspectives in Harry Potter studies* (pp. 19–32). Newcastle upon Tyne: Cambridge Scholars.

Westman, K. E. (2002). Specters of Thatcherism: Contemporary British culture in J. K. Rowling's Harry Potter series. In L.A. Whited (Ed.), *The ivory tower and Harry Potter* (pp. 305–328). Columbia: University of Missouri Press.

Willis-Rivera, J. L., & Meeker, M. (2002). De que colores: A critical examination of multicultural children's books. *Communication Education, 51*, 269–279. Doi: 10.1080/03634520216515.

The Prisoner of Gender: Masculinity in the *Potter* Books

LAUREN R. CAMACCI

"Rowling does not write a feminist novel.
She reflects a patriarchal, hierarchical world"
—Eliza T. Dresang (2002, p. 238)

Harry, Ron, and Hermione await their turn for water for their Quidditch World Cup campsite. They witness an argument between an old wizard, Archie, and a distraught Ministry wizard. According to the Ministry wizard, Archie is quickly becoming a spectacle, for he is wearing a woman's nightgown. The Ministry wizard is "almost crying with exasperation" as he tells Archie that he "can't walk around like that" and continues to emphasize fervently that Archie is wearing *women's* clothes (*GoF*, p. 83). Hermione suffers a giggle-fit so intense that she must leave the line. Why was the Ministry wizard so frustrated with Archie's choice of attire? Why does Hermione (and ostensibly, readers) find this so funny?

The simple answer is that Archie became a spectacle by flagrantly violating societal standards of "normative" masculine expression.[1] The Ministry wizard's logic is that "normal" men wear trousers. By wearing a flowery nightgown, however, Archie becomes "less manly" by taking on qualities traditionally associated with women (e.g., "delicate"). Maleness is nearly always defined by what it *is not*—that is, traditionally feminine characteristics (see Brooks & Gilbert, 1981). Indeed, one would likely find it easier to define "normative femininity" than if asked to define "normative masculinity." This comes from what R.W. Connell terms "hegemonic masculinity," or societal structures that reassert male dominance and normativity and female subordination and deviation (Connell, 2005). If society and scholars alike have a trained incapacity toward this concept of gender, one will be unsurprised that a substantial amount of gender studies scholarship has focused on femininity, rather than masculinity.

My research showed that *Harry Potter* gender scholarship is consistent with this trained incapacity; most studies of gender in *HP* examine female characters (e.g., Dresang, 2002; Gladstein, 2004; Heilman, 2003; Heilman & Donaldson, 2009; Weiss, 2013). The first installment of this very series of edited *HP* studies volumes dedicates itself to Hermione scholarship (Bell, 2012). Far fewer scholars attend to masculinity in the series, and the few who do have begun an important conversation on masculinity in the series that scholars should continue to plumb.

J.K. Rowling presents readers with artfully crafted characters that, rather than being homogenous, static archetypes (i.e., all good, all bad), are a rich amalgamation of many different traits and qualities. Noteworthy is the presence of both traditional and nontraditional expressions of masculinity, often within a single character. In this essay, I argue that, even for its richness and variety of masculine gender performance, however, the *HP* texts present a conservative statement on masculinity, often through other males reinforcing the superiority of traditional masculinity over nontraditional expression. The women of *Potter* shape the series in important ways, but the relationships between males are irreplaceable in creating such a complex world of masculine performance that characters negotiate as they mature through the series. My essay proceeds in four major parts: The first part briefly expounds the relevant scholarship on hegemonic masculinity, gender performance, and homosociality, concepts upon which the conservative hierarchy within the *Potter* texts heavily relies. I then take a close examination of the different performances of masculinity in the seven *Harry Potter* texts before engaging in an analysis of the roles of father- and brotherhood in the books. The fourth section explores homosociality at play in the *Potter* males' engagement with sexuality and "bro culture." The chief aim of this essay is to use textual evidence to understand and critique hegemonic masculinity at play in the series.[2]

Hegemonic Masculinity, Gender Performance, Homosociality

Edward H. Thompson Jr., and Joseph H. Pleck opine, "we now know far more about womanhood, femininity, and women's experiences than we know about manhood, masculinity, and men's experiences" (1981, p. 129). Second-wave feminism often emphasized scholarship on women, for such important scholarship was lacking greatly in the historical canon. Studies of masculinity, however, did not proliferate with similar rapidity or quantity.[3] Charlotte Kroløkke and Anne Scott Sørensen attempt to explain this phenomenon when they write: "Far less research has been carried out on male communication strategies, partly because 'male' has been the genderless norm, whereas 'female' has been the deviance in need of explanation" (2006, p. 105). A number of sociologists, noted for their contributions to masculinity studies, examine, at great length, masculinity as a social construct (for example, see Goffman, 1963; Kimmel, 2012; Stearns, 1990).

The assumption that maleness is normative can make active critique of masculinity and maleness a wooly effort. Pleck argues that "masculine ideology refers to beliefs about the importance of men adhering to culturally defined standards for male behavior" (1981, p. 19). Maleness is nearly always defined in contrast to traditionally feminine characteristics (see, for example, Brooks & Gilbert, 1981). For example, where society expects females to express "emotionality, warmth, and passivity," males should possess "independence, aggressiveness, and dominance" (Hardy, 1995, p. 431). What of a more passive man? In moments when he "acts tough," he is performing a different role, which, as Connell writes, "means enacting a *general* set of expectations which are attached to one's sex" (2005, p. 22). This illustrates Judith Butler's (2006) concept of "gender performativity," which insists that gender is not a static, natal quality, but is instead a series of performances carefully constructed as one navigates through society.

As Butler's concept notes, society has a hand in shaping a person's outward projection of gender. Similarly, Wilkerson argues that "identity is a *fusion* of the personal and the social," in which, according to Thompson, Jr., and Pleck, the societal expectations often outweigh personal desires (Wilkerson, 2001, p. 59, author's emphasis; Thompson & Pleck, 1981). Goffman's "gender role disparity" echoes these sentiments, suggesting that men constantly negotiate between want to do and what they are expected to do (Pleck, 1981, pp. 13–14). In *GoF*, Archie refuses to subordinate his own wishes to societal expectations of his gender performance. Rowling does not tell us whether the Ministry eventually *forced* Archie to don masculine Muggle attire, but the Ministry wizard's frustration and an urgent demand for change show how society polices gender performance.

Deviation from normative gender roles often has social consequences. Families, especially parents, begin to impose biological sex-defined gender roles on children—and mandate passing—from the child's natal day (Hardy, 1995; also see Adams & Coltrane, 2005). Schoolchildren confront the "hegemony of gendering," or the idea that society grooms boys and girls to prescribed gender roles in an attempt to maintain order and hierarchy (Whittle, 2005, p. 116; Swain, 2005). Hardy (1995) reports that educators expect high-achieving students to be male or to possess male qualities and poor students to be more feminine, something consistent with current statistics that girls pursue STEM degrees in later education than boys (also see Swain, 2005).

Furthermore, educators and parents often attribute boys' failures at school (and at home) to some outside force, whereas they consider females' failures to stem from lack of talent or intelligence (Hardy, 1995). Children also begin to expect certain gender performances from one another. In fact, Jordan, Vaughan, and Woodworth (1997) assert the high level of pressure to conform to a socially ascribed gender young people face in secondary school, increasing boys' level of desperation to create a traditionally masculine performance.

Such consequences, if anything, strengthen in adulthood. Kauth and Kalichman remark, "In a patriarchal society, men who are like women are less than 'men'" (1995, p. 85). In 2015 America, a woman wearing pants is no big deal, but a man, like Archie, going outside in a dress usually is. Conforming to such societal gender standards as clothing is part of "passing" as an unquestionable member of a certain gender (see Kroløkke & Sørensen, 2006, p. 131). For men, anxieties about passing are extremely deep-seated.

"Homosociality" is a common term within masculinity studies used to explain these anxieties. Sociologist Michael Kimmel writes:

> From fathers and boyhood friends to teachers, coworkers, and bosses, the evaluative eyes of other men are always upon us, watching, judging. As one Army general put it, every soldier fears "losing the one thing he is likely to value more highly than life—his reputation as *a man among other men*." Our real fear, writes the literary critic David Leverenz, "is not fear of women but of being ashamed or humiliated in front of other men, or being dominated by stronger men" [2012, pp. 5–6, author's emphasis].

Simply, homosociality refers to the practice among males as they police each other's masculinity and evince a certain anxiety that other men might perceive them as not masculine. Homosociality maintains a firm grip on Western men; rigid gender constructions, seated in ruggedness and independent achievement, abound (Kimmel, 2012). Acting "unmanly" risks perception as feminine or even gay, as gay men have been (unfairly) coded as "sissies" for centuries (see Battles & Hilton-Morrow, 2002; Edwards, 1991; Hardy, 1995; Harrison, 1981; Hershberger, 2001; Kimmel, 2012; Stearns, 1990). As such, Western men generally take pains to ensure their fellow men perceive them as manly.[4]

Boys and men of all ages struggle to reconcile their core emotional needs with their desire to conform to societal expectations of masculinity. Masculinity helps shape "men's involvement in social roles," such as their engagement in the act of fathering (Pleck, 1981, p. 18; also see Adams & Coltrane, 2005; Marsiglio & Pleck, 2005). If a man spent too much time in the home in 19th century America, society would see him as overly feminine (Kimmel, 2012; Adams & Coltrane, 2005; Marsiglio & Pleck, 2005). Modern fathers express great nurturing and affection for their children in home settings, but—at least until 15 years ago—often less so in public settings, indicating the same struggle to balance personal needs with social expectations (Kimmel, 2012; Adams & Coltrane, 2005). Hard work becomes a more normatively masculine expression of familial love than female-coded nurturing (Brooks & Gilbert, 1981; Kimmel, 2012). Men strive to be the "provider" for their families and believe themselves to be less masculine if they cannot provide or cannot provide adequately for the family (Brooks & Gilbert, 1981; Kimmel, 2012; Marsiglio & Pleck, 2005; Collinson & Hearn, 2005). While these different expressions of and tensions within masculine performance are consistent with the male characters in the *HP* series, most *Potter* scholars have not attended to these issues.

Some academic studies of *HP* focus on masculinity and the males of the series, but they are few. One such essay is Casey Cothran's (2005) "Lessons in Transfiguration," which explores the symbolism of sexual desire amongst the *Potter* males. Ximena Gallardo-C. and C. Jason Smith's (2003) "Cinderfella" examines "J.K. Rowling's Wily Web of Gender." These authors proceed with four basic premises:

> 1. that *HP* structurally echoes the classically feminine tale of Cinderella, which "allow[s] female readers to identify strongly with a male protagonist";
> 2. that Harry aligns more often with yonic than phallic symbols;
> 3. that the series features constant confrontation with "otherness"; and
> 4. that these premises yield not a radical feminist critique, but the possibility of feminist critique of a somewhat radical children's series [Gallardo-C. & Smith, 2003, pp. 191–92].

This essay offers a rich critique of the inherent sexism of the *HP* novels (e.g., analyzing the rhetoric of descriptions of female characters; also see Dresang, 2002) and of the ways in which Harry's actions and storyline align with more traditionally feminine gender expression. However, whether intentionally or not, Gallardo-C. and Smith do not radically challenge hegemonic masculinity: They define Harry by how he conforms not to traditionally masculine but to feminine standards.

Terri Doughty (2002), by contrast, engages in a comparative analysis of the first four books, and hold the *Harry Potter* books up against other "boys' literature" (like *The Outsiders*) to examine how it conforms to the constraints of the genre. Doughty notes the clear presence of sexism and hegemonic masculinity in the texts, pointing to the disparaging descriptions of girls in the books. She furthermore explores some of the roles boys play in traditional boys' literature, such as a reliance on sport for popularity. Similarly, Eliza T. Dresang (2002) offers a role analysis of Hermione, examining the different roles of historical Hermiones in literature. What follows combines the efforts and methods of Doughty and Dresang: I examine male roles in the *Potter* series, taking Doughty's assertions further to demonstrate the vital importance of male interaction and homosociality in *Harry Potter*'s world.

Masculine Appearance and Performance

As the preceding research has demonstrated, masculinity often comes to mean "that which is not feminine." Consistent with gender scholarship, vitality, strength, stoicism, and success are traits often coded masculine; therefore, advanced age, physical weakness, a quickness to emote, and lack of talent would come to indicate a lack of masculinity. J.K. Rowling creates dynamic male characters that simultaneously display both traditional and nontraditional masculinities, and in turn, challenges the reader to reconsider their normative assumptions about hegemonic masculinity.

A number of Rowling's male characters present readers with dissonant masculine performances. Young Albus Dumbledore leaves Hogwarts with a veritable laundry-list of prestigious honors and awards to his name and, in later life, earns the reputation for standing up against Dark wizards (*DH*, p. 353). These plaudits make sense for a young man. Dumbledore is, however, well over 100 years old by the end of his life, during which times he is still capable of great magic (*GoF*, p. 679; *OotP*, pp. 805–19). His sustained vivacity (even after his hand injury), skill, and intelligence contrast normative social stigma of old age as inept and decrepit.

Other characters have deceptive appearances as well. On the outside, Hagrid is the picture of traditional, rustic masculinity: physically enormous, "wild" of appearance, and without a strong sense of fashion. Interpersonally, however, Hagrid is an extremely sensitive person who displays many non-traditionally masculine traits and hobbies. Hagrid cries often, feels parental love for all sorts of animals, knits, and cooks (e.g., *SS*, pp. 15, 65, 235–36, 303; *PoA*, pp. 93, 121, 217–20). His character differs greatly from his appearances. By contrast, Rowling often describes Filius Flitwick nearly as childlike or feminine and rarely as a commanding presence (see *CoS*, p. 293; *PoA*, pp. 202–03; *OotP*, p. 582). In times of action, however, he produces exceptional magic (*DH*, pp. 599, 601). Physically, Flitwick is very nontraditionally masculine, but he possesses the strongly traditionally masculine trait of skill and power.

Gilderoy Lockhart's publicity contradicts reality: He is an ostensibly gifted wizard, while in reality, he is extremely untalented and foolish. Lockhart routinely expresses very nontraditionally masculine behaviors and appearances; he has the personality of a stereotypical beauty pageant participant: vain and shallow. Even the name "Gilderoy" has roots in the word "gilded," which means something that looks flashy or expensive but is actually worthless, like a plastic watch with gold paint over it.

Lockhart obsesses over his gilt to deflect attention away from his magical ineptitude. He is so narcissistic that he plasters his office with self-portraits, the occupants of which put their hair in curlers at night (*CoS*, p. 141). He also has a flamboyant sense of fashion. Throughout *CoS*, he wears robes in such vivid colors as forget-me-not blue, turquoise, deep plum, lilac, and lurid pink (*CoS*, pp. 59, 89–90, 235–37; *OotP*, p. 509). Lockhart's narcissism, hair curlers, and colorful robes are examples of nontraditionally masculine traits that one will certainly read as foppish, and which many socially code as homosexual. If this were the case, Lockhart would embody the "sissy," the previously mentioned stereotype that asserts that gay men are feminine and, therefore, cannot be masculine.

Lockhart's appearance and behaviors often horrify or are a source of laughter for other, mostly male, characters (*CoS*, pp. 100, 163). Rowling further exposes Lockhart's ineptitudes when he must face actual danger (*CoS*, p. 294); the gilt disappears. Lockhart is a phony and a joke, a social fate that especially the adolescent wizards hope desperately to avoid. Driven by homosociality, the boys of *Potter* deride those, like Lockhart, who do not conform to normative masculine gender expression.

Homosociality carefully shapes and polices male behavior for the boys of the *Potter* series; these adolescent males go to great pains to ensure that their peers view them as traditionally masculine. Harry, in particular, puts a lot of pressure on himself to appear traditionally masculine and to limit displays of nontraditional masculinity. After his friends drink Polyjuice Potion and take on Harry's appearance, Fleur-Harry looks at Bill in a "soppy, slavish" way "that Harry hoped with all his heart would never appear on his face again" (*DH*, p. 53). Harry's discomfort at this display illustrates his disinterest in ever appearing feminine (read: unmanly).

Harry, therefore, strictly polices his masculinity. For example, he only reluctantly expresses emotion, especially tears. Harry often feels frustrated with himself for crying, and the words Rowling uses to describe these scenes suggest a frustration born of not being in control of his "weak" physical reactions (e.g., *GoF*, p. 714; *DH*, pp. 67, 181). When he does openly emote, Harry often feels weak, using phrases like "ashamed" and "more humiliated by the moment" (*PoA*, pp. 86, 184, 257; *DH*, pp. 67, 285). In these cases, Harry is all the sourer when he feels his peers, especially Ron, might be coding him as nontraditionally masculine.

Others' perceptions of his masculinity are very important to Harry; he bristles at insinuations of nontraditionally masculine emotions, for they contradict the image he hopes to project. Harry becomes, for example, "cross" and "stony" when Hogwarts Madam Pomfrey and Professor Trelawney call him "delicate" and a "troubled soul" (*PoA*, p. 89). He positively prickles when Fleur suggests he is too juvenile to be a part of the Triwizard Tournament and when Rita Skeeter writes (falsely) that Harry still cries over his deceased parents (*GoF*, pp. 199, 274–75, 314–15).

Harry also often attempts to deny other emotions that might make him seem weak, such as fear, pain, and disappointment (e.g., *OotP*, pp. 165–68, 269; *HBP*, p. 547). Dumbledore reminds him, however, that such emotions do not indicate weakness, but a great strength and protection (*SS*, p. 299; *OotP*, p. 816; *HBP*, pp. 509–12). His ability to feel strong emotion increases his humanity and demonstrates the value of interpersonal connection (*OotP*, pp. 823–25; *HBP*, p. 78). By asserting love as Harry's "power the Dark Lord knows not," Rowling throws a wrench in the procession on normative masculine expression (*OotP*, p. 841). Harry's ability to triumph in the end is to embrace love for and interdependence on others, both nontraditionally masculine traits.

Emotional expression, for many of the adolescent males in the series besides Harry, becomes a signal of nontraditional masculinity. Draco Malfoy, for example, tries always to keep his aura of nonchalance, but often displays abject fear in the face of danger (*PoA*, p. 118; *DH*, p. 634). Once, when Harry catches Malfoy crying in the bathroom, Malfoy reacts violently, trying to curse Harry (*HBP*, p. 522). It is noteworthy that these young men have such intense, even violent, reactions to being caught emoting. The bathroom is a pseudo-private space, one of the few in Hogwarts. Thinking he was alone, but for Moaning Myrtle, Malfoy allowed his carefully crafted persona to slip; only in private does he risk nontraditionally masculine expression. Malfoy's violent reaction may show the quick escalation within his mind: Harry sees him acting "unmanly," which is embarrassing and, moreover, dangerous, for Harry could tell other students, who would then judge Malfoy as "unmanly," thereby ruining his reputation.

The anxiety of perceived unmanliness associated with homosociality thrives in the *Potter* series not only through emotions, but also through body image. Eliza Dresang noted the few instances of body image issues with the female characters in the first four books, but she did not discuss the males (2002, pp. 233–34; for more on body image and masculinity, see McKay, Mikosza, & Hutchins, 2005). The boys of *Potter* do often self-police any embodied non-masculinity. Ron, for example, sometimes struggles to conform to homosocial standards, in large part due to his family's financial situation. When his mother presents him with his second-hand dress robes, Ron's mortification for the dress-looking robes spurs him to declare that he would rather go to an event naked than in the robes, physical evidence of his family's poverty (*GoF*, pp. 155–57). However, he must wear them to the Yule Ball, and before the boys meet their dates, Ron looked "appalled" seeing himself in the robes. Rowling writes, "There was just no getting around the fact that his robes looked more like a dress than anything else," a statement with which Padma Patil agreed (*GoF*, pp. 411–12). These dress-like robes emasculate Ron, as does Ginny spreading the rumor that he has a tattoo of a Pygmy Puff on his body and his inconsistency on the Quidditch field (*HBP*, p. 536). Whereas Harry finds validation and praise for his performance in sport, Ron's inconsistency reflects the cultural anxiety that "real" men are good at sports (see Bederman, 1996; Swain, 2005). Later, however, Ron defeats the locket Horcrux with the sword of Gryffindor (a phallic symbol), asserting his manliness. Ron, therefore, represents another case of Rowling blending the traditional and nontraditional masculine roles males in the series play.

No character exemplifies Rowling's dynamic male characters that nonetheless emphasize the superiority of traditional masculinity more than Neville Longbottom does. Early in the series, Rowling describes Neville as "a round-faced and accident-prone boy with the worst memory of anyone Harry had ever met" (*CoS*, p. 86). By the end of the series, however, Neville transforms into a bold, rebellious hero in the Battle for Hogwarts (*DH*, pp. 573–82).

Neville is a remarkably poor wizard throughout the first four *Potter* books. Knowing Rowling's careful crafting of character names, even Neville's surname reveals his ineptitude. One can interpret "Longbottom" as "big ass," where "ass" means "dunce" or "screw-up." Neville certainly embodies this early in the series: he is forgetful, timid, quick to cry, and of ostensibly poor magical ability. Ron, commenting that blood status is not everything, says, "'Look at Neville Longbottom—he's pure-blood and he can hardly stand a cauldron the right way up'" (*CoS*, p. 116). In *SS*, Neville tells Harry and Ron an anecdote of how his family thought he was a Squib because he did not show magical ability until age eight. This late display of wizarding ability may reveal Neville as a late-bloomer, explaining why he is 15 years old before demonstrating a noteworthy change in personality and ability.

Until his transformation, however, other characters punish Neville for his nontraditionally masculine traits. Neville often blows up, Vanishes, or otherwise bungles tasks in his Hogwarts classes (e.g., *SS*, pp. 139, 144, 146; *CoS*, p. 283; *PoA*, pp. 125–26; *GoF*, p. 479). Professor McGonagall and Augusta Longbottom both often lament and even punish this lack of academic achievement, although both are kinder than Snape, who often humiliates Neville (e.g., *CoS*, p. 193; *PoA*, pp. 132, 271–72; *GoF*, p. 190; *OotP*, p. 513). This harshness from Neville's educators coincides with Hardy's (2005) report that teachers expect male students to be good achievers. In fact, Neville's only truly good subject is Herbology (*HBP*, p. 173; *DH*, p. 757). Neville's greatest academic achievement is in a not extremely masculine subject—as one may liken Herbology to botany or even the traditionally feminine pursuit of gardening.

Outside of lessons, other Hogwarts students punish Neville's nontraditionally masculine behaviors and traits (see Whittle, 2005). Pansy Parkinson, for example, teases Neville for being a "crybaby," and the Gryffindors howl with laughter when they learn Neville fears Snape more than anything else (*SS*, p. 148; *PoA*, p.137). Neville becomes the shame of Gryffindor twice, first for losing 50 House points in *SS* and again in *PoA* for accidentally allowing Sirius Black entrance into Gryffindor Tower (*SS*, pp. 243–44; *PoA*, pp. 268, 271–72). Although much kinder, even his friends do not take Neville seriously. Harry, in particular, often considers Neville an undesirable partner in lessons or adventures (*SS*, pp. 156–57, 171; *OotP*, pp. 393, 761).

Although Neville is the picture of nontraditional masculine early in the series, it is very important to note that he is a character who Rowling clearly wants her readers to like. Rowling's rhetoric surrounding Neville shows him to be kind-hearted, well-meaning, and hard-working. Neville's nontraditional masculinity never seems as insufferable as Lockhart's does or as sniveling as Wormtail's, in large part due to the few redeeming (read: traditionally masculine) qualities he possesses, such as his unwavering loyalty to Harry. Young Neville is a benign figure yet one whom a reader would likely pity rather than aspire to emulate.

The fifth book marks the start of Neville's mini hero-saga—in which the hero undergoes a major transformation to avenge a loss and stand up for good (think Luke Skywalker). Rowling writes, "Neville had improved beyond all recognition" in Dumbledore's Army lessons, especially in response to the traumatic news of the escape of his parents' torturers from prison (*OotP*, pp. 454, 553). That Neville's improvement springs forth from a desire for revenge highlights the violent streak associated with traditional masculinity (see Brooks & Gilbert, 1981).

Neville's character changes as much as his magical abilities. Where before Fluffy scared him speechless and he would stand quaking in his fluffy slippers, Neville now shouts at Harry not to relinquish the prophecy just to save his life, shrugs off others' horror that he was tortured by the Carrows, and vocalizes truth to power as Voldemort declares his victory at Hogwarts (*SS*, p. 161; *OotP*, pp. 800–01; *DH*, pp. 571–74, 731–33). Neville's crowning glory, of course, comes in *DH* when he issues the call to all free Wizarding people to join the Battle for Hogwarts and when Harry entrusts the destruction of the final Horcrux—the snake—to Neville as Neville carries bodies into Hogwarts castle. Neville's valor and loyalty allows him to pull the sword of Gryffindor from the Sorting Hat to decapitate Nagini (*DH*, p. 733). Neville reaches self-actualization by defeating the snake, a phallic symbol, with a different phallic symbol, the sword (also see Cothran, 2005; for more on phallic symbols and masculinity, see Plummer, 2005). He asserts his new, dominant persona through phallic power.

Rowling transitions Neville from being an already likeable, nontraditionally masculine male to an awe-inspiring portrait of traditional masculinity, once again revealing the hierarchy of masculinity present in Rowling's story. Neville changes remarkably through the series; he grows from "big ass 'fraidy cat crybaby" to a man of valor and achievement. How is such drastic change possible? How do boys learn to become "acceptable" men in the *Potter*verse?

Fathers and Brothers

Families are extremely influential in shaping a child's maturation, and masculinity helps shape fathering styles (D'Angelo, Weinberger & Feldman, 2000). The *Potter* males demonstrate just how influential a father's role can be (Damour, 2003; Grimes, 2002; Kornfeld & Prothro, 2009; Pharr, 2002).[5] Neville, for example, feels the constant presence of his absent father. Augusta often reminds Neville that is doing a poor job filling Frank's shoes, but, once he shows bravery and initiative in the final three books, she declares that Neville is "starting to live up to" Frank (*OotP*, p. 707; *HBP*, p. 137). Neville lacks fatherly guidance until the Azkaban prison break reawakens Frank's presence in Neville's life. Neville steps out of the shadow of this presence and starts to become his own man in *OotP*, symbolized by the breaking of his wand, Frank's old wand (*OotP*, p. 794).

The importance of paternal influence is especially relevant for characters with fathers who are neglectful or absent by choice. Lucius Malfoy, though present in Draco's life, is not a kind, loving father. Draco routinely parades around Hogwarts, boasting about his father's status and influence in Wizarding society (e.g., *CoS*, pp. 266–67). He is clearly proud to be Lucius's son, whereas Lucius appears to deem Draco an inadequate son and treats Draco coldly or with contempt (e.g., *CoS*, p. 52). It is not until he fears for Draco's life that Lucius shows any fatherly affection (*DH*, pp. 641–42). One could easily attribute Draco's attitude and behaviors to Lucius's poor fathering skills.

Lucius's fatherly indifference, and the resulting effect on his son, is but a shadow of the fatherly neglect demonstrated by figures like Barty Crouch, Sr., and Tom Riddle, Sr. Both men abandoned their sons, either emotionally or literally, and Rowling clearly implicates this abandonment in the subsequent psychopathy of the sons, who ultimately murder their fathers. Readers discover that Crouch, Sr., fell from grace when his son was exposed as a Death Eater (*GoF*, pp. 526–27). Sirius tells Harry, Ron, and Hermione, "people started feeling a bit more sympathetic toward the son and started asking how a nice young lad from a good family had gone so badly astray. The conclusion was that his father never cared much for him" (*GoF*, pp. 529–30). This passage simultaneously indicates that poor fathers deserve society's (and readers') disapproval and that sons without fatherly guidance are likely to go astray. The elder Crouch's abject cruelty to Barty during his trial indeed had a significant emotional effect on Barty (*GoF,* pp. 594–96, 684). The two Crouches demonstrate how a lack of fatherly love can lead a son to search for that love from any source possible, even one as evil as Voldemort. To become "closer than a son" to Voldemort, Barty does his bidding, murdering his unloving father to gain the favor of his father figure (*GoF,* pp. 678, 690).

Barty Crouch sought a father-figure when his father abandoned him emotionally; Voldemort, by contrast, chose to obliterate his absent father from his life. He reshapes his own name—from Tom Marvolo Riddle to Lord Voldemort—to rid himself of further connection with Tom Riddle (*CoS*, p. 314; *GoF,* p. 646; *HBP,* pp. 274–75). Dumbledore suggests to Harry that the murder of the Riddle family was Voldemort "'revenging himself upon the father who never wanted him'" (*HBP*, p. 367). Dumbledore's inference suggests that, even though Voldemort outwardly sought to remove all connection to Riddle, Sr., the abandonment irreversibly influenced the ruthless villain he became (see Bell, 2013). Crouch, Sr., and Riddle, Sr., made the choice to neglect or leave their sons; these fathers did not want them.

Rowling invites distinctly emotional responses from readers for characters like Crouch, Sr., Riddle, Sr., and Mr. Malfoy through her language choices surrounding these characters. Even though these men exemplify many traditionally masculine traits—such as power, status, and financial success—these men are cold, distant, disinterested, and cruel. Rowling's descriptions invite readers to develop a dislike or even antipathy for them for abandoning their sons—and by extension unleashing their sons' madness upon the Wizarding world.

Fathers absent by force, rather than by choice, influence their sons far differently. Harry, like Neville, feels the presence of his absent father, but unlike Neville, Harry has what Terri Doughty calls "a cast of 'fathers' who are there when he needs them" (2002, p. 253). A number of *Potter* scholars draw attention to the important relationship Harry develops with James throughout the series (e.g., Kornfeld & Prothro, 2009; Swanson, 2013). Harry travels through a number of stages, first idolizing his father, then resenting him, and ultimately accepting that James was a normal, not perfect man (*OotP,* p. 170). That Harry is nearly James's doppelganger but with Lily's eyes is significant. Harry sees the world through his mother's eyes—an experience that creates Harry as perhaps a more nuanced character than his very traditionally masculine father. In addition to James' part, Harry's father-figures play a formative role in Harry's maturation.

Harry's father figures each play different roles for him. Vernon Dursley is an extreme version of the disciplinarian, constantly finding ways to torment or punish Harry. Hagrid helps Harry with his emotional development; Harry often seeks Hagrid's company when he is upset. Lupin and Dumbledore are advice-givers; each help teach Harry vital magical skills and help him work through extremely important internal issues. In this way, Lupin and Dumbledore serve as (grand)father-figure mentors, and both men struggle to negotiate this role. Dumbledore, for example, loses himself in his grandfatherly affections for Harry and neglects his mentor duties. Lupin, by contrast, hopes to abandon his fatherly duties (to the unborn Teddy) to take on his role as Harry's mentor wholeheartedly (*DH*, pp. 211–16).

Harry's many father-figures and mentors are very important to him, and Sirius is doubtless the most important of all. Harry regularly writes to Sirius for advice and support when they are separated, and Sirius often risks his own safety and happiness to be present for Harry (*GoF*, pp. 290, 534, 698; *OotP*, pp. 180–81, 194–95). Such interdependence and self-sacrifice reveals the importance of the bond between Harry and Sirius. As with a real father, Harry sometimes becomes frustrated when Sirius lectures him about safety, but it is abundantly clear that the two men feel a great deal of affection and loyalty toward each other (*GoF*, pp. 572–73, 610, 713; *OotP*, pp. 83, 371, 523–24, 854–55). When Harry uses the Resurrection Stone, Sirius and Lupin appear alongside Lily and James, a tribute to the strength of their father-like influence (*DH*, p. 699). Harry's father-figures provide Harry emotional support and, in James and Sirius's cases, provide for Harry financially.

Traditional masculinity, especially in the West, relies heavily on a male's ability to be successful and to provide for his family. One way males provide for their families is, of course, financially. Lucius Malfoy and Arthur Weasley very differently exemplify the role of the provider in the *HP* series. Consistent with her presentation of other masculine traits, Rowling gives her readers dynamic male providers who represent a rich variety of subtleties to their performance of masculinity.

Rowling never identifies what Lucius Malfoy does for a living; rather, she implies that the Malfoys live off an inherited family fortune. Lucius uses his wealth to achieve a high social status, and Lucius and Draco regularly flaunt their family's high status and use their money to influence others, like Cornelius Fudge (e.g., *PoA*, p. 125; *GoF*, pp. 101–02; *OotP*, pp. 154–55). Lucius's fall from grace—both from Wizarding society and within Voldemort's ranks—demonstrates his inability to live up to his reputation; when words turn to action, Malfoy cannot meet expectations.

Rowling often draws attention to the contrast between the Malfoys and the Weasleys (*SS*, p. 196; *CoS*, pp. 62–63; *OotP*, pp. 154, 413). The Weasleys hold very low status in Wizarding society, despite being pureblood. They are very poor, for Arthur earns a limited income in an obscure, inglorious Ministry department, in large part due to his affinity for Muggle culture (*CoS*, pp. 30–31; *GoF*, pp. 46, 711; *HBP*, p. 84). In fact, this affinity is a deviance from normative Wizarding pastimes, and it earns him reprimand, both at work and at home (*CoS*, pp. 38–39, 88; *OotP*, pp. 506–07; *DH*, p. 93). It is with shame that the Weasley children often speak of their family's financial circumstances (*CoS*, pp. 41, 46–47; *GoF*, p. 156).

Perhaps the most notable similarity between Arthur and Lucius is their relationship with their wives. There are cases in which both demonstrate the more normative conception of traditional masculinity, acting as clear head-of-household (e.g., *GoF*, p. 101; *OotP*, p. 89). More often, however, Narcissa Malfoy and Molly Weasley appear to be the decision-makers and disciplinarians in their homes. Molly regularly bosses Arthur around (e.g., *CoS*, pp. 38–39, 67; *GoF*, pp. 53–54; *OotP*, pp. 70, 506–07, 522; *HBP*, p. 326; *DH*, p. 108); the words Rowling uses in these moments—for example, "meekly" and "guiltily"—show Arthur as nearly bullied. Narcissa's control over Lucius is tacit, coming in the form of silent instructions (e.g., *DH*, p. 8). One notes the circumstances of these reversals of normative expectations. Molly bosses Arthur in daily minutia, but Arthur takes a stronger stand in graver moments, whereas Lucius defers to his wife's instruction in moments of peril.

The clearest difference of character between Lucius and Arthur is their fathering ability. Lucius is hardly capable of being a good father to one child. Although he struggles to spread his finances amongst so many people, Arthur, by contrast, provides excellent fathering skills to seven children and surrogate fathering to Harry. Rowling's descriptions of Arthur invite readers to like him. Arthur is a nontraditionally masculine character; he is a poor achiever and a little goofy—and yet Rowling clearly wants readers to like this endearing character and affectionate father. Rowling makes clear in the text that, excepting Percy's defection, the Weasley children respect their father, even if they do laugh at his foibles. Furthermore, even if his children are mischievous and sometimes break rules, they are all, ultimately, good people—respectful, good-humored, responsible, and loyal.

One cannot contribute the crafting of these good qualities solely to a strong father; brothers (and brother figures) also play an important role. Like fathers, brothers help shape their siblings' personalities through the added element of peer pressure. Though perhaps counterintuitive, Dudley serves as a brother-figure in his capacity as the bully. Brothers do not always see eye-to-eye, and bullying does sometimes happen. If not for his endless experiences with Dudley, however, Harry would have been less prepared to deal with Malfoy, Crabbe, and Goyle when he arrived at Hogwarts. The Weasleys, by contrast, represent a much more positive influence.

The Weasleys constantly show that they support one another (e.g., *SS*, p. 305, *OotP*, p. 658). This is especially true in times of hardship, like the loss of George's ear and Fred's death (*DH*, p. 74, *DH*, pp. 637–40). The Weasleys also exemplify other elements of sibling relationships, like rivalry and competition (*SS*, p. 100; *GoF*, p. 290). The siblings do not just compete; they also tease each other a lot, usually good-naturedly. Fred and George incessantly tease Ron, Percy, and even Harry (*SS*, p. 204; *PoA*, pp. 63, 67; *GoF*, pp. 64, 567–68). At one point, the twins tease Ron about his romance with Lavender, rather than offering helpful advice from which Ron could certainly have benefitted (*HBP*, pp. 326–27, 338; also see Fisher, 2004). Why would such advice have helped Ron? By what standards are the twins able to tease him so badly?

Sexuality and Bro Culture

Amongst adolescent males, there is a tension between the physical and emotional sides of sexuality (see Plummer, 2005). Young men feel societal pressure to demonstrate success in physical sexual conquests and simultaneously seek to avoid being tied too closely to a female or (although societal standards are changing) be perceived as gay by their peers.[6] Ron and Harry, especially, struggle to negotiate their pubescence alongside societal standards surrounding sexuality. Neither, for example, advertises his lack of kissing experience. Ron becomes downright mean when Ginny yells that Ron is inexperienced with kissing (*HBP*, pp. 287–92). When that first kiss finally happens, Harry feels awkwardness more than anything other emotion, and Ron is awkwardly public about his kissing-based relationship with Lavender (*OotP*, pp. 457–62). What creates these awkward and uncomfortable pseudo-sexual situations?

Many American readers will likely recognize the term "bro code," or the code of ethics by which male friends should abide. One *College Humor* source provides men with the 20 most vital rules for successful bro life (Rebello, 2011).[7] These rules prescribe certain male behaviors while prohibiting others. For example, Rule VIII states that beer is an acceptable gift for optional birthday or Christmas presents. In this vein, Harry and Ron often gift each other food or sport-related gifts for these occasions (*SS*, pp. 200–01; *CoS*, p. 212; *GoF*, p. 28; *OotP*, pp. 8, 502). Rule XI proclaims that men should pay back their debts to friends as quickly as possible, a rule Ron attempts to follow in *GoF* (pp. 105, 545). Harry often follows the bro code by looking out for Ron—for example, scheduling Quidditch practice during Slughorn's parties so Ron will not feel excluded (*HBP*, pp. 243–44). He further keeps to the code when he takes Ron to Slughorn for a love potion antidote, rather than letting Ron "run amok" as revenge for Ron hitting him (*HBP*, p. 394). Male best friends, according to the bro code, must always look out for one another and let nothing come between them.

This part of the bro code asserts the uncouth aphorism "Bros before hoes." For the unfamiliar reader, this phrase means exactly what it sounds like: males should prioritize their male friendships over romantic relationships with females, because, "always remember, girlfriends come and go, but your boys are always there" (Rebello, 2011). Despite its sexism and blatant disregard for non-heterosexual people, the phrase maps well onto the balance *Potter* males seek between friendship and cross-sex romantic pursuit. Especially for Harry and Ron, there is a constant effort to find such a balance, exemplified by Ron's relationship with Lavender Brown and Harry's with Ginny.

"Bros before hoes" becomes salient when Ron begins dating Lavender. Ron immediately breaks Rule XIII of the bro code—"No Public Displays of Affection"—as Harry's first introduction to Ron's new romance is observing the pair making out in the Common Room (*HBP*, pp. 300–01). Rowling's language choices in the Ron/Lavender passages indicate Harry's disinterest in Lavender's company and his view that she is an intruder on the Harry/Ron friendship; Lavender is someone Harry has to "put up with" (*HBP*, p. 304). She routinely corners Harry to discuss Ron's feelings for her, which Rowling calls "a most uncomfortable experience that Harry would have happily foregone" (*HBP*, p. 410). However, when they laugh at her Christmas gift to Ron—the "My Sweetheart" necklace—Harry and Ron effectively emphasize that the Ron/Lavender relationship is insignificant and laughable, one clearly subordinate to the Harry/Ron friendship (*HBP*, p. 338).

Harry views Ron and Lavender's relationship not only as a nuisance to Harry, but more importantly as a negative influence on Ron. In response to Ron's emotional declaration after being dosed with love potion, Rowling writes, "Harry gaped at him. He had not expected this and was not sure he wanted to hear it. Friends they might be, but if Ron started calling Lavender 'Lav-Lav,' he would have to put his foot down" (*HBP*, p. 392). If Ron called Lavender "Lav-Lav," it would indicate that Ron was suffering undue influence from Lavender and putting Lavender before his "bro," which Harry will *not* allow. In this moment, Harry expresses his dedication to policing Ron's possible non-traditionally masculine behaviors.

Another element of the bro code from which "bros before hoes" comes is not dating a bro's sister (Rebello, 2011). Dating a friend's sister is taboo because it places strain on the male-male friendship. For example, in the case of a fight, would the brother take his best friend's side or his sister's? Additionally, male sex gossip would be limited, for the brother would not want to hear about his sister in sexual situations. Harry's crush on Ginny, therefore, creates anxiety for Harry, for it could ruin his friendship with Ron. Harry at one point thinks, "*She's Ron's sister. She's out-of-bounds*" (*HBP*, p. 290, Rowling's emphasis). Later, Rowling writes that "the battle still raged on inside his head: *Ginny or Ron?*" (*HBP*, p. 519, Rowling's emphasis). Harry's internal dialogue displays just how anxiety-producing this matter is for him: "*She's Ron's sister.* But she's ditched Dean! *She's still Ron's sister.* I'm his best mate! *That'll make it worse.* If I talked to him first—*He'd hit you.* What if I don't care? *He's your best mate!*" (*HBP*, pp. 515–16, Rowling's emphasis). The repetition of the phrase "best mate" highlights Harry's fears that to pursue a relationship with Ginny would be perhaps to strain his tight bond with Ron. Although Ron's shocked reaction to Harry and Ginny's first kiss—so unlike his jubilance at Harry's kiss with Cho—belies some strain to the friendship, balance returns to the Harry/Ron friendship when Ron gives the couple a lukewarm "blessing" (*HBP*, pp. 534, 536; *DH*, pp. 117–18).

Although overt depictions of puberty and sexuality are absent from the texts, *Harry Potter* gives readers a complex picture of boys maturing. The adolescent boys of *Potter* navigate a mire of social and personal pressures to conform to standards of "proper" masculine performance that could contradict how they might otherwise choose to act. In many cases, norms of homosociality enable males to monitor their male peers' masculine performances and attempt to enforce change in the event of transgressions. In the end, the most successful males in *Harry Potter* are those who learn to present a by-and-large traditionally masculine persona, peppered with a careful measure of socially appropriate non-traditional expression.

Conclusion: The Prisoner of Gender

In her genre analysis of the series, Terri Doughty posits, "The Harry Potter books do not problematize masculinity; this is, perhaps, one reason for their appeal for boy readers" (2002, p. 253). This assertion is nearly prophetic: Published before the series had concluded, Doughty makes a vital observation about masculine gender performance in *Harry Potter*. Sue Wharton argues that gender in children's literature is a "confirmation of dominant social discourses" (2005, p. 240). I have sought in this essay to demonstrate how, at their core, the *Potter* books maintain hegemonic masculinity and norms of homosociality in an effort to offer further analysis of masculinity as a gender performance worthy of scholarly inquiry.

The *Harry Potter* series is, in large part, a coming-of-age saga; readers watch Harry grow from boy to man, witnessing him negotiating his identity in a social world. Consistent with Grimes's (2002) assertion, Rowling's characters, especially Harry, provide a realistic picture of adolescent males that allows for deeper audience engagement. Diana Weiler's (2000) research agrees with this claim: she suggests that young readers identify best with stories that both challenge and confirm the *status quo*. *Harry Potter* is such a story, as Rowling creates nuanced characters that reflect the complexity of living humans. Harry is obviously the novels' hero, but he is not always the perfect picture of traditional masculinity (recall his self-pitying, teen angst phase in *OotP*). He demonstrates traditionally masculine characteristics like athleticism and success while simultaneously embodying nontraditionally masculine traits, such as expressing emotions like love.

Although many of her characters perform this varied masculinity, Rowling portrays nontraditional masculinity as subordinate to traditional masculinity. Those nontraditionally masculine characters in the series undergo some metamorphosis, allowing them to find a "proper" balance of masculine expression. The men and boys of the *Potter* series may perhaps appear quite different from other men and boys in Children's and Young Adult Fiction. However, the *Potter* males largely conform to standards of hegemonic masculinity, policed by homosociality. Some of Rowling's nontraditional males, like Arthur and Neville, are quite likeable; they only become admirable, though, when they transform into more traditionally masculine men.

Often, this transformation occurs through males' interactions with other males. Rowling's male characters exemplify homosociality: it takes men to make other men into "real men." Through norms of "proper" masculine performance and homosociality, fathers, brothers, friends, mentors, and intrapersonal selves carefully monitor and police masculine expression. Male-male bonds in the *Harry Potter* series become vital to healthy, masculine development in adolescent males. Male-female relationships in the series are doubtless important, but it is clear in the text that boys missing strong male-male bonds fail to become well-adjusted adult men.

Scholars have much to gain by studying the male characters of the *Harry Potter* series. Some scholars have examined the men as they relate to the women, while others have considered the *Potter* books as examples of boys' literature as a genre. Analysis of the *Potter* males on their own, however, provides critique of hegemonic masculinity and brings to the fore the socially constructed nature of masculinity and the power of homosociality. Men live in a constant state of self-monitoring: who knows what small action their male peers might see in them that would leave them as exposed as the flowery nightgown-clad Archie.

Notes

1. I use the word "normative" in place of the word "normal." "Normative" is a more acceptable term in gender scholarship, for it indicates the constructed nature of "normal." The word "normal" indicates a natural given. However, societal standards, like gender, are always constructed and negotiated. To assume a "normal" gender role is to reinforce the power of hegemonic masculinity and, thus, to stymie critique of masculinity. The term "gender" refers to societally constructed performances. I do not use "gender" synonymously with "sex," as term often associated with biology. Scholarship on intersex and trans*, however, have troubled this binary distinction

even further. Work by Anne Fausto-Sterling is a good starting place for those interested in more on the conversation on sex and gender.

2. The analysis that follows looks to canonical information only (i.e., information Rowling provided for readers in the original seven novels), rather than para-canonical (e.g., information from Pottermore) or non-canonical information (e.g., studies of fan culture).

3. Studies of masculinity are NOT the same as studies of masculinism. Masculinity studies, as specified above, seek to understand, interrogate, and critique masculinity. Sociology boasts a lot of masculinity scholarship. "Masculinism" is quite different. Defining it is difficult, due to lack of consistent scholarly presence, but "masculinism" generally indicates study towards the protection of hegemonic masculinity. An example of such a text is Mansfield, H.C. (2006). *Manliness*. New Haven: Yale University Press.

4. There are, of course, exceptions to every case. People of all sorts may choose purposely to ignore gender norms or even to flout their lack of conformity. However, the obsession with appearing "manly" is likely the source of the colloquialism "No homo!" uttered by often young men before they say or do something the fear their peers might perceive as overly feminine and therefore gay (for example, "I love you, bro ... no homo!").

5. Mothering in *Harry Potter* is indeed very important, but it is not the purpose of this essay. See Hidalgo, 2012, and Weiss, 2013, for analyses of *Potter* mothering.

6. Suman Gupta (2009) discusses the role of appearances and heterosexual desire in the series, with particular regard for Lockhart and for Veela/Fleur.

7. As with everything from *College Humor*, take "The Golden Rules of Manhood" with a grain of salt. The twenty-something writer purposefully trolls readers who will be easily offended by the essentialist, often sexist content.

References

Adams, M., & Coltrane, S. (2005). Boys and men in families: The domestic production of gender, power and privilege. In M. S. Kimmel, J. Hearn, & R. W. Connell (Eds.), *Handbook of studies on men & masculinities* (pp. 230–248). Thousand Oaks: Sage.

Battles, K., & Hilton-Morrow, W. (2002). Gay characters in conventional spaces: Will and Grace and the situation comedy genre. *Critical Studies in Media Communication, 19*(1), 87–105.

Bederman, G. (1995). *Manliness and civilization: A cultural history of gender and race in the United States, 1880–1917*. Chicago: University of Chicago Press.

Bell, C. E. (Ed.) (2012). *Hermione Granger saves the world: Essays on the feminist heroine of Hogwarts*. New York: McFarland.

Bell, C. E. (2013). Riddle me this: The moral disengagement of Lord Voldemort. In C. E. Bell (Ed.), *Legilimens! Perspectives in Harry Potter studies* (pp. 43–65). Newcastle Upon Tyne: Cambridge Scholars.

Butler, J. (2006). *Gender trouble: Feminism and the subversion of identity*. New York: Routledge.

Brooks, G. R., & Gilbert, L. A. (1981). Men in families: Old constraints, new possibilities. In R. F. Levant & W. S. Pollack (Eds.), *A new psychology of men* (pp. 252–279). New York: Basic Books.

Collinson, D. L., & Hearn, J. (2005). Men and masculinities in work, organizations, and management. In M. S. Kimmel, J. Hearn, & R. W. Connell (Eds.), *Handbook of studies on men & masculinities* (pp. 289–310). Thousand Oaks: Sage.

Connell, R. W. (2005). *Masculinities* (2nd edition). Berkeley: University of California Press.

Cothran, C. A. (2005). Lessons in transfiguration: Allegories of male identity in Rowling's *Harry Potter* series. In C. W. Hallet (Ed.), *Scholarly studies in Harry Potter: Applying academic methods to a popular text* (pp. 123–234). Lewiston, NY: Edwin Mellen Press.

Damour, L. (2003). Harry Potter and the magical looking glass: Reading the secret life of the preadolescent. In G. L. Anatol (Ed.), *Reading Harry Potter: Critical essays* (pp. 15–24). Westport, CT: Praeger.

D'Angelo, L., Weinberger, D. A., & Feldman, S. S. (2000). Like father, like son? Predicting male adolescents' adjustment from parents' distress and self-restraint. In G. Adams (Ed.), *Adolescent development: The essential readings* (pp. 139–170). Oxford: Blackwell.

Doughty, T. (2002). Locating Harry Potter in the "boys' book" market. In L. A. Whited (Ed.), *The ivory tower and Harry Potter: Perspectives on a literary phenomenon* (pp. 243–257). Columbia: University of Missouri Press.

Dresang, E. T. (2002). Hermione Granger and the heritage of gender. In L. A. Whited (Ed.), *The ivory tower and Harry Potter: Perspectives on a literary phenomenon* (pp. 211–242). Columbia: University of Missouri Press.

Edwards, T. (1990). Beyond sex and gender: Masculinity, homosexuality, and social theory. In J. Hearn & D. Morgan (Eds.), *Men, Masculinities, and social theory: Critical studies on men and masculinities 2* (pp. 110–123). London: Unwin Hyman.

Fisher, T. D. (2004). Family foundations of sexuality. In J. H. Harvey, A. Wenzel, & S. Sprecher (Eds.), *The handbook of sexuality in close relationships* (385–409). Mahwah, NJ: Lawrence Erlbaum.

Gallardo-C., X., & Smith, C. J. (2003). Cinderfella: J. K. Rowling's wily web of gender. In G. L. Anatol (Ed.), *Reading Harry Potter: Critical essays* (pp. 191–205). Westport, CT: Praeger.

Gladstein, M. R. (2004). Feminism and equal opportunity: Hermione and the women of Hogwarts. In D. Baggett & S. E. Klein (Eds.), *Harry Potter and philosophy: If Aristotle ran Hogwarts* (pp. 49–59). Chicago: Open Court.

Goffman, E. (1963). *Stigma: Notes on the management of spoiled identity*. Englewood Cliffs, NJ: Prentice-Hall.

Grimes, M. K. (2002). Harry Potter: Fairy tale prince, real boy, and archetypal hero. In L. A. Whited (Ed.), *The ivory tower and Harry Potter: Perspectives on a literary phenomenon* (pp. 89–122). Columbia: University of Missouri Press.

Gupta, S. (2009). *Re-reading Harry Potter* (2nd edition). New York: Palgrave MacMillan.

Hardy, M. S. (1995). The development of gender roles: Societal influences. In L. Diamant & R. D. McAnulty (Eds.), *The psychology of sexual orientation, behavior and identity: A handbook* (pp. 425–443). Westport, CT: Greenwood Press.

Harrison, J. (1981). Roles, identities, and sexual orientation: Homosexuality, heterosexuality, and bisexuality. In R. F. Levant & W. S. Pollack (Eds.), *A new psychology of men* (pp. 425–443). New York: Basic Books.

Heilman, E. E. (2003). Blue wizards and pink witches: Representations of gender identity and power. In E. E. Heilman (Ed.), *Harry Potter's world: Multidisciplinary critical perspectives* (pp. 221–239). New York: RoutledgeFalmer.

Heilman, E. E., & Donaldson, T. (2009). From sexist to (sort-of) feminist: Representations of gender in the *Harry Potter* series. In E. E. Heilman (Ed.), *Critical perspectives on Harry Potter* (2nd edition) (pp. 139–161). New York: Routledge.

Hershberger, S. L. (2001). Biological factors in the development of sexual orientation. In A. R. D'Augelli & C. J. Patterson (Eds.), *Lesbian, gay, and bisexual identities and youth: Psychological perspectives* (pp. 27–51). Oxford: Oxford University Press.

Hidalgo, A. (2012). Unstoppable force: Maternal power and feminism. In C. E. Bell (Ed.), *Hermione Granger saves the world: Essays on the feminist heroine of Hogwarts* (pp. 66–86). Jefferson, NC: McFarland.

Jordan, K. M., Vaughan, J. S., & Woodworth, K. J. (1997). I will survive: Lesbian, gay, and bisexual youths' experience of high school. In M. B. Harris (Ed.), *School experiences of gay and lesbian youth* (pp. 17–33). New York: Harrington Park Press.

Kauth, M. R., & Kalichman, S. C. (1995). Sexual orientation and development: An interactive approach. In L. Diamant & R. D. McAnulty (Eds.), *The psychology of sexual orientation, behavior, and identity: A handbook* (pp. 81–103). Westport, CT: Greenwood Press.

Kimmel, M. (2012). *Manhood in America: A cultural history* (3rd edition). New York: Oxford University Press.

Kornfeld, J., & Protho, L. (2003). Comedy, conflict, and community: Home and family in *Harry Potter*. In E. E. Heilman (Ed.), *Harry Potter's world: Multidisciplinary critical Perspectives* (pp. 187–202). New York: RoutledgeFalmer.

Kroløkke, C., & Sørensen, A. S. (2006). *Gender communication theories and analyses: From silence to performance.* Thousand Oaks: Sage.

Marsiglio, W., & Pleck, J. H. (2005). Fatherhood and masculinities. In M. S. Kimmel, J. Hearn, & R. W. Connell (Eds.), *Handbook of studies on men & masculinities* (pp. 249–269). Thousand Oaks: Sage.

McKay, J., Mikosza, J., & Hearn, J. (2005). "Gentlemen, the lunchbox has landed": Representations of masculinities and men's bodies in the popular media. In M. S. Kimmel, J. Hearn, & R. W. Connell (Eds.), *Handbook of studies on men & masculinities* (pp. 270–288). Thousand Oaks: SAGE.

Pharr, M. (2002). In medias res: Harry Potter as hero-in-progress. In L. A. Whited (Ed.), *The ivory tower and Harry Potter: Perspectives on a literary phenomenon* (pp. 53–66). Columbia: University of Missouri Press.

Pleck, J. H. (1981). The gender role strain paradigm: An update. In R. F. Levant & W. S. Pollack (Eds.), *A new psychology of men* (pp. 11–32). New York: Basic Books.

Plummer, K. (2005). Male sexualities. In M. S. Kimmel, J. Hearn, & R. W. Connell (Eds.), *Handbook of studies on men & masculinities* (pp. 178–195). Thousand Oaks: SAGE.

Rebello, J. D. (2011). The gold rules of manhood. Retrieved January 28, 2015, from http://www.pointsincase.com/articles/golden_rules_manhood.htm.

Spitzack, C., & Carter, K. (1987). Women in communication studies: A typology for revision. *Quarterly Journal of Speech, 73*(4), 401–423.

Swain, J. (2005). Masculinities in education. In M. S. Kimmel, J. Hearn, & R. W. Connell (Eds.), *Handbook of studies on men & masculinities* (pp. 213–229). Thousand Oaks: Sage.

Swanson, K. (2013). *Expecto pater*: Reading Harry's journey of identity in *Prisoner*. In C. E. Bell (Ed.), *Legilimens! Perspectives in Harry Potter studies* (pp. 95–111). Newcastle Upon Tyne: Cambridge Scholars.

Thomas, C. (2008). Re-enfleshing the bright boys; or, how male bodies might matter to feminist theory. In C. Thomas (Ed.), *Masculinity, psychoanalysis, and straight queer theory: Essays on abjection in literature, mass culture, and film* (pp. 19–62). New York: Palgrave Macmillan.

Thompson, E. H., Jr., & Pleck, J. H. (1981). Masculine ideologies: A review of research instrumentation on men and masculinities. In R. F. Levant & W. S. Pollack (Eds.), *A new psychology of men* (pp. 129–163). New York: Basic Books.

Weiler, D. (2000). Teenagers: A writing adventure. In M.C. Courtland & T.J. Gambell (Eds.), *Young adolescents meet literature: Intersections for learning* (201–210). Vancouver: Pacific Educational Press.

Weiss, M. (2013). The role of maternal females in Harry Potter's journey. In C. E. Bell (Ed.), *Legilimens! Perspectives in Harry Potter studies* (pp. 19–31). Newcastle Upon Tyne: Cambridge Scholars.

Wharton, S. (2005). Invisible females, incapable males: Gender construction in a children's reading scheme. *Language and Education, 19*(3), 238–51.

Whittle, S. (2005). Gender fucking or fucking gender? In I. Morland & A. Willox (Eds.), *Queer theory* (pp. 115–129). Houndmills: Palgrave Macmillan.

Wilkerson, W. S. (2007). *Ambiguity and sexuality: A theory of sexual identity*. New York: Palgrave Macmillan.

The HIV Metaphor: J.K. Rowling's Werewolf and Its Transformative Potential

Brendan G.A. Hughes

In addition to the official canon of seven books, eight films, and numerous companion books written by author J. K. Rowling, fans and readers have created their own theories, stories, forums and webpages to discuss the journey of their favorite boy wizard before and after the globally popular young adult saga's completion. It is from this fandom that a significant issue arose in 2007 as RDR Books attempted to publish a version of the popular website "The Harry Potter Lexicon" in book format. Warner Bros., Inc., who holds the media copyright ownership felt that the book threatened its monopoly on *Harry Potter* memorabilia and associated products, while J.K. Rowling was insulted by the lack of thorough reading and effort placed into the construction of the attempted encyclopedia. Judge Robert B. Patterson, Jr., eventually sided with Rowling and Warner Bros. stating that the work proposed by Steve Vander Ark, the creator and manager of the website and attempted author of *The Harry Potter Lexicon*, appropriated far too much of Rowling's creative material for the ill-fated book.

The above scandal in the world of *Harry Potter* fandom also revealed a few significant ideas and threads that were left untouched in the *Lexicon* and Rowling's various side-projects since they were edited out in the writing process. Perhaps the most stunning of these was described by Rowling in her testimony. Specifically, she described how painful it was to look at a badly constructed manuscript of the *Lexicon*; in her opinion as the creator of the world of *Harry Potter*, Vander Ark left far too many ideas and entries underdeveloped. In specific reference to Remus Lupin she stated:

> "I know that I said publicly that Remus Lupin was supposed to be on the HIV Metaphor. It was someone who had been infected young, who suffered stigma, who had a fear of infecting others, who was terrified he would pass on his condition to his son. And it was a way of examining prejudice, unwarranted prejudice towards a group of people. And also, examining why people might become embittered when they're treated that unfairly. There is not one single attempt to examine that, which is a key factor in the creation of the character" [*Warner Bros. Entertainment, Inc., and J. K. Rowling v. RDR Books*, 2008].

In less than two paragraphs of testimony, Rowling changed the way many people had perceived the character Remus Lupin and the werewolves of *Harry Potter*'s universe. Though Rowling stated that she had disclosed this previously, this moment was an official declaration by court testimony that that the Human Immunodeficiency Virus (HIV) had a space in the world of *Harry Potter*. However, since this complex metaphor was creatively used in a way that it did not make itself readily apparent to most readers, exploration of this metaphor and its transformative potential is needed.

A chronic medical condition that threatens 35 million people worldwide according to the World Health Organization (http://www.who.int/hiv/en/), HIV and Acquired Immune Deficiency Syndrome (AIDS) is a significant cultural and political issue to tackle in a children's book series—which potentially explains how the metaphor may have been missed by many readers. However, the overlay and comparison between the situation of people living with HIV[1] today and the situation of people infected with lycanthropy, or werewolves, in *Harry Potter* bear striking similarity. Such a similarity reveals a complex and well developed rhetorical strategy by the author to comment about a highly political medical epidemic which continues today. While the prevalence of lycanthropy is not discussed at length within the book series, readers only know that a community of werewolves exists at the margins of the wizarding world. The effects of a repressive and highly persistent stigma toward lycanthropy is made apparent through the character of Remus Lupin, Harry's Defense Against the Dark Arts teacher in *Harry Potter and the Prisoner of Azkaban* and mentor within the Order of the Phoenix from *Harry Potter and the Order of the Phoenix* onward. Similarities between the lives of werewolves and those living with HIV become highly visible once a reader uses this metaphor as a lens to examine the series itself.

Rowling's use of the metaphor of lycanthropy and its stigmas as a stand-in for HIV and its stigmas as social commentary within a book series written for children, but consumed by all ages and across all continents, renders this metaphor a powerful object for critical study and exploration. Though Westman (2002) and Stypczynski (2009) briefly discussed the relationship between HIV and the prejudice faced by Lupin, neither discussed the metaphoric comparison between the HIV and lycanthropy at length—Westman addressed the relationships between Thatcherism and the wizarding culture of Harry Potter and Stypczynski addressed Lupin's role as educator, not his power as an indexical symbol and metaphor for HIV. As such, this essay will fill that need by analyzing the "new metaphor" (Lakoff & Johnson, 1980) *Lycanthropy as HIV* using a methodology of metaphor critique and rhetorical criticism widely used for the examination of rhetorical metaphor within the field of Communication Studies. As a new metaphor (Lakoff & Johnson, 1980), *Lycanthropy as HIV* serves as a powerful intervention by Rowling into the sphere of moral allegory through her werewolf character Reumus Lupin; this metaphor creates powerful opportunities for educational and social intervention against pervasive HIV stigma that continues today. This essay will first discuss metaphor theory and how metaphoric connections and cognitive links are constructed and used within communication discourse. Second it will prove that the werewolf meets Osborn's (1967) criteria for an archetypal metaphor. Next, it will explain the process of how such rhetorical uses of metaphor are critiqued by communication scholars by providing specific examples of how metaphor has been used in communication critique specific to instances surrounding HIV and viruses/sicknesses. After providing this theoretical understanding and constructing a lens of metaphor critique specific to the werewolf archetypal metaphor, the essay will progress to perform an analysis of various moments primarily within the books *PoA* and *HBP*, the two books of the series with significant discussion of the context of werewolves within Rowling's world. Specifically, powerful connections and metaphoric entailments between the stigmas faced by Remus Lupin and the use of the "Wolfsbane Potion" as rhetorical devices for commentary about HIV will be illuminated along with other powerful moments of rhetorical transference that the *Lycanthropy as HIV* metaphor provides the reader.

Metaphor, the Werewolf and Metaphor Criticism

In their hallmark book *Metaphors We Live By*, Lakoff and Johnson (1980) address the theoretical position of metaphor within the human conceptual system of meaning making. They point out that metaphor exists beyond stylistic and poetic language usage—metaphors influence and structure our very cognitive systems, which are "metaphorical in nature" (p. 3) Of these systems of cognition, we (as members of a Western society) are mostly left unaware as we go about our lives communicating and acting through a system built on metaphoric blocks of language. As such, we "experience one kind of thing in terms of another" which fosters an understanding of the world around us that is both complex metaphorically and taken for granted cognitively (p. 5). Lakoff and Johnson begin their discussion with the metaphor *Argument is*

War to show how culturally the way of individuals winning or losing an argument or debate is framed cognitively and linguistically as warfare between nations—simply reduced in scale and perceived as ordinary, which leads the viewer/speaker to be hardly conscious of the differences. Metaphors such as *Argument is War* are both cognitive and conventional, which means it structures our daily life and processing of cultural knowledge; however metaphor functions on much more complex cognitive and experiential levels. Lakoff and Johnson note that "creative and imaginary" metaphors exist outside our conventional system and that these "new metaphors" allow us to reshape our processing of experience in order to produce new meaning, new experiences, and new cognitive layers for metaphorical understanding (p. 139).

The framing and understanding of reality based on the metaphorical linking of one thing in terms of another is called an entailment; entailments from more complex metaphors and may chain together to dramatically reshape our understanding of experiences and language. "New metaphors" have the ability to reshape the reality in which we perceive them as we also interact with their entailments and each other. Lakoff and Johnson use the metaphor *Love is a Collaborative Work of Art* to demonstrate a coherent structure to a wide range of experiences that produce similarities and produce new kinds of understandings—which in their example, *Love is a Collaborative Work of Art,* helps the individual understand that their frustrations in producing a work of art with another person is very similar to a romantic relationship and its challenges (p. 151). This new understanding is both partly culturally determined, meaning it is shaped by the cultures and systems in which we live our lives, and partly by our past experiences; it is the frustrating experience of a past collaborative art project that helps the metaphor user understand the challenge of a romantic relationship and negotiating its tensions (p. 143).

From a perspective of communication practice and enactment, we choose our words according to systems of metaphoric connection that are built into our lexicon of language use that shapes both the "what" and "how" of our communication systems (Steuter & Wills, 2008, p. 3). Steuter and Wills note that metaphors "operate through the interplay of languages denotative value, what it says clearly and obviously, and its connotative value, what it evocatively and often subjectively calls up, its overtones, allusions and associations" (p. 3).

Significantly, metaphors serve an influential function within communication that moves beyond the decorative function metaphors are often given in language use (Steuter & Wills, 2008). Since metaphors structure our understanding and cognitive systems, when we refer to one thing or idea in terms of another, we slowly begin to conflate them, a process called metaphoric transference; such transferences of properties can lead to either new and deeper understandings of our reality (as stated previously) or possibly the merging of dangerous ideas and ideologies into persuasive messages and appeals (Steuter & Wills, 2008). Thankfully, despite some critical entailments made within the writings of J. K. Rowling and her boy wizard, the former, and not the latter, is the case for *Lycanthropy is HIV*.

As a practice, metaphor criticism is the critical act of looking at the rhetorical implications of a specific metaphor, the way it may influence or persuade an audience's thoughts or actions (Burkholder & Henry, 2009). As a rhetorical function, metaphors have two specific parts: the *tenor*, or the focus of the metaphor, and the *vehicle*, or the framing of the rhetorical comparison (p. 98). When these two categories of experience—argument and war, love and art, Lycanthropy and HIV—are brought together, certain relevant characteristics of the vehicle "carry over" and define parts of the tenor, thus shaping the comparison of the two concepts. In Lakoff and Johnson's *Argument is War*, the vehicle "war" and its violent imagery carries over to the way we understand "argument" and creates a system of battle and antagonism around the exchange of ideas. However, it is also important that the reader/listener understand these two words and their conceptual link in order to grasp the "jump" from one concept to the next. Specifically, the metaphor may fall apart if certain characteristics of the vehicle do not carry over for the framing of the tenor.

Built upon the communal and collective understandings of a culture and its associations between words, or simple cognitive metaphors, the audience's cooperation—they must "get it"—is required for the metaphor to "work" and if the rhetor and audience come from different speech communities or cultures, the rhetorical force of the metaphor may fail (Burkholder & Henry, 2009). *Argument is War* succeeds in Lakoff and Johnson's example because in our current cultural understanding of argumentation, specifically political debate, the metaphor and imagery of warfare—two sides with differing opinions fighting, often explosively—"fits" what we understand and have experienced; however, someone from a culture based on consensus understanding or collective decision making, may not "get it" and for them this metaphor would be both confusing and shocking. Complex metaphoric relationships, according to Leff (cited in Burkholder & Henry, 2009), provide us with the possible means of "synthesizing our reactions to the ongoing flow of events in time" and "[localize] our attention" on specific rhetorical issues within political and social discourse. Such metaphors, which Lakoff and Johnson would call "new metaphors," can help us draw comparisons between complex political issues (the tenor) and more simplistic issues we understand either holistically or comprehensively (the vehicle) in order to render politics understandable (Burkholder & Henry, 2009, p. 100).

Lycanthropy as Archetypal Metaphor

In exploring and outlining the ways in which politics and "archetypal" metaphor use may vary "according to the rhythms such as crisis and calm or development and deterioration within a culture," Osborn (1967) lays out four categorizing features of archetypal metaphors and their use: these metaphors are exceedingly popular within rhetorical discourse, this popularity is immune to changes over time, they are grounded in prominent features of experience inescapable from human consciousness, and are contingent upon embodiment of basic human motivations. These four characteristics influence the "persuasive potency" of the metaphor (Osborn, p. 349). I question Osborn's claim that these conditions only pertain to archetypal metaphors of speeches, since he also claims that it is possible to study the "public address of different ages" to "determine patterns of visual imagery." As a book series, film franchise, and popular culture phenomenon, it is arguable that the world of Harry Potter and its various means of addressing consumers carries the important cultural patterns of understanding and experience that renders metaphors such as Rowling's persuasively potent.

Standing alone, Rowling's *Lycanthropy is HIV* metaphor does not meet Osborn's (1967) requirement for an archetypal metaphor, however Osborn notes that *disease-remedy* does function as an archetypal metaphor for its persuasive appeal toward accepting reassurance at a solution (the remedy) to a problem (a disease). It should be noted that the metaphor of this project is more complex than Osborn's vague example metaphor (that of a solar system, and seasonal cycles), though it fits the third and fourth component easily. The third requirement for inescapable human experience is easily achieved since both the tenor and vehicle are diseases and disease, and fear of it, is a prominent feature of human life. Additionally, the werewolf is described often as the manifestation of or release for sexuality and sexual desire (Bernhardt-House, 2008; DuCourday, 2006), making the requirement for embodiment of basic human emotions easy to meet as well—desire, specifically for sex, is a basic motivation for human existence. And yet, what of the other two requirements of Osborn's archetypal metaphors: popularity and resistance to time? By briefly tracing some of the evolutions and discussions about werewolves and lycanthropy it becomes apparent that the werewolf itself may function as an archetypal metaphor.

DuCourday (2006) traces the evolution of the female werewolf or wolf woman in popular fiction of the 20th century. Focusing specifically on the ways in which female sexuality was reframed through these literary texts in a positive light regarding characteristics traditionally regarded as feminine, DuCourday notes how modern feminism critiques the relationships that female authors have in regards to deconstructing the traditional (male) subject of the enlightenment. Bernhardt-House (2008) also states that popular culture contains countless iterations of werewolves in film, fiction, and other media; Calafell (2012) states that modern representations of werewolves in film and on television reveal a popularity that has not been seen since the 1980s. From this, it is easy to see that the werewolf is a popular metaphor within society and has been for generations. Bernhardt-House, Calafell, and DuCourday's commentary and critiques reveal that werewolves also function as a prominent metaphor for developing feminism's rehabilitation of sexuality for women—thus, the werewolf meets the first of Osborn's archetypal requirements for being a prominent and popular rhetorical metaphor. Bernhardt-House further reveals from a queer theory analysis of several ancient and medieval myths and legends surrounding werewolves in comparison with modern queer interpretations on the werewolf legend and story are in fact not as queer or transgressive as initially believed.

Since the modern popular culture discourse of werewolves reflects the medieval and ancient discourses of werewolves as hybrids (Bernhardt-House, 2008; Calafell, 2012; Ward, 2010) in nature and are always seeking of community but excluded from human society, the second requirement of Osborn's archetypal metaphor—immune to changes over time—is met as well. If the werewolf is an archetypal metaphor that allows for the exploration of human experience in order to produce deeper understanding and meaning, this strengthens Calafell's "[reflection] on the *archetype* [of the werewolf] to begin a conversation about the ways women of color in the academy are marked as monstrous Others" in order to continue the problems of racism, homophobia, and sexism that are still endemic to academic systems today (p. 114). Calafell's assertion that this metaphor archetypally applies to women of color in the academy as other strengthens the use of the metaphor in this analysis.

Scholars of *Harry Potter* have also said various threads of important conversation about the werewolves in Rowling's texts. Ward (2010) describes the horror of Rowling's secondary werewolf character—antagonist Fenrir Greyback. In contrast to this chapter's primary focus on Remus Lupin, Ward addresses the fact that Greyback is not entirely an unsympathetic character himself. Ward further notes that Greyback's "cannibalistic and predatory behavior," combined with his sexually predatory behavior—as his attacking of Remus Lupin as a child can be read as a childhood sexual assault—connects his actions to both classic and medieval narrative about werewolves (p. 104), which strengthens the validation for Osborn's (1967) requirement that metaphors remain unchanged over time. This connects to Westman's (2002) relationship of prejudice faced by Lupin as similar to the situation of people with HIV and AIDS during Margaret Thatcher's time as prime minister of Great Britain. Stypczynski (2009) and Anatol (2003) spend a great amount of energy discussing the various moments of prejudicial discourse espoused against Lupin, but primarily addresses them in relationship to racism and suggest that this connection could relate to HIV. Since this metaphor and connection has been discussed by other scholars of *Harry Potter*, but has not been critiqued for its benefits and drawbacks within the complex web of entailments that Rowling weaves regarding HIV, such a criticism must be performed. The means of this critique is described below.

Metaphor Criticism as Method: A Re-Examination

Burkholder and Henry describe metaphor criticism to begin with an exhaustive and close textual reading of the artifact in question (2009). Though they advise against the selection of a method of critique that focuses on theory before criticism, preferring the metaphor to develop out of the close reading itself as the most significant method available, for this analysis I reject this claim for its over-specific focus on acts of public address specific to speeches and simpler cognitive metaphors. Though also focused on speeches, Ivie (1987) noted that metaphors used by rhetors often serve as "motivating perspectives" which repeat throughout the text in question. Alternative texts filled with metaphor creation may have similar motivating perspectives. Rowling's attempt to create a sympathetic werewolf character in Remus Lupin, and the marginalized werewolf community at large, moves beyond allegory to a complex cognitive metaphor according, which according to Ivie (1987) has the power to reveal the "untapped potential as sources of invention" (p. 361). Additionally, Butterworth (2007) reveals in his analysis of the media and political discourses about the Iraqi soccer team for the 2004 Olympics that metaphors may exist outside of traditional public address situations, though influential people still are involved in making these metaphors circulate and the circulation has political ramifications.

The narrow view that metaphor criticism reveals impact on "policy decisions" made by influential individuals restricts the transformative potential of Rowling's metaphor and other new metaphors that may exist in popular culture texts that are not speeches, and yet such texts can help transform human experience and understanding of experience (Burkholder & Henry, 2009, p. 111).

Angeli (2012) addresses the relationship that metaphors used in electronic and wide-reaching media play in societies' understanding of dangerous medical pandemics, specifically flu outbreaks, the "war on drugs," and significantly the HIV epidemic and AIDS crisis. Angeli also notes that popular culture such as the radio, internet, television, and newspapers are essential in disseminating health messages and metaphors to billions of people, and citing Susan Sontag, she states that these metaphors play a strong role in shaping the public understanding of disease and illness. Sontag (1988) specifically notes that as the disease spread, it became a metaphor for anything highly contagious, pervasive, and not understood. Examples of these contagions taking on AIDS metaphors could include computer virus pandemics, or the Feline Leukemia Virus (FeLV) and the Feline Immunodeficiency Virus (FIV). Though the latter shares a similar classification and viral structure (though it is not transferable to humans), both often engender in cat owners imagery of their pets dying from AIDS like symptoms and pain. Gronnvoll and Landau (2010) discuss the powerful associations that viruses can play metaphorically in discourses of health. In their study of metaphoric connections between genes and disease as explained by lay people, a prominent metaphor of genes as disease—something one already has—was highly prominent, creating a challenge for health and science education in underserved populations. Brown (2009) explores the way in which metaphors of biomedicine and female pleasure permeate pharmaceutical culture. This permeation create the possibility of understanding female sexual dysfunction as both a problem and something that can be treated with medication, but also creates a rhetorical code that frames the biological woman as incompatible for pleasure when framed through a similar metaphor of "body-as-machine" used for erectile dysfunction in men. The problems raised by this metaphor and its entailments raises complex questions about who is qualified to help women answer their sexual concerns.

As it is inarguably clear from these examples, metaphor is a vastly more complex form of language use than initially proposed by Osborn (1967), and the conceptual systems that humans develop and shift using metaphors cannot be simplified to just political policy decisions; simply stated, metaphor criticism must move beyond the realm of speeches and into the mass mediated 21st century of texts and popular culture. As stated above, the werewolf as an archetypal metaphor allows for the exploration of various pieces of the human experience, and it is important to note that most of these representations exist outside of public policy speeches and are more apparent in our films, television shows, books, and video games. From this discussion, it is clear that metaphor allows readers to experience the unfamiliar through the familiar (Brown, 2009), and that it can play an immeasurably effective role when discussing issues related to healthcare, medicine, prejudice, and the relationships of institutional power that marginalize. Through metaphor criticism, this essay will explore how the familiar fiction of the werewolf-other in *Harry Potter* allows us to discover and explain the prominently unfamiliar (and yet familiar for many) reality that is HIV.

As rhetorical critic whose goal is to advance the knowledge of the

Humanities in the study of rhetoric, specifically as both a method of criticism of popular culture texts and means of fighting pervasive stigmas, specifically stigma surrounding HIV—I believe that Rowling's own claim that Remus Lupin was an HIV metaphor in her testimony (*Warner Bros. Entertainment, Inc., and J. K. Rowling v. RDR Books*, 2008) serves as evidence that such an advanced "new" metaphor—*Lycanthropy is HIV*—exists within her books. The existence of this metaphor and its entailments reveals specific information about the world of *Harry Potter* and how it may be used to educate and facilitate conversations about HIV with young adults that do not have experience with HIV, its epidemic, or who struggle to cast off stigmatizing opinions about people living with HIV. In the following section of analysis, I will explore the complex entanglement of rhetorical entailments, or the parts of reality highlighted by the metaphor which we perceive as true and the "perceptions and inferences" that arise from it (Lakoff & Johnson, 1980, p. 158) that connect the vehicle *Lycanthropy* to our tenor *HIV*.

A Perspective of Metaphoric Entailments: The Disease, the Stigma and the Potion

Within Rowling's book series, *PoA* and *HBP* discuss the nature of Lycanthropy more than any other media sources in her canon. As such, these two texts will be explored primarily in order to reveal and analyze the entailments of *Lycanthropy is HIV*. Specifically, from this reading of the texts there are three very specific areas of entailments that deserve careful attention. These entailments, or the ways in which similarities between the tenor and the vehicle draw attention to certain characteristics and obscure others, can be viewed as a matter of "perspective" for identification and persuasion according to Kenneth Burke (1945). Burke notes that these similarities are a "juncture on two levels" (p. 424) that allows the viewer to see one characteristic in the terms of another characteristic and that both perspectives of similarity carry over to the other. While most forms of metaphor analysis describe entailments as the ways language or word use is intentionally or instrumentally used to draw two distinct categories of things together in terms of the other, this analysis instead draws from Burke and describes entailments as the language use as argument of similarities, or as Burke calls it, the perspective that Rowling subtly weaves into the text of her canon to create the new metaphor *Lycanthropy is HIV*.

The three primary perspective entailments, or secondary metaphors (Burkholder & Henry, 2009), can be conceived of as threads that build the perspective of similarities in *PoA* and *HBP* are: *the disease of lycanthropy is the disease HIV*, further called the "disease" entailment, which focuses on specific characteristics of the two conditions; *lycanthropy stigma is HIV stigma*, or the "stigma" entailment, which addresses the ways in which prejudices faced by werewolves mirrors may prejudices faced by people living with HIV; and *the potion for lycanthropy is HAART for HIV*, or the "potion" entailment, which connects the ways in which medical advancements for treating HIV and preventing its spread are similar to the Wolfsbane Potion's impact on the werewolf community within *Harry Potter*.

These perspectives are built specifically around the writing of two specific characters, Remus Lupin and Fenrir Greyback, one incidental victim of a werewolf bite (in *OotP*) and the larger werewolf community that sides with Voldemort during the second wizarding war and the Battle of Hogwarts (Rowling, 2007). The primary character of this analysis is Remus Lupin, Harry's defense against the dark arts teacher for *PoA* and mentor figure until his death at the Battle for Hogwarts in *DH*. Readers are first introduced to Remus Lupin on the Hogwarts Express in *PoA*. Lupin is described as being particularly shabby in appearance, his possessions revealing a high degree of wear and mend, and that even "a good hex might finish him off" (Rowling, 1999). Throughout *PoA*, the Gryffindor students of Harry's year become attached to Lupin, who they feel is a much better instructor than both of their previous teachers. Lupin is shown to be empathetic and supportive of his students, during their confrontation of their fears vis-à-vis a boggart. The revealing of his status as a werewolf, however, ends his term as a professor at Hogwarts, as he feels he may threaten the wellbeing of the students and that the parents wouldn't want a perceived dangerous person teaching their children (Rowling, 1999). As the reader follows Harry's point of view in the narrative provided by Rowling, the reader, too, becomes attached to Lupin—a kind, intelligent, and frail man with a past connected to Harry's own who wants only to teach despite the prejudice toward his condition as a werewolf. However, Remus Lupin stands in stark contrast to the second werewolf character in the *Harry Potter* franchise: Fenrir Greyback.

Fenrir Greyback has already been given a thorough reading by Ward (2010), who reveals that much like Lupin's search to be included within mainstream society, Greyback wants to find and make a place where he belongs—though Greyback's place is among the lower-levels of the Death Eaters and a community of werewolves that he has either infected or has drawn to his aggressive and dangerous philosophy for dominance. It is important to note that the connection between Greyback and Lupin is established within *HBP*, as Lupin states that it was Greyback who bit him (Rowling, 2005). Lupin also informs Harry that Greyback positions himself near potential victims in order to spread his condition to as many people as possible (Rowling)—a tactic that Barnhardt-House (2008) notes is comparable to the malign belief that members of the queer community may intentionally and indiscriminately spread STIs including HIV. This greatly contrasts to Lupin, who was assured a monthly brewing of the Wolfsbane potion, brewed by Potions master Snape, as part of his tenure as Defense Against the Dark Arts professor at Hogwarts rendering him no risk to the students. Further contrast to Greyback can be found in *DH* when Lupin declares his anguish at potentially passing his condition along to his unborn child, something he would never want to do. Readers first hear of Greyback in *HBP* when Malfoy uses his name to threaten the proprietor of Borgin and Burkes into acquiescence, and then readers meet him at the top of the Astronomy tower prior to the Battle of the Astronomy Tower in *HBP*. Much like our meeting of Lupin, Greyback is ragged, but his appearance is further marked as unclean as his hair is long and unkempt, his nails sharp like talons, and he smells of earth and blood.

Other werewolves, potential or actual, are only hinted at in Rowling's books. In *OotP* we see a victim of a werewolf attack in St. Mungo's Hospital for Magical Maladies and Injuries who looks "pale" and in a state of shock; Lupin quietly goes to calm him and reassure him—though it is unknown if the individual becomes a werewolf in Greyback's army (Rowling, 2003). In *HBP* a potential werewolf is introduced by name only. Marcus Belby, the nephew of Damocles, the creator of the Wolfsbane potion (detailed below), is introduced at the first meeting of Horace Slughorn's revived Slug Club. However, Belby states that his father and his uncle do not get along very well, and that the family is not very close with him; which is rendered peculiar by Slughorn's commentary that the discovery of the potion could not have come without hard work and a great deal of sacrifice (Rowling, 2005). Based upon the extreme prejudice that werewolves receive, and despite Damocles receiving an Order of Merlin award for creating the means by which werewolves could integrate themselves into wizarding society, it is possible to read this shunning as the reveal, the outing, that Damocles himself was a werewolf. At the least, this comment by Belby opens the possibility that Damocles had personal or romantic connections with werewolves and the stigma of the disease carried over to him and then his family.

The werewolf community is only made visibly apparent during the Battle for Hogwarts, as they side with Voldemort in the siege of the castle. However, their existence cannot be one of comfort or stability, as during the events of *HBP*, Remus Lupin is sent to live among them in order to persuade them not to join Voldemort's cause. However, they reject Dumbledore's offer for the sake of a new world that might instead let them live openly, rather than reliant upon a difficult to brew potion. This is a clear reference to "why people might become embittered when they're treated that unfairly" that is mentioned in *Warner Bros. Entertainment, Inc,. and J. K. Rowling v. RDR Books* (2008).

After describing the characters that are central to this metaphor's construction, it is important to discuss the details of the similarities between both Lycanthropy and HIV, otherwise known as "the disease" entailment. As mentioned above, the power of a metaphor comes from the ways in which the tenor is influenced by the entailments of the vehicle which carry back over onto the tenor (Burkholder & Henry, 2009). These entailments become stronger when there are both similarities and dissimilarities to the vehicle and the tenor. Both HIV and Lycanthropy are described as a virus or disease that affects people and wizards, respectively. In the Pottermore website (Rowling, n.d., "Werewolves"), Rowling notes that in order for a person—usually a wizard because muggles do not normally survive being bitten—to become a werewolf, the werewolf's saliva must mix with the blood of the bitten, on the night of the full moon when the werewolf is transformed. This occurrence cements the infection and foretells future transformation should the victim survive. This is similar to the transmission of HIV, as bodily fluids (semen, blood, breast milk, or vaginal fluids) must come into contact with a person's mucus membranes, as described by the Centers for Disease Control and Prevention (http://www.cdc.gov/hiv/basic/). This infection occurs most often in intimate settings, such as sexual intercourse, or the sharing of needles for drug use. Though the bite of werewolf is an attack, which is dissimilar, it is still an intimate action and requires a proximal connection to a werewolf that has been transformed.

A specific dissimilarity is seen in the "Werewolves" note from Pottermore that reveals that there has never been a case where the offspring of a werewolf is also a werewolf. This is a marked difference from HIV, which can be spread from mother to child during pregnancy, though advances in medication and treatment have reduced this possibility dramatically (Mark et al., 2012). A third dissimilarity is the potential and opportunities for infection by both diseases. A werewolf is only infectious and a danger to others on the night of the full moon and when he or she is transformed—the danger of which may be negated due to the Wolfsbane potion. When transformed, a werewolf will do just about anything to bite or scratch or infect another living being—which passes on the virus (Rowling, 1999; Rowling, 2005). However, a person living with HIV or AIDS does not have the luxury of only being infectious and dangerous on the night of a full moon; he or she carries the active virus with them at all times. However, the trade-off is that a person living with HIV or AIDS who is aware of their infection can take steps to prevent the infection from spreading to relational partners—a marked difference from the mindless monster the werewolf becomes on the full moon.

These constructed similarities show in many ways both how the metaphor of HIV, the vehicle, allows the reader to understand the tenor, Lycanthropy, in a new light. There is however a final similarity between the two diseases: the commentary on humanity. On Pottermore, Rowling states that in human form, a werewolf is no different or kind or malevolent than any other witch or wizard within the magical community (Rowling, n.d., "Werewolves"). This is perhaps the most powerful similarity, as people living with HIV are also human, and have hopes, dreams, desires, and families; they are also as potentially questionable of character as people not infected with HIV. Just as werewolves in Harry Potter could be just as good or murderous as non-werewolves Hermione Granger or Bellatrix Lestrange, so too are people living with HIV in the spectrum of human (or wizarding) morality. This again fits into Rowling's testimony (*Warner Bros. Entertainment, Inc., and J. K. Rowling v. RDR Books*, 2008) where she states that the situation of the werewolf community was important to the context second wizarding war and what lead up to it; the prejudice of wizarding society and not an inherent flaw of moral character, is what drove them into Voldemort's army. It is important to now expound upon this prejudice, which correlates with stigma toward HIV, and how this part of Rowling's metaphor is constructed.

There are three social institutions where the metaphoric entailments for the "stigma" of the *Lycanthropy as HIV* metaphor are made apparent to the reader: education, employment, and the family. Within *PoA*, all of these play into the double-bind of Lupin's security in access to the Wolfsbane potion and the intimidation by Snape while at Hogwarts as a teacher. This reveals many of the stigma entailments for Lycanthropy that carry over related to stigma of HIV and homophobia are encountered in educational contexts. Lupin also states in *PoA*, that the Whomping Willow was planted when he started his first year at Hogwarts in order to protect the other students from him on the night of the full moon. Additionally, Lupin kept his condition secret from his friends at school because he feared their reprisal and animosity would threaten the opportunity for education provided by Dumbledore. Lupin's access to the spaces of education is made complex by his being a werewolf, and that complication is mirrored by many reactions to and the treatment of people with HIV or AIDS during the early years of the epidemic. Pryor, Reeder and Landau (1999) address this as a fear if social contamination by secondary association, and that such secondary associations often reveal visceral and complex network of subconscious connections based in stigma. During the initial meeting of Lupin, the markers of economic disadvantage are clear in his apparel, his possessions, and his placement on the student train. Though great strides have been made in treatment of HIV, many people living with the chronic condition experience economic hardship (Ibrahim, Anderson, Bukutu & Elford, 2008). Lupin states that he was very grateful for Dumbledore to offer him the job as a teacher, and implies that chances for employment for werewolves is hard to come by, which mirrors the challenges may people living with HIV faced prior to the Americans with Disabilities Act expanding to protect them from discrimination in service or employment of major life activities (*Bragdon v. Abbot*, 1998).

Further, in both *HBP* and *DH*, we see Lupin's lover and later wife Nymphadora Tonks at the Burrow with Molly Weasley, the mother figure of the entire series. It is made clear that Molly is inviting her over regularly as a potential romantic foil for Fleur Delacour. Additionally, Tonks has lost her ability to change her appearance at will, which is said to be from depression over the loss of her cousin Sirius Black in the Battle at the Department of Mysteries at the end of *OotP*. However, it is later revealed that it is instead her feelings for Remus that are causing her stress, and that after the death of Dumbledore, she and Lupin married in private away from the magical community, due to the prejudice toward werewolves marrying non-werewolves. This mirrors the way in which stigma surrounding HIV carries over to people not infected with HIV when they are dating someone living with HIV; the quick assumption and "secondary association" is that the other person must also "be positive" or that the disease can still spread through them (Pryor, Reeder & Landau, 1999). In *DH*, Lupin further mentions his anxieties around having a child with Tonks; though Rowling states on Pottermore that this anxiety was unfounded (Rowling, n.d., "Werewolves"). Lupin claims that his child also deserves a father that he could be proud of, and one that does not pose a danger to him. These challenges expressed by Lupin and visible in *HPB* with Tonks reveal the means by which challenges in familial relationships, specifically around children and childbirth, that carry over onto Lycanthropy from the experiences of people living with HIV, specifically before medication was developed to prevent the spread of the disease from mother to child—a time period that coincides with the *Harry Potter* novels chronologically.

The final entailment thread revolves around the treatment for werewolves first mentioned in *PoA* and discussed further in *HBP*, the Wolfsbane Potion. Distilled from aconite and developed by the wizard Damocles in the 1970s, this potion dramatically changed the possibilities available for werewolves in wizarding society (Rowling, n.d., "Werewolves"). The potion, much like medication for HIV, allows for the individual to "pass" for a normal wizard in wizarding society, and prevents them from being a risk to others on the night of the full moon (Schlossberg, 2001). Such a pass, however, is always something that is difficult to maintain and may be fleeting if the performance, in this case, the access to the potion, is not maintained. In *HBP*, Slughorn notes that it is very difficult to brew, and in *PoA* Lupin notes that it must be consumed for a few evenings, each night, before a full moon in order to stave off the horrific parts of the transformation. Lupin notes that when he takes the potion correctly, he would simply transform into a wolf and retain his human consciousness, and then curl up in his office to sleep (Rowling, 1999). This is similar to the way in which Highly Active Antiretroviral Therapy, or HAART, controls the viral load or viral reservoir of HIV in a person's blood—

making them both dramatically less likely to infect others with a bodily fluid exchange and staves off damage to the immune system that leads to AIDS[2] (Rodger et al., 2014).

Additionally, in *HBP*, while Harry is skeptical of Snape's intentions with Malfoy, Lupin reminds Harry that Snape dutifully brewed the potion for Lupin's use every month and that Snape kept Lupin healthy; Lupin states he would always be grateful for that service. Here we see another reference to the treatment for Lycanthropy containing a similarity which "carries over" from HAART. Successful treatment for an HIV infection uses a complex battery of drugs, often called a cocktail, to suppress the viral infection to an "undetectable" level (Rodger et al., 2014). As stated previously, not only does lower the possibility for potential infections to single-digit percentiles (Rodger et al.), it essentially reduces the immune system's decline and the progression to AIDS to a glacial crawl. This facilitates a form of the ability of a person living with HIV to perform in society with almost no barriers or restrictions—essentially he or she may "pass" for a healthy individual (Schlossberg, 2001).

In this way, Snape's providing of the Wolfsbane potion to Lupin to keep him healthy, mirrors an insurer or government health agency providing a person living with HIV the means to not only stave off a painful and debilitating death, but to remain productive and healthy in life. However, Lupin's access to the Wolfsbane potion is not a normal situation for most werewolves. The difficult-to-brew potion does not appear to be accessible to many of the werewolves in the magical community, as the prejudice surrounding them apparently had not changed in the nearly twenty years since the potion's invention. This challenge of access to the Wolfsbane potion by the werewolf community in *Harry Potter* reflects a similar problem faced by people living with HIV in the United States, for challenges exist(Ed) for people diagnosed with HIV and finding access to care and lifesaving medication. Through the passage of the Affordable Care Act, and before it the Ryan White CARE Act, this situation has changed dramatically, though challenges navigating bureaucracy may prevent people seeking or accessing care in a timely manner—much like finding a potions master to brew the Wolfsbane potion.

Metaphoric Implications of Lycanthropy as HIV

Having explored the threads of entailments for disease, stigma, and treatment, it is now important to assess the transformative potential this metaphor creates for readers and those who see HIV in *Harry Potter* as a means to promote change. The metaphor *Lycanthropy is HIV* has multiple consequences, both productive and problematic, in its deployment and execution within the *Harry Potter* franchise. Primarily, it is important to note that Rowling's metaphor is very well crafted, and prior to her interview and *Warner Bros. Entertainment, Inc., and J. K. Rowling v. RDR Books* (2008) few readers picked up on the metaphoric connection between werewolves and people living with HIV, though some critics and scholars had some idea of the connection. This leads to the metaphor providing a very unique reading of the book series, and shows a deeper, academic reading of Rowling's wizarding world can yield rewarding insights. Second, being a highly political topic, discussing HIV in a children's book series about magic and the defeat of evil is no small task. However, Rowling's sympathetic portrayal of Remus Lupin succeeds in crafting this metaphor in a way that addresses a complex political issues in children's literature, and addresses it quite well. The previously shown attention to detail in crafting these similarities of perspective provides a strong and positive representation of a character (Lupin) who struggles against stigma and oppression and has very human desires, goals, and failures. When viewed through the HIV metaphor, Lupin becomes a heroic representation of what someone living with HIV could be, and this creates a possibility for a sympathetic and emotional connection to a disease that is often considered unclean and undesirable by those who are not familiar with its complexities. This will be expounded upon further below.

However, it is important to note the ways in which Rowling's metaphor does limit the possibilities for a transformative reading of HIV in her series. While Rowling's depictions of the prejudice that Remus, Greyback, and the werewolf community at large faced seem appropriate and not hyperbolic when compared to experiences of people living with HIV, it still reproduced an environment of pervasive stigma that paradoxically continues despite advancements in medicine (or potioncraft), and that has been shown to remove individuals from the workforce or society at large (Ibrahim, Anderson, Bukutu & Elford, 2008). If readers follow Rowling's statement in *Warner Bros. Entertainment, Inc., and J. K. Rowling v. RDR Books* (2008), she constructed the werewolves as a way of showing how systems of oppression and prejudice pressures push people and groups into undesirable actions—specifically the werewolves joining Voldemort in *DH*. However, in attempting to construct this argument, she also associates the werewolves, which stand in for people living with HIV, as associates of the central evil of the entire series. The associated aura of evil-by-proxy of joining Voldemort's army is not a pleasant association for this critic.

Most importantly, the metaphor's greatest challenge is Rowling's killing of Remus and Tonks—which she claims is a trade-off for sparing Arthur Weasley in *OotP*—during the battle of Hogwarts, with Remus receiving a posthumous awarding of the Order of Merlin First Class (Brown, 2007;

Rowling, n.d., "Remus Lupin"). Rowling claims on Pottermore that the awarding of the Order of Merlin, First Class to Remus resulted in reducing the pervasive stigma surrounding werewolves. Despite her claim that she wanted to kill the parents of her characters, which she showed by killing the mother of Hufflepuff Hannah Abbot, it is important to address that Rowling spared another parent—Arthur Weasley, father of Ron Weasley and a comic relief character. By saving Arthur from Nagini's deadly bite in *OotP* as a trade for the deaths of Tonks and Lupin in *DH*, Rowling potentially activates the very stigma she contests in order to protect the family man. While Rowling's decision leaves Teddy Lupin, Remus and Nymphadora's child, in a similar situation to Harry after the first wizarding war reveals the horrors that war can bring, this critic wonders what might have happened if Rowling had instead let Reumus and Tonks survive despite her claim that "he had to die" (Jensen, 2011). Would Remus Lupin have made a better example of what a werewolf could be in the *Harry Potter* universe as a living, celebrated example and father to his child? If we switch the vehicle and tenor of Rowling's metaphor, does this mean the only people with HIV who are worth of praise are those who are dead? Further, Rowling's portrayal of Greyback as the deranged and devious individual who wishes to infect as many people as possible strays into the realm of dangerous stereotypes about members of the gay male community. Coupled with a possible interpretation of Lupin's childhood bite as surviving sexual assault, which is supported by Ward's (2010) assertion that Greyback is a sexual predator, the use of stereotypes to build her two central werewolf characters reveals further limits of the metaphors potential.

Implications: Bringing HIV into Educational Settings through Metaphor in Literature

These considerations, when considered with Rowling's conclusion of the series, are important for the potential transformative power of the *Lycanthropy is HIV* metaphor and its use in dispelling stigma through readership. Despite the serious concerns stated above that problematic issues of stigma are recreated subtly in the conclusion of the series, the benefit of having a strong, heroic character in Remus Lupin serves a critical purpose. If read as a person living with HIV, Remus Lupin serves as a powerful point of entry for other people living with HIV to read themselves into the text of *Harry Potter*. Additionally, with HIV education a taboo and controversial subject in schools, the possibility of this metaphor to shape conversations is incomparable to the deficits of the metaphor mentioned prior. It is because of this reason, and that *Harry Potter* as a franchise circulates widely, I argue that the metaphor *Lycanthropy is HIV* can bring discourse about HIV into spaces and to reach individuals—specifically younger children and adults—it could not enter before.

Vezzali et al. (2014) noted in their study of school children reading *Harry Potter* that many children "may have learnt to take the perspective of discriminated group members" and then applied this identification with real-world targets of prejudice (p. 12). In a powerful affirmation of the role fantasy can play in circumventing defensiveness and political correctness, the authors note that most fantasy novels do not explicitly refer to any real-world group or category of people that are oppressed. By going about discussing these oppressed groups in terms of general issues of prejudice, students who may be reactionary to specific identities of political issue may rethink their perspectives about prejudicial behaviors specifically because those groups are not mentioned by name. This feeds the argument of this chapter, as it shows how using Burke's (1945) ability to see metaphoric "perspectives" that allow characteristics to carry over can promote critical thinking that does not fall into defensive reactions.

Strimel (2004) notes this potential in her reading of Rubeus Hagrid and the prejudice that the Malfoys show him. Strimel also goes as far as to show that even as Hagrid faced with prejudice for being part giant, he has the strength of character to determine that one cannot connect a creature's (or person's) value with their actions—which is shown by Hagrid's fondness for dangerous creatures such as Norbert(a) the baby dragon and Fluffy the three-headed dog in *SS*, the acromantula Aragog in *CoS* and *HBP*, the noble hippogriff Buckbeak in *PoA*, and that Hagrid probably maintains the Thestral herd in *OotP*. The purpose of Hagrid and his pets, Strimel argues, is for Rowling to show readers that individuals should be separated from stereotypes about their racial identity. The perspective about Hagrid's love for his pets carries over to the reader's love for Hagrid and the rethinking of him as both large and dangerous, rather than large and caring. In a reverse of Pryor, Reeder, and Landau (1999) who focused on stigma around HIV, this affection can serve as a secondary association and carries over to the individual rethinking their assumptions about other identities often conflated with danger or disease, such as people living with HIV, and reshape perspectives surrounding their treatment by society.

This essay has provided a unique and informative discussion about how Rowling's metaphor, *Lycanthropy is HIV*, creates a powerful opportunity for conversation and education about the current context of HIV in 2014. As Vezzali et al. (2014) has described, individuals—specifically younger adults and children—who identify with the protagonists of the *Harry Potter* series are more likely to be tolerant of diverse and different peoples. I have argued in this essay that Rowling's metaphor creates the potential for readers to creatively explore and confront their own stigmas and reshape their rhetorical perspectives about HIV through the archetypal metaphor of the werewolf. This argument also provides a point of entry for critical conversations about HIV to happen in a way that often circumvents the defensiveness and resistance that often accompanies HIV discussions and other political topics since the channel uses fantasy or science fiction, as Vezzali et al. (2014) made clear. This analysis of *Harry Potter*'s werewolves as constructed by J.K. Rowling reinforces the potential for fantasy and fiction to reshape the way we view the world (Strimel, 2004).

Noctor (2006) notes the inspirational power of using this creative medium for addressing group processes and discussions. In his review of the potential for *Harry Potter* to be used in a clinical psychology setting he reminds us that "as we think we have escaped from the world, [the books] help us to find the power to live in it" and find courage or meaning (p. 588). Wallace and Pugh (2007) further support the use of Harry Potter for teaching critical thinking and engagement with complex topics such as class, gender, sexual orientation and race; they note that fans expend great amounts of energy in order to create fan content, and this content shows that there is a desire to apply characteristics of close reading and critical thinking to this popular text.

Significantly, since most young adults in this second decade of the 21st century were born after both the darkest days of HIV's scourge in the 1980s and 1990s and the advent of Highly Active Antiretroviral Therapies (HAART), this metaphoric intervention creates a powerful and transformative opportunity. J. K. Rowling has given HIV prevention professionals, young adult educators, and scholars of communication a powerful tool for having important conversations about the current state of HIV. By providing an avenue to bring HIV into discussions within literature courses, not only can stigma and prejudice against people living with HIV be contested, students exposed to this metaphor and line of argument will potentially leave with a deeper understanding of power of fantasy literature, for any age range, to reshape society and fight prejudice. Though her metaphor is not perfect, and few metaphors "carry over" the entailments of the vehicle and tenor perfectly (Burkholder & Henry, 2009), Rowling has changed the way scholars and fans of *Harry Potter* should forever view Remus Lupin, his love for Nymphadora Tonks, and the plight of victims of prejudice across the globe.

Additionally, this chapter's analysis of the *Lycanthropy is HIV* metaphor has provided scholars of Communication Studies and scholars who study metaphor the impetus to move metaphor criticism into more complex analysis of the popular texts of our time and to show that such examples of heroic characters do, as Black (2003) tells us, help young adults make and find meaning in the world. With this knowledge, though the mischief is not yet managed, it is now possible for readers of *Harry Potter* to fight the prejudices in our world, against HIV stigma or the prejudices against peoples of difference, just as Rowling's trio fought against Voldemort.

Notes

1. In order to avoid the culturally divisive and medically technical terminology in the binary HIV positive/HIV negative when discussing serostatus (a person's HIV status) for this essay, I employ person-centered language in order to focus the attention on the people who live with the chronic manageable condition of HIV, rather than the virus itself—a rhetorical and linguistic move away from technical discourses centered in fear of disease and toward discourses of acceptance, change, and love for people. As such, I will use the terms "people living with HIV" and "people without HIV," respectively.

2. Generally speaking, AIDS is the final stage of the immune system's compromise as a result of failed treatment to manage the HIV virus. With modern medical treatment, reducing the viral load to an undetectable level in a person's bloodstream, AIDS may be staved off almost indefinitely. As long the person remains in treatment and the treatment does not fail, the person living with HIV may have a normal lifespan. See the CDC and WHO sources in the references list for more information.

References

Anatol, G. L. (2003). The fallen empire: Exploring ethnic otherness in the world of Harry Potter. In L. G. Anatol (Ed.), *Reading Harry Potter: Critical Essays* (pp. 163–178). Westport, CT: Praeger.

Angeli, E.L. (2012). Metaphors in the rhetoric of pandemic flu: Electronic media coverage of h1n1 and swine flu. *Journal of Technical Writing and Communication 42*(3), 203–222. Doi: 10.2190/TW.42.3.b.

Bernhardt-House, P. (2008). The werewolf as queer, the queer as werewolf, and queer werewolves. In N. Giffney and M. J. Hird (Eds.), *Queering the non/human* (pp. 159–181). Hampshire: Burlington.

Black, S. (2003). The magic of harry potter: symbols and heroes of fantasy. *Children's Literature in Education 34*(3), 237–247.

Bragdon v. Abbott, 524 U.S. 624 (1998).

Brown, J. (July, 7, 2007). Rowling: I wanted to kill parents. *Today*. Retrieved from http://www.today.com/.

Brown, M. (2009). Woman as mysterious machine: metaphor, rhetoric, and female sexual dysfunction. *At the Interface/Probing the Boundaries, 55*, 125–134.

Burke, K. (1945). *A grammer of motives*. New York: Prentice-Hall.

Burkholder, T. R., & Henry, D. (2009) Criticism of metaphor. In J.A. Kuypers (Ed.), *Rhetorical criticism: Perspectives in action* (pp. 97–115). Lanham, MD: Lexington Books.

Butterworth, M. L. (2007). The politics of the pitch: Claiming and conquesting democracy through the iraqui national soccer team. Reprinted in C. R. Burgchardt (Ed.), *Readings in Rhetorical Criticism* (4th edition, 2010) (pp. 377–394). State College, PA: Strata.

Calafell, B.M. (2012). Monstrous femininity: Constructions of women of color in the academy. *Journal of Communication Inquiry 36*(2), 111–130. Doi: 10.1177/0196859912443382.

Centers for Disease Control and Prevention. (2015). HIV/AIDS. Retrieved from http://www.cdc.gov/hiv/.

DuCourday, C.B. (2006). *The curse of the werewolf: Fantasy, horror, and the beast within.* London: I.B. Tauris.

Gronnvoll, M., &. Landau, J. (2010). From viruses to Russian roulette to dance: A rhetorical critique and creation of genetic metaphors. *Rhetoric Society Quarterly 40*(1), 46–70. Doi: 10.1080/02773940903413415.

Ibrahim, F., Anderson, J., Bukutu, C., & Elford, J. (2008). Social and economic hardship among people living with hiv in London. *HIV Medicine 9*, 616–624. Doi: 10.1111/j.1468-1293.2008.00605.

Ivie, R. L. (1987). Metaphor and the rhetorical invention of cold war "idealists." Reprinted in C. R. Burgchardt (Ed.), *Readings in Rhetorical Criticism* (4th edition, 2010) (pp. 359–357). State College, PA: Strata.

Jensen, J. (November 1, 2011). Harry Potter: J.K. Rowling on why Hagrid was spared, and what sealed lupin's fate. *Entertainment Weekly*. Retrieved from http://www.ew.com/.

Lakoff, G., & Johnson, H. (1980) *Metaphors we live by*. Chicago: University of Chicago Press.

Mark, S., Murphy, K. E., Read, S., Bitnun, A., & Yudin, M.H. (2012). HIV mother-to-child transmission, mode of delivery and duration of rupture of membranes: Experience in the current era. *Infectious Diseases in Obstetrics and Gynecology 2012*, 1–5. Doi: 10.1155/2012/267969.

Noctor, C. (2006). Putting harry potter on the couch. *Clinical Child Psychology and Psychiatry 11*(4), 579–589. Doi: 10.1177/1359104506067879.

Osborn, M. (1967). Archetypal metaphor in rhetoric: The light-dark family. Reprinted in C. R. Burgchardt (Ed.), *Readings in Rhetorical Criticism* (4th edition, 2010) (pp. 348–359). State College, PA: Strata.

Pryor, J. B., Reeder, G. D., & Landau, S. (1999) A social-psychological analysis of HIV stigma: a two factor theory. *American Behavioral Scientist, 42*(7), 1193–1211.

Rodger, A., Brunn, T., Cambiano, V., Vernazza, P., Estrada, V., & Lunzen, J. (2014). HIV transmission risk through condomless sex if hiv+ partner on suppressive art: PARTNER study. In *Conference on Retroviruses and Opportunistic Infections* (pp. 3–6).

Rowling, J. K. (n.d.) Remus lupin: New from J.K. Rowling. Retrieved from Pottermore: A unique online experience from J.K. Rowling, http://www.pottermore.com/en-us/book3/chapter22/moment1/remus-lupin.

Rowling, J. K. (n.d.) Werewolves: New from J.K. Rowling. Retrieved from Pottermore: A unique online experience from J.K. Rowling, http://www.pottermore.com/en-us/book3/chapter20/moment1/werewolf.

Rowling, J.K. (1998). *Harry potter and the sorcerer's stone*. New York: Scholastic Press.

Rowling. J.K. (1999a). *Harry potter and the chamber of secrets*. New York: Scholastic Press.

Rowling, J.K. (1999b). *Harry potter and the prisoner of Azkaban*. New York: Scholastic Press.

Rowling, J.K. (2003). *Harry potter and the Order of the Phoenix*. New York: Scholastic Press.

Rowling, J.K. (2005). *Harry potter and the half-blood prince*. New York: Scholastic Press.

Rowling, J.K. (2007). *Harry potter and the deathly hallows*. New York: Scholastic Press.

Schlossberg, L. (2001). Introduction. In M. C. Sánches and L. Schlossberg (Eds.), *Passing: Identity and interpretation in sexuality, race, and religion* (pp. 1–12). New York: New York University Press.

Sontag, S. (1988). *AIDS and its metaphors*. New York: Farrar, Straus, and Giroux.
Steuter, E. & Wills, D. (2008). *At war with metaphor*. Lanham, MD: Lexington Books.
Strimel, C.B. (2004): The politics of terror: Rereading Harry Potter. *Children's Literature in Education, 35*(1), 35–52.
Stypczinski, Brent. (2009). Wolf in professor's clothing: J. K. Rowling's werewolf as educator. *Journal of the Fantastic in the Arts, 20*(1), 57–69.
United States Department of Health and Human Services. (n.d.) Who was Ryan White? Retrieved from http://hab.hrsa.gov/abouthab/ryanwhite.html.
United States Department of Health and Human Services. (2014). The affordable care act and hiv/aids. Retrieved from https://www.aids.gov/federal-resources/policies/health-care-reform/.
Vezzali, L., Stathi, S., Giovannini, D., Capozza, D. Trifiletti, E. (2014). The greatest magic of Harry Potter: Reducing prejudice. *Journal of Applied Psychology*. Doi: 10.1111/jasp.12279.
Wallace, D. L., & Pugh, T. (2007). Playing with critical theory in J.K. Rowling's Harry Potter series. *English Journal, 96*(3), 97–100.
Ward, R. (2008). J.K. Rowling's Fenrir greyback: Identity, society, and the werewolf. In S. K. Goetz (Ed.), *Terminus: Collected papers on Harry Potter*. Sedalia, CO: Narrate Conferences.
Warner Bros. Entertainment, Inc., and J. K. Rowling v. RDR Books, 575 F.Supp.2d 513 (SDNY 2008).
Westman, K. E. (2002). Specters of Thatcherism: Contemporary British culture in J. K. Rowling's Harry Potter series. In L. A. Whited (Ed.), *The ivory tower and Harry Potter* (pp. 305–328). Columbia: University of Missouri Press.
World Health Organization. (2015). HIV/AIDS. Retrieved from http://www.who.int/hiv/en/.

Heroes and Horcruxes: Dumbledore's Army as Metonym

Christopher E. Bell

One of the more useful concepts in my field (critical rhetoric) and the study of popular culture is that of *metonymy*, or the *metonym*. Kenneth Burke (1941) describes metonymy as "to convey some incorporeal or intangible state in terms of the corporeal or tangible" (Burke, 1941, p. 424). The metonym is a "terminological reduction" (Burke, 1941, p. 426); it is a "metaphorical extension ... borrowing from the corporeal, visible, [and] tangible and applying by analogy to the realm of the incorporeal, invisible, intangible" (Burke, 1941, p.425). Metonymy is when one figure replaces another in representation, which means that a metonym is when one object stands in for the figure being represented.

We can think about this in terms of phrases like "Wall Street," for example. When we say, "Wall Street is doing this" or "Wall Street is doing that," we don't mean the actual, physical street. "Wall Street," as a phrase, *stands in for* all of the businesses housed there, for the stock market in general, and for the range of ideas and values and practices of large corporations. "Wall Street" is a classic metonym. Or, one could say, "I bought a Picasso." That does not mean that one actually bought the man, Pablo Picasso, and he is sitting in the living room. It means that that one painting *stands in for* not just Pablo Picasso as a person, but all of his work, what his work stood for, what his work might mean, where he might fall in a lineage of painters, and so on. This concept has been applied to literally hundreds of objects and phrases, from political contexts such as "9/11" (McQuillan, 2012) and President Obama (Corrada, 2011) to poetry (Eldridge, 2014), nationalism (Canziani, 2015), health care (Buchanan, 2013) and the Holocaust (Shneer, 2014). Metonyms can be found all around us.

In *OotP*, Rowling introduces Dumbledore's Army—a small cadre of students dedicated to learning Defense Against the Dark Arts, despite the unreasonable and oppressive restriction of the subject by Ministry of Magic stooge Dolores Umbridge. Initially made up of nearly two dozen students from all four houses (or, at least, three of the four—it is unclear if any Slytherins sign up); at its core, Dumbledore's Army is foundationally constituted by six Hogwarts students: Harry Potter, Ron Weasley, Ginny Weasley, Luna Lovegood, Neville Longbottom, and the club's founder and de facto president, Hermione Granger. These six are the front line fighters who, from beginning to end, represent Dumbledore. Those six characters, and Dumbledore himself, are the real, core, seven members of Dumbledore's Army—Dumbledore and his six best lieutenants, in a manner of speaking. Each of those seven characters serves as a metonym for some essential personality trait or characteristic that is crucial to the eventual victory over Lord Voldemort. That is to say, each member of Dumbledore's army is specifically representative of one of seven virtues necessary to triumph over "the ultimate evil." (Note that all seven members possess some measure of each of the seven virtues in varying degrees. However, each has an overwhelming affinity with one of the seven virtues, such that it becomes the defining feature of the character.)

Additionally, Voldemort creates seven Horcruxes, in order to preserve and conceal his immortal soul. Each of these Horcruxes also represents an essential personality trait or characteristic that Voldemort possesses in a perverted capacity. Voldemort fancies himself as brave, as a hard worker, as someone who inspires loyalty from his subjects. However, he can only reflect diminished or tainted versions of these virtues—in him, they become vices. These seven vices are directly connected to the seven virtues—they are the mirror opposites of each of the seven virtues.

Interestingly, as each personality trait is the defining characteristic of one of the members of Dumbledore's Army, and each Horcrux is the objective representation of those personality traits, then each Horcrux can be matched to a particular and specific member of Dumbledore's Army. Not only that, but that character is the member of Dumbledore's Army who specifically leads to the destruction of that Horcrux. Further, each Horcrux is destroyed in order of the importance of its virtue to overall, eventual victory—not necessarily in the order of the importance of the *character* but of the *personality trait* to the defeat of Lord Voldemort.

Pair each Horcrux with the character most directly tied to its destruction—Albus Dumbledore with the Ring of Gaunt, Luna Lovegood with Ravenclaw's Diadem, Ron Weasley with the Locket of Slytherin, Hermione Granger with Hufflepuff's Cup, Ginny Weasley with the Diary of Tom Riddle, Neville Longbottom with the serpent Nagini, and, of course, Harry Potter with himself—and we begin to see that J.K. Rowling has created an intensely complex environment of metonymy that fits together like an extremely well-crafted, intricate puzzle.

Ginny Weasley, the Diary of Tom Riddle and Youth

Tom Marvolo Riddle's diary, it is important to remember, is the first Horcrux he makes. The Horcrux is created when Tom Riddle is still a student; he makes it by killing Moaning Myrtle. Myrtle's death is an accident (Riddle certainly meant to kill someone, but Myrtle was not an intentional target; she happened to be in the wrong place at the wrong time), but he does kill her and creates the Horcrux in that moment. It is the first one he makes, and it is certainly the clumsiest and the one that makes the least sense—Tom Riddle does not kill Myrtle; the basilisk kills Myrtle. It is unclear how this could lead to the creation of a Horcrux, as Riddle does not perform the murder himself. Nonetheless, it is Riddle's first Horcrux, and he is still (for all intents and purposes) in high school when he makes it.

Ginny Weasley is the direct conduit for the destruction of the Diary of Tom Riddle in *CoS*. Ginny is also the youngest member of Dumbledore's Army. She is the first to fall under the power of one of the Horcruxes. It is Ginny who is pulled by Riddle into the Chamber of Secrets; Riddle uses her as a lure to draw in Harry Potter.

The defining characteristic, both of the particular Horcrux at hand and of Ginny Weasley, is the idea of *youth*. That is to say, descriptions of Ginny Weasley and of her behavior are filled with markers that define her as young. Beginning in *CoS*, Ginny is often described in terms of her crush on Harry Potter: "You don't know how weird it is for her to be this shy. She never shuts up normally—" (*CoS*, p. 40). Later in the same volume, Ginny "accidentally knock[s] her porridge bowl to the floor with a loud clatter" and "seemed very prone to knocking things over whenever Harry entered a room" (*CoS*, p. 43). This sort of childish shyness and awkward puppy love pervades Ginny's character for her first two years at Hogwarts.

As she enters teenage life, Ginny's markers of childishness give way to more adolescent descriptions of youth. She begins to embody the dual tropes of the "tomboy" and the "prettiest girl in school" simultaneously—both cultural expressions of youth. By *OotP*, Ginny is made seeker on the Gryffindor Quidditch team when Harry is banned from playing by Dolores Umbridge (*OotP*, p. 453). Ginny's relationship with Dean Thomas drives Ron into a misguidedly paternalistic anger ("I don't want to find my own sister snogging people in public … d'you think I want people saying my sister's a—" [*HBP*, p. 287]); when she breaks up with Dean, Harry "had the nagging worry that if he didn't do it, somebody else was sure to ask Ginny out soon: He and Ron were at least agreed on the fact that she was too popular for her own good" (*HBP*, p. 519). Ginny is brash and funny and popular, in the ways only a teenager full of youthful vibrancy can be.

Ginny is also the last of the Weasley children Molly is still able to control:

in *OotP*, it is Ginny who is sent to bed when she is reminded Fred and George are too old to be disciplined and that Harry would likely repeat every word of a secret conversation to Ron anyway (*OotP*, p. 91); in *DH*, Molly demands that Ginny promise not to leave the Room of Requirement while the entire rest of the family engages in the Battle of Hogwarts (*DH*, p. 606). It should also be noted that Ginny, in yet another display of youthful action, disregards that command almost immediately. Incidentally, it is Ginny, and nobody else, who leads Harry away from Dumbledore's body when he dies. The majority of the Order of the Phoenix is in the hospital wing with Bill Weasley, and everyone else is frozen in shock. Ginny, it is repeatedly shown, is not really afraid of anything, due to the sort of aura of youthful rashness and sense of invulnerability around her.

The dark side of youth, displayed both by Ginny in her worst moments and by Voldemort (and, by extension, the Diary as Horcrux), is *rage*. The term "rage" here is more appropriate than the simple term "anger" because "rage" contains an implication that it is, at some level, adolescent, unfocused, and uncontrollable. Ginny Weasley has a very short fuse. Her temper is both legendary and rather childish; she gets mad about a great deal of childish kinds of things. For example, in *HBP*: "You remember that idiot from Hufflepuff who was in the D.A.? He kept on and on asking about what happened at the Ministry and in the end he annoyed me so much I hexed him" (*HBP*, 147). Ginny's quickness and skill with the Bat-Bogey Hex is commented on no less than five times throughout the series; her brothers, in particular, are mildly terrified of her hexing abilities. At her least rational, Ginny is an incredibly temperamental teenager, particularly in interactions with her mother.

This short temper and subsequent rage permeates the character of Voldemort. It is the manifestation of the negative side of the positive trait, and it is clearly seen in the Diary as Horcrux, and in its subsequent effect on Ginny Weasley. The Diary of Tom Riddle is an object of *rage;* it is born from Riddle's own rage toward the dystopian and discriminatory society in which he lives and the abandonment issue he has with his own parents (covered extensively in Bell, 2013, p.43–66). At the culmination of the Diary's master plan, teenage Tom Riddle verbalizes a wide variety of sources of rage: his Muggle father, Dumbledore's mistrust, Ginny's increasing unwillingness to carry out his plans, and, most of all, "how is it that *you*—a skinny boy with no extraordinary magical talent—managed to defeat the greatest wizard of all time?" (*CoS*, p. 313).

It is not the old who win the day in Rowling's story. Rowling makes that point in the end—the young have to save the world, not the old. Dumbledore does not destroy Voldemort; Snape does not destroy Voldemort. McGonagall does not destroy Voldemort. Kids destroy Voldemort. In fact, there is only one Horcrux out of the seven that is not destroyed by a child. All of the other Horcruxes are destroyed by children. Youth is the first of the seven virtues necessary for victory over Voldemort, and Ginny Weasley is the metonym for youth. The Diary of Tom Riddle is the objective manifestation of that metonym, and Ginny is the integral part of the Diary's position in the story. It makes perfect sense that it is the first Horcrux that gets destroyed (youth is fleeting) and that Ginny is the one who directly leads to its destruction.

Albus Dumbledore, the Ring of Gaunt and Pride

The Ring of Marvolo Gaunt is the second of the three Deathly Hallows, given to the middle Peverell brother by Death himself in *The Tale of the Three Brothers*. The second brother is described in the story as "an arrogant man" (*DH*, p. 407) who "decided that he wanted to humiliate Death ... and asked for the power to recall others from Death" (*DH*, p. 407). Although the second Peverell uses the Resurrection Stone to bring the girl he was once going to marry back from the grave, it is important to remember that this is not *why* he asks for the Stone. He asks for the Stone in order to humiliate Death.

This arrogance is reflected in the man who comes to possess the heirloom—Marvolo Gaunt. Gaunt is the descendant of a great wizarding family that was marred by both incest and by a lack of fiscal responsibility. This, as Dumbledore points out to Harry, left Marvolo Gaunt "in squalor and poverty, with a nasty temper [and] a fantastic amount of arrogance and pride" (*HBP*, p. 212). This arrogance is fully displayed when the Ministry of Magic sends Mr. Ogden to question Morfin Gaunt about misuse of magic in front of Muggles. Marvolo Gaunt is outraged, and waves the Ring of Gaunt in his face, screaming, "See this? See this? Know what it is? Know where it came from? Centuries it's been in our family, that's how far we go back, and pureblood all the way! Know how much I've been offered for this, with the Peverell coat of arms engraved on the stone?" (*HBP*, p. 207). He is proud of his lineage, he is proud of that ring, and it is not the kind of pride that one takes in accomplishment. It is the kind of pride that one takes in *birthright*.

Pride is also the defining characteristic of Albus Percival Wulfric Brian Dumbledore. His list of titles often precedes him: "Headmaster, Order of Merlin, First Class, Grand Sorc., Chf. Warlock, Supreme Mugwump, International Confed. of Wizards" (*SS*, p. 51). He is "considered by many the greatest wizard of modern times," especially for "the discovery of the twelve uses of dragon's blood" (*SS*, p. 102). Dumbledore's pride is revealed over and over in the myriad of self-congratulatory side comments he is prone to making. He is constantly commenting on what a better, more accomplished wizard he is than other people, in ways both obvious—"It was one of my more brilliant ideas, and between you and me, that's saying something" (*SS*, p. 100)—and subtle—"Which goes to show that the best of us must sometimes eat our words" (*CoS*, p. 331). Make no mistake; by "the best of us," Dumbledore is explicitly referring to himself. While he often couches his self-aggrandizing in apology—"Had it not been—forgive me the lack of seemly modesty—for my own prodigious skill" (*HBP*, p. 503)—Dumbledore's incredible pride always shines through.

Voldemort's perversion of the virtue, *arrogance*, mirrors that of his grandfather, Marvolo, and that of the middle Peverell as displayed, by extension, by the Resurrection Stone. Voldemort repeatedly uses the statement "I, who have gone further than anybody along the path that leads to immorality" (*HBP*, p. 501), revealing the arrogance in his assessment of his own achievements. This arrogance, apparently, had been brewing since Tom Riddle was a child; in Dumbledore's first encounter with Riddle, after revealing to the boy that he is a wizard, Riddle whispers to himself, "I knew I was different.... I knew I was special. Always, I knew there was something" (*HBP*, p. 271). Of course he would choose, as a Horcrux, the ring which his grandfather treasured above all else as a symbol of the Gaunts' noble lineage, even without the knowledge that it contained one of the three Deathly Hallows. It is the very exemplification of the arrogance of "purebloods" that Riddle so desperately craves.

However, it is not just Riddle who displays the arrogance of blood status. Dumbledore himself, in his youth, was much like Tom Riddle. It is revealed, in *DH*, that Dumbledore was once great friends (perhaps even lovers) with the dark wizard Gellert Grindelwald. At 17 years of age, Dumbledore wrote a letter to Grindelwald claiming that "wizard dominance" was for "Muggles' own good" and that "power gives [wizards] the right to rule" (*DH*, p. 357). While it may be tempting to blame Dumbledore's arrogance on his age, Harry himself points out, "They were the same age as we are now. And here we are, risking our lives to fight the Dark Arts, and there he was, in a huddle with his new best friend, plotting their rise to power over the Muggles" (*DH*, p. 361). Additionally, Dumbledore, at the time of the writing of the letter, was the same age as Tom Riddle was when he made his first Horcrux.

It is Aberforth Dumbledore who makes the most pointed, and perhaps most astute, claim about Dumbledore's pride. Essentially, Aberforth's assessment paints a very different picture of Dumbledore as an incredibly arrogant person who trusts nobody's knowledge except for his own, puts no faith into the people he is sending off to die, and so wrapped up in himself that he couldn't even take care of his own family. When Harry tells him that Albus has given him a job to do, Aberforth laughs and asks, "Nice job, I hope? Pleasant? Easy? Sort of thing you'd expect an unqualified wizard kid to be able to do without overstretching themselves?" (*DH,* p. 561). Aberforth's speech is tinged with a fair bit of jealousy, but it also seems like a reasonable assessment, given what we already know about Dumbledore's personality.

Whether one views Dumbledore's pride as rightfully-earned confidence or as dangerous arrogance, it is the defining feature of Dumbledore. This makes the perverted form, as embodied by the Ring of Gaunt, his ideal objective metonym. As Dumbledore is the living metonym for pride himself, the destruction of the Ring of Gaunt by Albus Dumbledore creates a perfect circle.

Ron Weasley, the Locket of Slytherin and Bravery

The Locket of Salazar Slytherin is one of the more interesting Horcruxes. It is the only one of Voldemort's Horcruxes that was not destroyed either in or near Hogwarts. The Locket is destroyed away from Hogwarts, in the Forest of Dean. All other Horcruxes are destroyed either in or near Hogwarts, depending on how one views Dumbledore's destruction of the Ring of Gaunt—we do not know exactly when and where that happened, so that is, admittedly, an educated presumption.

The Locket of Slytherin is surrounded in stories of *bravery*, from the first time we hear about it chronologically (not necessarily in the pages of the book). The first time readers hear the story of Slytherin's Locket is when Tom Riddle's mother, Merope, steals it from her father, Marvolo Gaunt, and runs away from home. It is probably the bravest act she ever performed in her life; perhaps, even, the last brave act she ever performed. Merope breaks free of an intensely abusive household, in which she is shouted at, derided and physically abused. Marvolo Gaunt calls her "pointless lump" (*HBP,* p. 205), "useless sack of muck" (*HBP,* p. 205), a "disgusting little squib" and a "filthy little blood traitor" (*HBP,* p. 210) over the span of a single conversation that ends with Marvolo's hands around Merope's throat. Marvolo Gaunt, and Merope's brother Morfin Gaunt, are sent to prison and Merope is, for the first time in her life, free of abuse. Even though it does not end up well for her, the act of stealing the Locket of Slytherin and running away before her father and brother return is, itself, an incredibly brave action.

The Locket of Slytherin, thereafter, becomes the conduit by which others must show bravery in overcoming their fears in order to possess it. In order to retrieve the Locket as Horcrux, both Regulus Black and Albus Dumbledore were forced to drink a potion that manifested their deepest fears. Regulus was able to steal the Locket from Voldemort's hiding place, an act of fantastic bravery that ultimately cost Regulus his life. When the Locket comes into the possession of Dolores Umbridge, the Trio must display extraordinary bravery in sneaking into the heavily guarded Ministry of Magic to retrieve it.

Ron Weasley's patronus is a representation both of companionship and of protective kinds of bravery. In the *OotP* film, it is portrayed as a Jack Russell terrier, which is an incredibly protective breed. The Jack Russell Terrier Club of America describes the breed as "aggressive … fearless, often challenging other dogs three times their size … and can become very possessive of their owner to the point of showing aggressive protective behavior" (JRTCA, 2015). This is an important facet of Ron Weasley's character—the patronus is a reflection of the "hope, happiness, the desire to survive" (*PoA*, p. 237) of the wizard who conjures it—because Rowling intentionally, continually depicts Ron as a whiner and a crybaby. Ron is afraid of *everything*; he whimpers (*PoA*, p. 345; *OotP*, p. 545; *DH*, p. 173) and moans (*SS*, p. 159; *CoS* p. 75; *PoA* pp. 226, 253, 338; *GoF*, pp. 57, 175, 180, 399; *OotP*, pp. 168, 264; *HBP*, p. 395; *DH*, pp. 273, 293, 500) constantly. More than any other character in the books, Ron Weasley is full of fear. However, at the end of the day, Ron is braver than he thinks he is. He may cry, whine, or cower, but he will be at the side of Harry and Hermione when needed. This is why Ron is a Gryffindor and not a Hufflepuff, which he should be (Each member of the Trio should be in one of the other houses, by personality traits and behavior: Ron should be in Hufflepuff, Hermione should be in Ravenclaw, Harry should be in Slytherin. None of them are because each chose Gryffindor, a fact Hermione confirms in *OotP* [p. 399], Ron in *SS* [p. 106] and Harry in *CoS* [p. 206].) Ron, who does not think he is a tough guy or a brave guy, is actually the bravest of the three of them because he has the farthest to go—he has more to overcome in terms of fear than the other two do, which makes him in many ways the bravest of the three.

The perversion of this virtue, as displayed throughout the series by Ron Weasley, and as manifested by Voldemort, is *jealousy*. Ron is an intensely jealous person, particularly of Harry Potter, and that jealousy steadily increases throughout the early part of the series, culminating in *GoF*. In fact, it is this jealousy that the Locket of Slytherin attempts to exploit to break Ron's resolve: "*Least loved, always, by the mother who craved a daughter … least loved, now, by the girl who prefers your friend … second best, always, eternally overshadowed*" (*DH*, p. 376). Voldemort's own jealousy—of Albus Dumbledore—is also repeatedly referenced, as "Dumbledore was the only wizard Voldemort had ever feared" (*GoF*, p. 679). Harry throws this in Tom Riddle's face on several occasions, including during their first meeting in the Chamber of Secrets: "Sorry to disappoint you and all that, but the greatest wizard in the world is Albus Dumbledore. Everyone says so. Even when you were strong, you didn't dare try and take over at Hogwarts" (*CoS*, p. 314) Voldemort is always jealous of Dumbledore, attempting (and failing) to best him at every turn.

Thus, bravery and jealousy surround the story of Slytherin's Locket. That is why the Locket, which manifests one's deepest fears and uses them against a would-be adversary, could only be destroyed by Ron Weasley. No one else, including Regulus Black, Albus Dumbledore, or Harry Potter himself, is brave enough to face the fear induced by the Locket of Slytherin. Ron has to be the one to do it, because he is the bravest of the lot. To paraphrase Bruce Banner in Marvel's *The Avengers* (2012), Ron is the best at overcoming fear because "that's the secret: [he's] always [afraid]" (Whedon, 2012).

Hermione Granger, Hufflepuff's Cup and Hard Work

Hufflepuff's Cup is a golden chalice, which is traditionally the very representation of femininity: the chalice symbolizes the source of life, "the generative, nurturing, and creative powers of nature" in benefit to all people (Eisler, 1988, p. 43). It is important to note, therefore, that Hufflepuff's Cup is the only Horcrux destroyed by a girl. Every other Horcrux is destroyed by boys. That the object representing the sacred feminine is destroyed by the character who represents the mothering figure of the Trio (covered in great detail in Hidalgo (2012) and Weiss (2013)) is not coincidental. Hermione's destruction of the Horcrux is couched in Ron's problematic "Hermione stabbed it. Thought she should. She hasn't had the pleasure yet" (*DH*, p. 623), as if it was entirely his idea. This is apropos, as it is often how Hermione's role is diminished and devalued throughout the series.

Hermione Granger represents the one thing that she never gets credit for, and that is her *hard work*. Hermione Granger is the hardest working witch in show business. She is the most important member of Dumbledore's Army by far—she is more important than Ron, she is more important than Harry (Bell, 2011). Harry and Ron without Hermione are dead on several occasions. Hermione without Ron and Harry eventually does kill Voldemort—it takes her longer, but she gets him (Waters, 2012). She is the only member of the Trio who can actually do things. She casts all the protective charms (*DH*, p. 272), she knows all the healing spells (*DH*, p. 210), she remembers all of their gear (*DH*, p. 162), she disapparates them away from danger on several occasions when they are stupefied by the situation (*DH*, pp. 161, 364). She does most of the heavy lifting during the entire series; she solves most of the problems and most of the puzzles. She carries the load for a mostly otherwise inept team and without her, they are doomed; even Harry is forced to say, "I'd be dead if you hadn't been there to help me" (*DH*, p. 352).

But the fascinating thing about Hermione Granger is that we, the readers and *Potter* scholars, never seem give her credit for her labor. We always call her smart (Armstrong, 2015; Dresang, 2002; Foster, 2012; Kellner, 2010; Klingbiel, 2012). This treatment of Hermione mirrors what, societally, we do to girls: we overvalue their innate qualities and undervalue their conscious effort. It is why girls get called bossy and boys get called leaders (Baer, 2014): leading is a thing one *does*, bossy is a thing one *is*. It is why studies show that girls fall off in math and science development right around sixth grade when it starts getting significantly harder (Keller, 2013)—because boys learn math is a thing they *can do* and girls learn that math is a thing they are *good at*. When math gets harder, around the age of 13–15, boys *work harder* and girls think they're not *good enough*.

The perversion of hard work is the utter *insufferability* that a workaholic can muster. Hermione Granger displays this incessantly from the very beginning—Ron remarks, "She's a nightmare, honestly ... she must've noticed she's got no friends" (*SS*, p. 172). It takes months before Harry and Ron accept Hermione into their friendship circle, and even then, her work ethic can be overwhelming. At her worst, she can be impossible to even be around; for example, in *PoA*, Ron and Harry stop talking to her after she snaps at them with, "'Well isn't it *obvious*?' said Hermione, with a look of maddening superiority" (*PoA*, p. 236). Voldemort's own perversion of this virtue is in the ceaseless, relentless pursuit of immortality, even at the expense of his own happiness, love, and soul. This insufferability of inflated work ethic is mirrored in the curse placed upon Hufflepuff's Cup by Voldemort: "Everything you touch will burn and multiply, but the copies are worthless—and if you continue to handle the treasure, you will eventually be crushed to death by the weight of expanding gold!" (*DH*, p. 537). The harder one works to retrieve the Cup, the more futile the effort becomes. The trick to retrieving the Cup is to work only as hard as absolutely necessary, and the Trio is nearly killed in the process of recovering it. (Another significant note: it is Hermione, as per usual, who comes up with the plan to escape from Gringotts by freeing the captive dragon and riding it to safety.)

It is important to recognize that Rowling makes this match between Hermione Granger and Hufflepuff's Cup intentionally because Hermione's hard work *matters*. She destroys the Cup because it is a recognition not that she is only the smartest one of the bunch, but she is the one who works the hardest. That, more than her innate intelligence, is why she continues to have success. She always does her homework; Ron and Harry repeatedly cheat by copying from her. This says everything one needs to know about the relationship among the Trio and Hermione's place in it.

Luna Lovegood, the Diadem of Ravenclaw and Wisdom

Luna Lovegood is directly responsible for the destruction of the Diadem of Ravenclaw, as it is she who brings Harry to the Ravenclaw common room and gives him all of the necessary clues to find the Diadem's hiding place. In the film version of *DH,* it is, in fact, Luna who tells Harry exactly who would know where the Diadem is located. "Wit beyond measure is man's greatest treasure" (*DH,* p. 588) is the motto of Ravenclaw House. This is usually applied to Ravenclaws in terms of them being smart, but there is an element of wit that has less to do with intelligence and more to do with intelligence *applied.* Applied intelligence is the very definition of *wisdom.* Luna is wise; she is the voice of reason for the group. Luna looks at the world in ways other people do not, and she sees things no one else sees (which, of course, occasionally includes nargles [*OotP,* p. 453]). This ability is literally applied in *OotP,* as she is the voice of reassurance to Harry when he sees the thestrals for the first time—"I've been able to see them ever since my first day here. They've always pulled the carriages. Don't worry. You're just as sane as I am" (*OotP,* p. 199).

While Luna, as just demonstrated, is often depicted as comedy relief, if one goes back and takes the comedy out of the situations, her insights are almost always incredibly sophisticated. It is Luna who gets Dumbledore's Army to London by suggesting, "Well, we'll have to fly, won't we?" (*OotP,* p. 761); Luna also recommends using the thestrals to get to the Ministry of Magic (*OotP,* p. 762). It is Luna's words of comfort that help Harry get past the loss of Sirius Black; she is the only other person who can hear the voices of the dead behind the veil in the Department of Mysteries, and she consoles Harry with the knowledge that "it's not as though I'll never see Mum again, is it? ... You heard them, just behind the veil ... they were just lurking out of sight, that's all" (*OotP,* p. 863). Luna's wisdom is both surprising and endearing.

The perversion of this virtue as embodied by Voldemort and displayed regularly by Luna, is *madness.* While wise and insightful, Luna is referred to often by her peers as "Loony"; in fact, this is how Ginny introduces her upon Harry's first meeting (*OotP*, p. 185), while Luna reads an upside-down magazine. Luna's insistence upon the existence of everything from the Crumple-Horned Snorkack (*OotP*, p. 762) and Wrackspurts (*HBP,* p. 140) to conspiracy theories about the Minister of Magic's assassinations of goblins (*OotP,* p. 393) and private army of heliopaths (*OotP*, p. 345) infuriates the Trio; Hermione, in particular. Hermione's constant refrain of "But where's the *proof* in that?" (*OotP,* p. 345) is normally ignored by Luna. Harry observes that Luna often says "uncomfortable things" that make him "feel a squirming mixture of pity and embarrassment" (*HBP,* p. 138). When Harry invites Luna to Slughorn's Christmas party, Ron is mortified: "'You could've taken *anyone!* ... And you chose Loony Lovegood?'" (*HBP,* p. 312).

Madness, of course, also defines Voldemort from beginning to end. Once the brightest student at Hogwarts, Tom Riddle's pursuit of power and immortality drove him into lunacy, turning him into a mass murderer. Dumbledore characterizes Voldemort as "the most dangerous Dark wizard of all time" (*HBP*, p. 276), which is saying a lot, considering he was best friends with Grindelwald (who quite possibly murdered Dumbledore's sister). From a young age, Tom Riddle displayed tendencies toward "cruelty, secrecy, and domination" (*HBP*, p. 276), and these were only amplified as Riddle transformed into Lord Voldemort. This madness also pervades the story of Rowena Ravenclaw's lost Diadem. Her daughter, Helena, stole the Diadem from her mother to "make [her]self cleverer, more important than [her] mother" (*DH*, p. 616). Rowena sent the Baron, a notoriously volatile man, to find Helena, knowing the Baron had been madly in love with Helena for years. When the Baron located Helena, she spurned him, and, mad with jealousy and grief, the Baron stabbed her to death. Distraught by what he had done, the Baron then committed suicide. Madness surrounds the Diadem, and it is in the madness of Crabbe's ill-advised and out of control Fiendfyre curse, devouring everything in its path, that the Diadem Horcrux is destroyed.

When Harry goes off to find the Diadem in *DH*, Cho volunteers to accompany him, but Ginny demands that Luna go instead (*DH*, p. 585). This is played as an act of jealousy, as though Ginny does not want Cho alone with Harry, but thematically, only Luna can help Harry find the Diadem. Only Luna sees the world in the way that it needs to be seen in order to clue Harry in to where the Diadem resides. Wisdom is one of the most important traits to victory for Dumbledore's Army, and Luna possesses it in spades.

Neville Longbottom, Nagini and Loyalty

When ranked in order of importance, the second most crucial trait Dumbledore's Army needs to triumph over Lord Voldemort is personified by Neville Longbottom. Dumbledore first provides foreshadowing to Neville's ultimate importance at the end of *SS*, where he reminds the students of Hogwarts that, "there are all kinds of courage" (*SS*, p. 306).

Neville's particular brand of courage, that which is his defining characteristic, is *loyalty*. There is nobody who embodies loyalty more than Neville Longbottom, who has few discernable skills, is considerably weaker than the others, cannot seem to do anything right, and yet is always charging into the middle of the fight—knowing every single time, he is probably going to die, because he doesn't know how to do anything.

Neville's character is fueled by both his loyalty to his friends and his loyalty to his parents, who were tortured to the point of institutionalization by Bellatrix LeStrange. It takes three people to hold Neville back from pummeling Draco Malfoy when Malfoy makes an off-handed comment about

Neville's parents (*OotP,* p. 361), and Harry learns that Neville regularly visits his parents in St. Mungo's Hospital for Magical Maladies and Injuries (*GoF*, p. 603). It is Neville who demands that he, Luna, and Ginny accompany the Trio to the Ministry of Magic in *OotP,* declaring, "We're all in the D.A. together ... or was that all just a game or something?" (*OotP,* p. 761). Despite the fact that it takes Neville ages to learn defensive spells that others pick up rather quickly—Harry admits that "if he could have chosen any members of the D.A. ... to join him in the attempt to rescue Sirius, he would not have picked ... Neville" (*OotP*, p. 761)—Neville is willing to risk his life for his friends. In the Department of Mysteries, Neville's wand and nose are both broken by Antonin Dolohov (*OotP,* p. 792), and yet it is he who carries Hermione's unconscious body out of harm's way (*OotP*, p. 795).

This loyalty is both reflected and perverted in Nagini, who is the closest thing Tom Riddle has to a friend. For Nagini, and the rest of the Death Eaters surrounding Voldemort (as evidenced particularly by Bellatrix LeStrange), the perversion is *blind allegiance.* The negative side of Neville's loyalty perverts itself into foolhardiness, forcing him into situations he clearly cannot handle, but Voldemort's version of loyalty is perverted into the objective form of Nagini. She is his most valuable and most treasured Horcrux, and the one he keeps closest to himself. Voldemort's return to corporeal form is fueled by Nagini's venom; she provides the equivalent of mother's milk that nurses him back to full strength (*GoF,* pp. 7, 656). Even Dumbledore notes that "he is perhaps as fond of her as he can be of anything; he certainly likes to keep her close, and he seems to have an unusual amount of control over her" (*HBP,* p. 506). If fact, it is Nagini who comes the closest to actually killing Harry Potter on Voldemort's behalf (*DH,* p. 341). When everyone else has been sent away, it is only Nagini who remains by Voldemort's side (*DH,* p. 729), and she is the last of Voldemort's most trusted followers to die (*DH,* p. 733). Because she is an animal and cannot dissent, she is a direct metonym for blind allegiance; she is the only servant Voldemort has that he completely trusts, and she defends Voldemort up to the very moment she gets her head cut off, without questioning.

In *CoS*, Dumbledore tells Harry that he "must have shown [Dumbledore] real loyalty down in the Chamber. Nothing but that could have called Fawkes to you" (*CoS*, p. 332). This loyalty allows Harry to wield the Sword of Gryffindor and kill the basilisk. In *DH,* it is this same loyalty that brings the Sorting Hat to Neville, allowing him to draw from it the Sword of Gryffindor and decapitate Nagini (*DH,* p. 733). This makes perfect sense—only Neville can kill Nagini because they are symbolic counterparts. They are two sides of the same coin. They are metonyms of each other and of the value (and vice) of loyalty.

Harry Potter, Harry Potter and Trust

Over and over, constantly, all the time in this series, love is referred to as the most important thing in the world. However, it is not love that wins the day against Voldemort, despite what everyone (including Harry) seems to think. It is *trust* that definitively sees Harry through to the end, and to ultimate victory. Despite the fact that people lie to his face *all the time*, Harry still has complete trust in the people that are around him. People betray him. People keep things from him. In the case of Mad Eye Moody, individuals are sometimes entirely differently people disguised as his friend, and he still puts his trust in the people around him. The person he distrusts most in the world, Severus Snape, is actually his biggest defender—"the bravest man [Harry] ever knew" (*DH*, 758). In the end, the person he puts the most trust in, Albus Dumbledore, is the biggest liar. Aberforth Dumbledore pegs Albus Dumbledore clearly and cleanly: "I knew my brother, Potter. He learned secrecy at our mother's knee. Secrets and lies, that's how we grew up, and Albus ... he was a natural" (*DH*, p. 562). Dumbledore repeatedly withholds crucial information from Harry for years, only revealing the truth about the prophecy concerning Harry and Tom Riddle after his negligence gets Sirius Black killed (*OotP*, p. 841). Yet Harry continues to trust Dumbledore implicitly, despite numerous reasons not to do so. Dumbledore's trust in Severus Snape—"Dumbledore trusts Severus, and that ought to be good enough for all of us ... it comes down to whether or not you trust Dumbledore's judgment. I do; therefore, I trust Severus" (*HBP*, p. 332)—is the pinnacle of Harry's undying faith in Dumbledore. Snape has been borderline cruel to Harry for years, and yet, it is Harry's trust in Dumbledore that prevents Harry from mistakenly exacting vengeance upon Snape.

The perversion of this virtue is *gullibility*, which both Harry and Tom Riddle display on multiple occasions. It is Harry's gullibility—his unending trust—that directly leads to the death of Sirius Black. Voldemort was well aware that the "one person whom [Harry] would go to any lengths to rescue was Sirius" (*OotP*, p. 831), and uses Harry's gullibility to lure him to the Department of Mysteries and nearly kill him. This same gullibility, again, nearly results in Harry's death when he follows a clearly enchanted Balthilda Bagshot to her home, where Nagini almost kills him and Hermione (*DH*, p. 342). Tom Riddle demonstrates the same gullibility in his trusting of Severus Snape. Only Bellatrix LeStrange (rightfully, it turns out) questions Voldemort's trust of Snape: "The Dark Lord is ... I believe ... mistaken" (*HBP*, p. 21). There are a litany of reasons Bellatrix mistrusts Snape: his disappearance at the original falling of Voldemort, his lack of attempt to find Voldemort after the fall, Snape's effort to stop Voldemort from retrieving the philosopher's stone, Snape's refusal to join the other Death Eaters in the Department of Mysteries (*DH*, p. 25). Yet, despite all of these valid concerns, Voldemort continues to trust Snape implicitly. This gullibility backfires spectacularly on Tom Riddle, as Snape withholds the information that he, not Dumbledore, possessed the Elder Wand that eventually passed to Harry Potter. That crucial information directly leads to the death of Tom Riddle, in the end.

Trust surrounds this entire epic story at all times. It is only when Harry kills off the lies that live in his head—the repeated omissions and obfuscations of Albus Dumbledore—and makes peace with Dumbledore at King's Cross Station that he can finally kill Tom Riddle and move on. Dumbledore is given an opportunity to resolve his own issues: "I was offered the post of Minister of Magic, not once, but several times. Naturally, I refused. I had learned that I was not to be trusted with power" (*DH*, p. 717) and admit that he is not as trustworthy as Harry believes. With this admission from Dumbledore, Harry is able to reconcile his gullibility with true trust, and that enables him to return to the world and win the game. In the end, who does Harry trust the most? Harry. Harry's defining characteristic is his ability to trust. This is why Harry works both as a Horcrux and as a metonym both trust and of himself.

Conclusion

One of the drums I have been beating the loudest over the course of my *Harry Potter* scholarship is that it is not Harry Potter that Lord Voldemort is battling (Bell, 2014; Bell, 2011). The major mistake that Tom Riddle makes is believing Harry Potter is the main opposition of his plans, because he is not. What enables Harry Potter to defeat Lord Voldemort is that Harry is a part of a *team*, each member of which brings a specific element—a specific virtue—to the team that is *specifically designed* to kill off a part of Voldemort. Each Horcrux is destroyed by the character who best embodies the virtue needed to correct the perverted form created by Voldemort. Thus, at the end, when Harry says, "There are no more Horcruxes. It's just you and me" (*DH*, p. 737), he is correct, but he fails to mention this is only possible because everyone else has already done their jobs. Ginny has grown up, Dumbledore has put aside his arrogant pride, Ron has overcome his jealousies, Hermione has learned how not to alienate people, Luna has tamed her madness, Neville has channeled his loyalty, and Harry has surmounted his own gullibility. He is, then, free and clear to vanquish Voldemort, once and for all.

References

Armstrong, R. (2015). Sexual geometry of the golden trio. In C.K. Farr (Ed.), *A wizard of their age: Critical essays from the Harry Potter generation.* Albany: State University of New York Press.

Baer, D. (2014). Here's why banning the word "bossy" is great for women. *Business Insider*. Retrieved 4 May 2015, from http://www.businessinsider.com/what-bossy-words-says-about-gender-at-work-2014-3.
Bell, C. (2011). Three is a magic number: The trinity archetype in Harry Potter. *Journal of Literature and Art Studies, 1*(3), 209–218.
Bell, C. (2014). Riddle me this: The moral disengagement of Lord Voldemort. In C.E. Bell (Ed.), *Legilimens! Perspective in Harry Potter studies*. Newcastle Upon Tyne: Cambridge Scholars.
Buchanan, D. A. (2013). The austerity bargain and the social self: Conceptual clarity surrounding health cutbacks. *Nursing Philosophy, 14*(1), 38–44.
Burke, K. (1941) Four master tropes. *The Kenyon Review, 3*(4), 421–438.
Canziani, B. F. (2015). Power in tourism research: The tourist gaze as metonym. *International Journal of Tourism Anthropology, 4*(1), 13–24.
Corrada, R. L. (2011). Synecdochic perils & opportunities for Latina/os in the academy. *Harvard Latino Law Review, 14*, 257.
Dresang, E. T. (2002). Hermione Granger and the heritage of gender. In L.A. Whited (Ed.), *The ivory tower and Harry Potter: Perspectives on a literary phenomenon* (pp. 211–242). Columbia: University of Missouri Press.
Eisler, R. T. (1988). *The chalice and the blade: Our history, our future*. New York: Harper & Row.
Eldridge, A. F. (2014). "I long for my mother's bread": Poetry as integrative, historical practice in the Palestinian context. *Multilingual Discourses, 1*(2).
Foster, T. (2012). Books! And cleverness! In C.E. Bell (Ed.), *Hermione Granger saves the world! Essays on the feminist heroine of Hogwarts*. Jefferson, NC: McFarland.
Hidalgo, A. (2012). Unstoppable force: Maternal power and feminism. In C.E. Bell (Ed.), *Hermione Granger saves the world! Essays on the feminist heroine of Hogwarts*. Jefferson, NC: McFarland.
"JRTCA." (2015). *Bad dog talk for Jack Russell terriers*. Retrieved 4 May 2015, from http://www.therealjackrussell.com/breed/baddog.php.
Keller, E. (2013). Girls and science: Why the gender gap exists and what to do about it. *The Guardian*. http://www.theguardian.com/world/us-news-blog/2013/feb/05/girls-science-gender-gap-fix.
Kellner, R. T. (2010). JK Rowling's ambivalence towards feminism: House elves-women in disguise-in the "Harry Potter" books. *The Midwest Quarterly, 51*(4), 367.
Klingbiel, C. (2012). Hermione Granger: Insufferable know-it-all or superhero? In C.E. Bell (Ed.), *Hermione Granger saves the world! Essays on the feminist heroine of Hogwarts*. Jefferson, NC: McFarland.
McQuillan, M. (2012). Deconstruction of the Idiom "9/11." *Belgrade Journal of Media and Communications, 2*, 47–56.
Rowling, J. K. (1998). *Harry Potter and the sorcerer's stone*. New York: Scholastic.
Rowling, J. K. (1999a). *Harry Potter and the chamber of secrets*. New York: Scholastic.
Rowling, J. K. (1999b). *Harry Potter and the prisoner of Azkaban*. New York: Scholastic.
Rowling, J. K. (2000). *Harry Potter and the goblet of fire*. New York: Scholastic.
Rowling, J. K. (2003). *Harry Potter and the Order of the Phoenix*. New York: Scholastic.
Rowling, J. K. (2005). *Harry Potter and the half-blood prince*. New York: Scholastic.
Rowling, J. K. (2007). *Harry Potter and the deathly hallows*. New York: Scholastic.

Shneer, D. (2014). Ghostly landscapes: Soviet liberators photograph the Holocaust. *Humanity: An International Journal of Human Rights, Humanitarianism, and Development*, 5(2), 235–246.

Waters, T. (2012). Is Hermione Granger the real chosen one? In C.E. Bell (Ed.), *Hermione Granger saves the world! Essays on the feminist heroine of Hogwarts.* Jefferson, NC: McFarland.

Weiss, M. (2013). The role of maternal females in Harry Potter's journey. In C.E. Bell (Ed.), *Legilimens! Perspective in Harry Potter Studies.* Newcastle Upon Tyne: Cambridge Scholars.

Whedon, J. (2012). *The avengers.* [Motion picture]. Marvel Studios.

"I'm a wizard too!" Identification and Habitus

HILLARY A. JONES

The first Harry Potter book had an initial print run of 6 million copies in 1997. Within 10 years, the first six books sold over 325 million copies (Jordan, 2007). The series has been merchandised extensively, selling film rights to Warner Bros. and toys to Mattel (Gelder, 2004, p. 34). The first film (whose soundtrack was crafted by industry giant John Williams) skyrocketed to become the second-highest grossing film of all time; as of 2015, all of the films ranked in the top 50, with the final film highest, at fourth. The *New York Times* created a new bestseller list for children's fiction in 2000, due solely to the Potter series dominating so many spots on the list. Fans have created bands, websites, and copious fan fiction; people hold academic and fan conferences. The books catalyzed controversy; parents campaigned to keep it out of school libraries, spiritual leaders vilified it from pulpits, and academics scorned and critiqued it (e.g., Bloom, 2001; Byatt, 2003; Pennington, 2002; Schoefer, 2000). Rowling was accused of witchcraft and Satanism, and Harry Potter has been derided by a variety of religious organizations (e.g., Boffetti, 1999; Komschlies, 2000). On the flip side, the Potter series has received overwhelmingly positive reviews, many academics (including the authors of this volume) have engaged with the text substantively, and it has been credited with increasing literacy levels—especially for boys (Gelder, 2004, p. 35). Harry, Ron, and Hermione have joined Alice, Huck, and Frodo as instantly recognizable characters. In short, the Harry Potter franchise is a cultural juggernaut.

From magazines at the grocery store to runaway Billboard hits to the books children read, popular culture permeates our lives. Even those seeking to avoid mass-mediated texts are exposed to texts as touted as *Harry Potter*. Analyzing a widely circulated text, like the Potter series, enables scholars to evaluate the themes, desires, and fears extant in a culture. In addition to drawing large audiences, popular culture texts provide identity scripts that influence and reflect everyday life. A popular cultural text's banality justifies sustained scholarly attention because it teaches us about culture.

Children's popular culture is particularly useful for discovering the ideological and cultural work performed by mass-mediated texts; kids are less likely to seek or question a text's ideological ramifications. However, they are socialized significantly by these reading experiences. George Orwell once observed that the most important books "are usually the ones read earliest in life" (as cited in Rosenberg, 1986, p. xxi). Popular young adult fiction such as the Potter series thus facilitates scholarly identification and evaluation of embedded ideology and identity scripts that shape the lives of a large segment of the population. The focus on adolescents (both the characters and targeted readers) makes the Potter books even richer resources; identity formation features prominently in adolescence and thus recurs as a theme in young adult fiction.

Like much genre fiction, fantasy fiction invites readers to lose themselves in the fancy. As both fantasy and bildungsroman (a novel focused on an individual's formative years), the Potter series invites imagination, not critical reading. Because readers focus on the page-turning plot and the fantastic world, most of the novels' ideological work may be even more potent as it evades direct detection (Gelder, 2004, pp. 33–37).

Although I draw examples from the series as a whole in order to demonstrate some of the ways the characters present and model ideology and identity scripts, I submit the first Harry Potter novel (abbreviated throughout as *SS*) to sustained, focused rhetorical criticism. Not to be confused with criticism reviewing the readability, accessibility, and literary quality of texts, rhetorical criticism examines the cultural and persuasive work a text does by evaluating its situated context, internal construction, and indicators of effect on an audience. "Rhetoric" is the persuasion, identification, or invitation a text does to and with an audience. In this essay, I consider primarily *SS* because it introduces readers, and the characters, to the wizarding world and the identity scripts and norms that typify it. I enrich the rhetorical analysis with two theoretical tools: Bourdieu's habitus and Burke's identification. Analyzing *SS* with this method and these theories, I show how characters in the novel strategically construct, change, and navigate identifications with various habiti (the plural of habitus). The ways the characters negotiate three of the most prominent structuring binaries in this book (Muggle/wizard, Gryffindor/Slytherin, and rule-breaking/rule-following) reveal some of the text's ideological and identity scripts, as well as the utility of combining habitus with identification for rhetorical analysis.

The narrative construction of identity has sustained cultural scholars' interest for some time. Hall (1990) defines identity as "a 'production,' which is never complete, always in process, and always constituted within, not outside representation" (p. 222). Other scholars focus on specific identities. For example, Mac an Ghaill (1994) considers narrative identity, education, and the formation of masculinity, observing that "students are active makers of sex/gender identities" (p. 90). Walkerdine (1990) looks at identities defined by roles; she relays how student and teacher identities are "produced as a nexus of subjectivities in relation to power which are constantly shifting" (p. 3). Narrative, in other words, informs identity production, performance, and power relations. By explicating how identity is (re)presented in narrative, fictional texts, scholars illustrate how identity is formed, negotiated, resisted, and revised. Representations are not determined entirely by nor do they completely reflect real-world experiences, but they do promulgate shared cultural mores. In turn, these fictional narratives and identity scripts shape and reflect cultural values. Booth (1983), one of the foremost theorists of rhetoric and fiction, notes:

> All narratives both depend on and impose what I called "beliefs" and "norms," what modern jargon calls "values," what Bakhtin and other continental critics call "ideology".... In fictional forms most of the important facts are simultaneously values [p. 419].

This fusing of narrative with values and ideology reinforces the link between everyday life and the culture inside books. Examining the rhetoric of fiction thus allows textual critics to uncover possible influences those narratives could have upon audiences and upon culture.

Linking rhetoric with fiction, particularly the rhetoric of myth and narrative, has significant precedent (Booth, 1974, 1983; Burke, 1969a; Chatman, 1990; Fisher, 1984, 1985, 1988, 1989; Lucaites & Condit, 1985; Mendelsohn, 2008; Phelan, 2007; Roberts, 2004; Rushing, 1983, 1985; Rushing & Frentz, 1980, 1993, 2000; Stroud, 2001, 2002). For Burke (1969b), rhetoric is the "symbolic means of inducing cooperation in beings that by nature respond to symbols" (p. 43). Symbolic means encapsulates a broad range of material. Burke delineates the division between rhetoric and fiction based on end-goals. He observes, "Whereas poetic language is a kind of symbolic action, for itself and in itself ... rhetorical language is inducement to action (or to attitude, attitude being an incipient act)" (p. 42). This differentiation enables critics to examine the rhetorical dimensions of poetic texts, including novels like the Potter series. Rhetorical aspects of fiction include the narrative construction of identity and a relationship between audiences and representations (like fictional characters) that Burke terms identification.

Burkean Identification

Burke (1969b) argues that "metaphysically, a thing is identified by its *properties*" (italics original), leading him to define identity as "uniqueness as an entity in itself and by itself" (pp. 21, 23). Individuality emerges from and interacts with cultural values in fictional texts. Burke explains that an individual tries "to form himself in accordance with the communicative norms that match the cooperative ways of his [*sic*] society" (p. 39). This attempt to match representations with identity scripts, as lived, constitutes the "rhetoric of identification" (Burke, 1969b, p. 39). Identification operates both consciously and unconsciously (p. 35). Even when identification is not intentional or conscious, the individual's identifications contribute to "social cohesion" (p. 44). The formation of individual identities relies on identification with collective identities. Identification balances and enables the formation of both individual and collective identity scripts. Such identification requires consubstantiality, a uniting of natures or essences. Burke (1969b) defines consubstantial as "an *acting-together*" (italics original) in which people have "common sensations, concepts, images, ideas, [and] attitudes" (pp. 21, 46). Individuals seek consubstantiality with others via identification. Thus, identification links the individual to a larger community and in turn relies on and fosters communal values and shared ideology.

Burke classifies identification and identity formation as a rhetorical act. He (1969b) contends that "we are clearly in the region of rhetoric when considering the identifications whereby a specialized activity makes one a participant in some social or economic class. 'Belonging' in this sense is rhetorical" (pp. 27–28). By identifying with a group and assimilating communal values and ways-of-being, an individual crafts identity. Like all rhetorical acts, identification depends on contingency. Burke (1969b) argues that "only insofar as men are potentially free, must the spellbinder seek to persuade them" (p. 50). The individual exercises agency when s/he chooses to identify (or not) with a representation, identity script, or ideology.

Although identification with collective identities twines people together, it relies equally upon division from others. Burke (1969b) clarifies that identification "confront[s] the implications of *division*" (italics original) and involves "matters of socialization and faction" (pp. 22, 45). By identifying with one group, faction, or set of values or ideologies, one necessarily deselects others. Therefore, identifications are neither singular nor isolated. Individuals opt to identify with some identity or group scripts and reject others. They face persuasion to join (or not) at every turn, with much of it mediated via popular culture (like the Potter series), about who (and who not) and how to (and not to) be. Burke (1969b) emphasizes how "often we must think of rhetoric … as a general *body of identifications* [italics original] that owe their convincingness much more to trivial repetition and dull daily reënforcement [*sic*] than to exceptional rhetorical skill" (p. 26). Rhetoric, particularly as popular culture, is pervasive. It can be banal and repetitive. As such, identification with rhetorical messages about who and how to be in the world can persuade even more effectively than overt persuasion.

Encouraging identification with an identity script relies on another rhetorical tenet: audience adaptation. Claiming that identification is "perhaps the simplest case of persuasion," Burke (1969b) connects his concept to ancient rhetoric; he reminds us "opinions or assumptions (perhaps today they would be treated under the head of 'attitudes' or 'values') are catalogued as available means of persuasion" in Aristotle's work (pp. 55–56). Aristotle terms this form of widespread public opinion doxa. Bourdieu draws upon this concept, as well; he (1990b) defines doxa as the "relationship of immediate adherence that is established in practice between a *habitus* [italics original] and the field to which it is attuned, the pre-verbal taking-for-granted of the world that flows from practical sense" (p. 210). At its most basic, Burke (1969b) points out, identification entails the "translation of one's wishes into terms of an audience's opinions" (p. 57). By defining identification in terms of doxa, Burke centers the relationship, the interaction between the social field (the audience) and the individual. He concludes, "you persuade a man [*sic*] only insofar as you can talk his language by speech, gesture, tonality, order, image, attitude, idea, *identifying* [italics original] your ways with his" (p. 55). Identification bridges the gap between the individual and the social field by aligning two habiti.

Bourdieu's Habitus

Like doxa, habitus can be traced to ancient Greece, as hexis. In the *Nicomachean Ethics*, Aristotle (trans. 1999) presents hexis as "those things in virtue of which we are in a good or bad condition with respect to the feelings" (pp. 25–26). He champions temperance, fortitude, justice, and prudence in his ethical treatises. In his *Categories* (trans. 2002) and *Metaphysics* (trans. 2000), Aristotle establishes that hexis lasts longer and is more steady than dispositions (2000, Chapter 8; 2002, pp. 27–28). Through life-long preparation, Aristotle suggests, a person fosters the potential to choose to act virtuously. Hexis is not just a capacity or feeling, however. Hexis is both the potential, the capacity, to act virtuously and the acts as enacted, constantly adding to or detracting from that embodied virtue. In short, hexis is a constellation of dispositions and experiences that comprise a person's moral character over time.

When hexis was translated to Latin, it was rendered as habitus. As happened to many classical texts and ideas, hexis/habitus lapsed into obscurity temporarily. Aquinas resurrected the concept and designated the potential virtues as art, science, understanding, and philosophic wisdom (Pegis, 1948, pp. 578–596). After Aquinas, the concept diminished again. The sociologist Pierre Bourdieu reinvigorated and expanded it in the 20th century. Although Celenza (2004) asserts that Bourdieu would reject defining habitus as analogous to the formalist Aristotelian hexis, Bourdieu (1990b) grants Aristotle's hexis was a theoretical precursor for habitus in its present iteration (Bourdieu, p. 53; Celenza, p. 77). Hexis and habitus share several features, including simultaneous flexibility and permanence, engagement with doxa, and emphasis on individual choice.

Bourdieu (1990b) defines habitus as "systems of durable, transposable dispositions" (p. 53). These dispositions create practices and representations, as well as providing a structure that organizes them. Bourdieu differentiates habitus from Wittgenstein's version of dispositions and Chomsky's generative grammar (Bourdieu, 1992, pp. 178–180). The constellation of dispositions that define habitus "incline agents to act and react in certain ways. The dispositions generate practices, perceptions and attitudes which are 'regular' without being consciously co-ordinated or governed by any 'rule'" (Thompson, 1991, p. 12). Dispositions, Wittgenstein suggests, precede and predicate action. So far, dispositions fit with Bourdieu's explanation of habitus. For Wittgenstein (1932), however, dispositions are "something always there" (pp. 91–92). Bourdieu excludes the always-there from habitus. Instead, habitus is indeterminate and vague, always in flux, always changing. He (1990a) explains that habitus functions "as a generative spontaneity which asserts itself with an improvised confrontation with ever renewed situations, it obeys a practical, inexact, fuzzy sort of logic, which defines one's normal relation to the world" (p. 78). Repetition insists upon duplication while transcending the rote predictability of habit or set dispositions. Margolis (1999) explains that Bourdieu's version of habitus focuses on the "spontaneous activity of speech and behavior in ordinary human life" (p. 68). He summarizes the concept as a "ubiquitous feature of ordinary … highly ritualized forms of life" (Margolis, 1999, p. 69). Thus, habitus retains shadows of precipitating action without being collapsible into mere disposition or a rule or grammar.

Habitus functions more like rhetoric than grammar. Like identification, habitus adapts to an audience but can do so "without presupposing a conscious aiming at ends or an express mastery of the operations necessary in order to attain them" (Bourdieu, 1990b, p. 53). Habitus can be unintentional enactments derived from existing dispositions, which emerge from experience. Furthermore, claiming he wanted to "demonstrate the active, inventive, and 'creative' capacities of the *habitus* [italics original] and the agent," Bourdieu (1992) argues that habitus, like Aristotle's hexis, is acquired, changing, and not universal (p. 179). Bourdieu (1992) expands this point, arguing that habitus does not have a "direct and mechanical explanation" because the "dispositions constitutive of the *habitus* [italics original] depend on the state of the field of production" (p. 83). If the state of the field changes, "very different if not contrary positions" may emerge (Bourdieu, 1992, p. 83). Habitus cannot be reduced to habit or to dispositions. It is not repetitive, mechanical, or unreflective; it fluctuates and responds to the state of the field, what we rhetoricians term context.

This continual negotiation of the social field's dispositions further links rhetoric to habitus. Because habitus is practiced, realized, and (re)formed in response to its context, it also can "engender assumptions and anticipations which, ordinarily being confirmed by the course of events, ground a relation of immediate familiarity or ontological complicity with the familiar world, a complicity totally irreducible to the relation between a subject and an object" (Bourdieu, 1992, pp. 328–329). In other words, habitus is not simply a single position or character trait. Rather, it is a constellation, a system, of identity scripts and dispositions developed due to one's "social trajectory" such that any act depends on identifying the possibilities extant in the social field that intersect with one's current identities and dispositions (Bourdieu, 1992, pp. 214–215). Habitus depends on choice and contingency. The reliance on the social field, the context, moves habitus beyond a single individual, however. Considering how an individual's identities and habiti are implicated in a society allows scholars to assess the interaction between the "structures of the social world" and how a particular identity or individual habitus changes over time via lived experiences (Bourdieu, 1992, pp. 265, 328).

Although an individual's habiti are acquired across the lifespan, individual dispositions or identities may not be acquired consciously or intentionally. Margolis (1999) explains that habitus' unconsciousness increases its utility. He (1999) writes, "it is because agents never know completely what they are doing that what they do has more sense than they know" (p. 68). Agents negotiate ways-of-being in the world in inventive, creative, and infinite ways. Although they choose those acts, they may not always consider the ways those acts entangle them with larger ideological and sociological systems. Bourdieu (1990a) reiterates that "types of behavior can be directed towards certain ends without being consciously directed to these ends, or determined by them" (p. 10). The habitus, Bourdieu continues, is the "source of cognition without consciousness, intentionality without intention, and a practical mastery of the world's regularities which allows one to anticipate the future" (p. 12). Habitus enables individuals to negotiate identities and communal values precisely because it is so banal that we may not notice we are enacting cultural and individual dispositions and scripts. Furthermore, habitus "produces strategies which, even if they are not produced by consciously aiming at explicitly formulated goals on the basis of adequate knowledge of objective conditions ... turn out to be objectively adjusted to the situation" (Bourdieu, 1990a, p. 11). The ongoing adaptation between habitus and a social field makes each action inherently contingent—and therefore rhetorical.

Contingency introduces space for agency; Bourdieu expands habitus beyond dispositions to implicate banal ways-of-being. Celenza (2004) explains that habitus, for Bourdieu, is a "complex and intersubjective web of concerns and assumptions shared by a group of people" that creates a field of doxa (p. 14). Articulations of habitus reflect a familiarity with cultural habiti and contribute to the unconscious construction of a cultural doxa. Habitus' flexibility enables one to act, purposefully, without the need for conscious intent or awareness of what drives the choice. Bouveresse (1999) maintains that this intent paradox is positive. He notes, "*habitus* [italics original] allows one to explain how the subject of practice can be determined and yet be acting too" (p. 53). The subject deploys agency by exercising judgment and discernment about the particular situation. The habitus provides the agent fluency with a culture's (and hence audience's) norms, values, and identity scripts—their ideology. Thus, the individual is both constrained by the habitus and contributing to it as s/he acts, even if the individual does not reflect upon or notice the habitus shaping or emerging from the act. Bouveresse (1999) clarifies that agents can act spontaneously because the "action is not the result of an external constraint, but of a disposition whose seat is in the agent himself" (p. 47). Habitus provides a path between the determinism and rules inherent in structural objectivism and the agency and free will of post-structuralism (Bourdieu, 1990a, p. 61; Bouveresse, 1999, p. 51). If individuals internalize or form a given habitus, they are influenced by collective norms even when the agent chooses and negotiates the particulars of each articulation. This in turn contributes to the collective's ongoing habitus, indirectly affecting the actions of others. The concept prevents fixity of social conventions and structures because it fluctuates as individuals act.

Margolis (1999) argues Bourdieu's habitus is distinct from structuralism because of Bourdieu's insistence upon three themes. First, Bourdieu views humans as subjects, not as automatons who follow precepts or rules (although they do not exercise total autonomy). Second, Bourdieu explains human actions as exploitation of the possibilities presented rather than as obedience to societal precepts. Finally, Bourdieu supports binarism in a way distinct from structuralism. Although he rejects hidden totalizing structures, Bourdieu does not reject binaries as structuring principles. Instead, he allows that individuals are faced with binaries and insists they have the capacity, the agency, to respond strategically.

Bourdieu (1984) observes that "*habitus* [italics original] is not only a structuring structure, which organizes practices and the perception of practices, but also a structured structure" (p. 170). It is a symbiotic system of relations between constraints, dispositions, and actions. He emphasizes the agent, who is governed by and creates social norms; he (1984) notes that the "principle of division into logical classes which organizes the perception of the social world is itself the product of internalization of the division into social classes" (p. 170). By emphasizing positions in particular structures, Bourdieu retains binaries as structuring principles. He (1984) contends that the "most fundamental oppositions in the structure (high/low, rich/poor, etc.) tend to establish themselves as the fundamental structuring principles of practices and the perception of practices" (p. 172). Thus, individuals are governed by collective binaries, a structured habitus. As individual agents, they are not merely "us" or "them." Instead, they act in ways that construct, deconstruct, and reconstruct the categories, structuring the individual and collective habiti. The characters in the Potter series negotiate a number of binaries that illustrate the connections between habitus, identification, and narrative forms of identity. The characters must negotiate a series of identity scripts, constrained by binaries, including (but not limited to) Muggle/wizard, Gryffindor/Slytherin, and rule-breaking/rule-following.

Muggle/Wizard Binary

The word Muggle appears seven times in *SS*'s first chapter. This coaches readers, from the outset, with whom to identify. When Harry asks what Muggle means, Hagrid explains, it is "what we call nonmagic folk" (*SS*, p. 53). Not what *they* call themselves, but what *we* call them. Curious what Muggles are like, Ron asks Harry; he responds, "horrible," although he immediately qualifies that not every Muggle is bad (*SS*, p. 99). Within 100 pages, readers understand that Muggles constitute the derogated half of the Muggle/wizard binary. The word wizard always appears in lowercase. Unlike the capitalized Muggle, it is not a proper noun. We are to view "wizard" as ordinary and normal. Modifiers such as "our" and "Muggle" permeate the books, adding us/them connotations to banal items ranging from photographs to chess sets to jelly beans. Following Harry's story, readers learn to identify more with the wizarding world as Harry increasingly identifies with it. Before he encounters the wizarding world, Harry, walking in London with Hagrid, describes the street, and its inhabitants, as "ordinary" (*SS*, p. 68). As he assimilates, however, readers transfer alliances, as well. Harry accomplishes this transition early, learning to view wizards as ordinary folk and to describe non-magic folk, "them," as Muggles.

The characters all must negotiate this binary. Their strategies form habiti responding to individuals' identifications. They demonstrate four strategies in *SS*: (1) avoiding and abjecting the Other, (2) being near "us," (3) relying on inborn talent, and (4) working hard to identify with the desired group.

Avoidance and Abjection of "Them"

The Dursleys identify with the Muggles and abject wizards. To reinforce their identification, they avoid the wizarding world and try to deny that magic exists. All three of the Dursleys bully Harry, to the point that they have tried to erase him—by placing no photos of him in the house, hiding him from guests, and housing him alternately in their smallest room or in a closet beneath the stairs. They speak about, rather than to, him, and Harry is not allowed to ask questions. The Dursleys even pretend Harry's mother, Petunia's sister, never existed. Their avoidance and erasure of magic mirrors the Dursleys' overall strategy for navigating and reinstantiating the binary: they deny, avoid, and abject wizards and magic.

As a child, Harry has unusual events happen around him. He does not intend to create strange events, but his magic manifests even without his conscious intent. The Dursleys attribute these events to Harry, even though he denies it, and they repeatedly discourage him from discussing anything out of the ordinary. After Hagrid reveals Harry's magical nature, the Dursleys avoid Harry, a synecdoche for magic, even more assiduously. They pretend Harry's chairs are empty, and Dudley runs away from Harry (*SS*, pp. 52, 88–89).

They also try to keep magic away from Harry (and vice versa). In order to avoid discussing Harry's acceptance to Hogwarts, his Uncle Vernon attempts to keep acceptance letters out in every possible way, refuses to talk to Harry about it, and moves the family repeatedly, trying to run away. When Hagrid finally finds them and begins to tell Harry about magic, Uncle Vernon tries to intimidate Hagrid and, failing, yells, "I FORBID YOU!" (*SS*, p. 50).

When forced to acknowledge magic's existence, the Dursleys reveal their derision, using words like "rubbish," "peculiar," "weirdos," "dangerous," and "barking, howling mad" (*SS*, pp. 91, 3, 56, 36, and 90). Any time they discuss wizards, they never use we, opting instead for the third person: her, them, they (*SS*, pp. 2, 3, 7, 8). The Dursleys actively construct wizards as the Other. Whenever and however they can, they avoid magic and they handle (and in turn form) the Muggle/wizard binary with their rejection, denial, and avoidance.

Their active avoidance and Othering reflects the Dursley's hatred of magic and highlights a fear of association with an abject Other. Vernon asserts, "they're not like you and me" (*SS*, p. 40). The Dursleys desperately fear that other Muggles will discover they are related to magic. Being associated with the Other is so unspeakable, Vernon even resists thinking it: "If it got out that they were related to a pair of—well, he didn't think he could bear it" (*SS*, p. 8). Thus, the Dursleys deal with the Muggle/wizard binary by constructing a habitus whereby they actively deny and abject the wizarding community. Their proud identification as Muggles (although they would not use that word) works to prevent their (and readers') identification with this half of the binary.

The wizarding community also maintains this Muggle/wizard division through avoidance and abjection. One purpose of the Ministry of Magic, for example, is to hide all evidence of magic from Muggles (*SS*, p. 65). Hagrid and Minerva McGonagall are appalled by the Dursleys in particular. Hagrid asserts the Dursleys are the "biggest Muggles" and McGonagall tells Dumbledore, "you couldn't find two people who are less like us" (*SS*, pp. 53, 13). They both urge Dumbledore to reconsider leaving Harry with them. Avoidance sometimes occurs less purposefully, however. Molly Weasley has a Muggle cousin, Ron notes, but admits they "never talk about him" (*SS*, p. 99). Whether or not they seek to avoid the other, most wizards choose not to interact with Muggles frequently.

Furthermore, anti-Muggle prejudice pervades the wizarding world. Wizards express contempt even for those, like Ron's father, who are interested in Muggles. When Draco Malfoy and Harry Potter first meet, Draco inquires about Harry's lineage, seeking to discover if Harry's parents were "*our* kind"; moreover, Muggle-born wizards, Draco asserts, lack familiarity with societal norms ("*our* ways") (*SS*, p. 78). He values old families, wealth, and social rank more than magical ability (*SS*, p. 108). Hagrid rejects Malfoy's snobbery, but reassures Harry that "yer not from a Muggle family" and "some o' the best I ever saw were the only ones with magic in 'em in a long line o' Muggles—look at yer mum!" (*SS*, p. 79). Ron echoes this sentiment, noting that many Muggle-born wizards succeed (*SS*, p. 100). Rowling coaches us, through Harry's socialization, to identify with wizards but to resist anti-Muggle prejudice. The prejudice reinforces the importance of this binary in the wizarding world. If it were not important, it would not attract so much attention. The binary is maintained by the habitus of avoidance and abjection from both sides. By maintaining the binary, each group reinforces their identification with their own identity.

Being Near "Us"

Hagrid seeks to identify with the wizards, but, as a failed wizard (a squib), Hagrid is liminal. He negotiates the Muggle/wizard binary by being as near as possible to wizards. He lives at Hogwarts, surrounded by aspiring wizards, and works as the Hogwarts gamekeeper, surrounded by magical creatures. This proximity helps to reinforce his identification with wizards instead of Muggles.

Although he identifies with the wizards, Hagrid is self-conscious. When he first meets Harry, he fumbles with the pronouns: "About our world....

Your world. My world. Yer parents' world" (*SS*, p. 50). He includes himself in "us" and immediately distances himself. He desperately wants to be included but realizes he cannot identify fully with the wizards. Moreover, despite being near magic, he is allowed minimal use of it because he was expelled from Hogwarts. The first spell readers and Harry see Hagrid attempt does not work as intended, buttressing his in-between, squib status. Hagrid is between the students and the teachers, the two worlds, and even wizards and magical creatures. He supervises the woods and students' detention well enough, but he fails as a teacher. He acts as Harry's friend, but his age and position separate them. As a half-giant, he is magical but neither a wizard nor a creature. Rowling reinforces his status by depicting Hagrid as physically out of place. When he visits the Hogwarts library, his manner is skulking and self-aware. When he visits Harry in the infirmary, he is described as "too big to be allowed" (*SS*, p. 303). Throughout, Rowling makes readers aware of Hagrid's liminal status.

To increase his identification with the wizards, Hagrid exhibits undying loyalty to Hogwarts and to Dumbledore. Despite his intense commitment, however, Hagrid often lets important information slip. Someone manipulating his attachment to dragons endangers the entire wizarding world (*SS*, p. 266). Due to his mistake, Hagrid feels responsible for Harry's injuries and cries, "I should be chucked out an' made ter live as a Muggle!" (*SS*, p. 303). He accordingly reminds readers both of his desire to be near the wizarding world and the strict division between the two by imagining the ultimate punishment as social exile to the Muggle world.

Hagrid negotiates his status by employing a habitus comprised of seeking proximity to magic. Thus, he finds ways to demonstrate loyalty to wizards, live near wizards, work with magical creatures, and include magic in his life. By doing so, he identifies with the "wizard" half of the binary and helps to reinforce the binary's existence by rejecting life as a Muggle.

Rely on Inborn Talent to Identify with "Us"

Harry's habitus relies on using inborn talent to identify as a wizard. Throughout the series, Harry exhibits magic, ability, and courage that depends on inborn talent and instinct. Anxious to prove himself, he identifies as a wizard not through effort but by relying on his genetics.

From the first moment Harry learns he is a wizard, people's comments establish the strength of his genetic, inborn talent (*SS*, pp. 50, 53). Hagrid shares that Harry's parents were Head Boy and Head Girl when attending Hogwarts, proving both were talented magically (*SS*, pp. 51, 55, 58). Indeed, because Harry's parents were brave, he has additional familial protection (*SS*, pp. 294, 299). Bravery, like his status as a wizard, is his heritage. By the end of *SS*, Harry faces Voldemort alone, relying on his inborn ability and his mother's love. Within a single year, Harry fully identifies as a wizard through this habitus.

Flying provides another example of Harry's inborn talent. It comes naturally to him, making Quidditch instinctual, as well. Harry becomes a Quidditch star overnight. The team captain (Wood) crows that Harry exhibits promise to do as well as (or better than) Charlie Weasley, who was talented enough he could have played professionally. McGonagall observes that Harry's father was quite good at the game as well, again attributing Harry's skill to genetics. Harry need not need exert himself to prove he belongs. His inborn talent becomes his habitus; it requires little work and establishes his identification with the wizard half of the binary as inevitable.

Work Hard to Identify with "Us"

Hermione Granger is unquestionably one of the most talented wizards at Hogwarts. Nevertheless, because both of her parents are Muggles, Hermione works very hard to identify as part of the wizarding world. She is portrayed as worried and feeling inadequate (*SS*, pp. 228, 234). Her hard work helps to show readers that she belongs and that the binary depends on ability as much as birthright.

Hermione's hard work establishes her identification. Simultaneously, it supports her male friends. She helps to prepare the boys' study schedules, insists they attend class, and gets Harry through his exams when he spends most of his time at Quidditch practice. The boys mock her dedication to her studies, despite relying on her knowledge, guidance, and skill. Her studiousness even prevents them from getting in trouble when they need a cover story (*SS*, p. 269). Granted, Hermione completes her homework primarily to enrich her own knowledge. The boys undeniably ride her coattails, however, with the luxury of appearing not to care or working hard. Indeed, Ron and Harry want to put her in her place. For example, they think it is good for her to lose at chess (*SS*, p. 217). Despite their weak work ethic and condescension, Hermione continues to help them to stay on track throughout the series. She works so hard that she manages to get all three of them through school, in other words.

Hermione's extensive knowledge saves them repeatedly. For example, she gets all of them past the first challenge at the end of *SS*. Despite her considerable magical knowledge and talent, though, Hermione's main task in this final sequence is not magical at all. She solves a logic puzzle—a task even a Muggle could contribute (*SS*, p. 285). She is rewarded for her reasoning. Readers are invited to see Hermione as extraordinarily able, but her ability emerges from hard work rather than spell-casting or innate ability. As such,

Hermione appears as a talented and hard-working Muggle rather than a gifted witch. She illustrates characteristics akin to those familiar for a good student in the Muggle world. Her magical skill is so under-played and under-celebrated that even she does not highlight her ability as a witch.

Instead, Hermione emphasizes her ability as a student. She performs well on exams, earns the best grades (including a 112 percent on a Charms exam), and is given the time-turner not to change events (as she and Harry eventually do) but so she can take more classes—so that she can work even harder. Her hard work re-instantiates the binary. Hermione's habitus also genders the binary; "masculine" is aligned with natural talent and inclusion (even Neville comes into his genetic heritage, in the end) and "feminine" is aligned with needing to work harder to belong. Because she must endeavor to be a witch, instead of relying on talent as others do, Hermione's Muggle-born and female identities further reinforce the Muggle/wizard divide because Muggle-born wizards must work much harder than wizard-born (and male) wizards.

All of the characters face the Muggle/wizard constraint as they construct their identities. Their identity scripts emerge from identifications formed with or in reaction to the binary. They adopt habiti that avoid and abject, seek proximity, rely on inborn talent, or work hard in order to craft these identities.

Gryffindor/Slytherin Binary

Upon the students' initial arrival at Hogwarts, McGonagall tells them that houses are like family (*SS*, p. 114). Interpellation into each house's traditional habitus shows up in a number of ways. First, a genetic linkage to the houses is suggested. Identification for many derives from transferring familial commitment to the house. The Weasleys are all in Gryffindor; the Malfoys are all Slytherin (*SS*, pp. 106, 79). The Sorting Hat, with its unfettered access to students' thoughts, naturalizes placement in various houses; it associates particular characteristics with each house (*SS*, p. 118). Students believe they belong in Hufflepuff, for example, if they are loyal, just, and patient. The students then seek to enact their house's habitus, a set of dispositions that seek to embody those virtues. These identifications become so strong that students are conflated with the adjective; they are not Ravenclaw students but Ravenclaws. The ways the characters construct, mobilize, and resist their house habiti demonstrate how official scripts and identification come together to form habitus and identity scripts.

Although readers gain occasional glimpses at Hufflepuff and Ravenclaw, the books' central rivalry between Gryffindor and Slytherin creates a binary.

In case readers needed reinforcement, the first Quidditch match between these two houses firmly establishes us/them in a venue that celebrates competition and division. The characters negotiate this binary with two strategies: (1) following and contributing to the scripts forming the existing habitus, and (2) actively re-creating the habitus through repeated and sustained identification and enactment. Some create the binary by following a house's traditional habitus. Others, through remarkably similar actions, seek to differentiate "us" from "them." Both approaches reify the binary.

Follow the Scripts Provided

Neville Longbottom performs an official habitus to identify with his house. In the beginning of the series, Neville appears weak in every possible way. He cries, expresses fear, snores, and falls off his broom (*SS*, pp. 191, 144–149). He is forgetful and accident-prone (*SS*, pp. 144, 171). When readers first encounter him, he has lost his pet toad, and his grandmother gives him a Remembrall because he cannot remember to complete even the most basic tasks. He struggles with most magic; he messes up a potion badly during their first lesson, teaching readers to associate him with failure (*SS*, pp. 248–249). He admits his family feared he might be a Muggle (*SS*, pp. 243, 125). Readers are encouraged to question why Neville is placed in Gryffindor, but Neville's colleagues urge him to internalize the house's habitus.

The sorting hat struggled to place Neville, but the Gryffindors trust the hat and help him to adopt the house's habitus. In *SS*, Draco curses him and Neville protests to his classmates that he does not belong. Harry reassures Neville and uses the sorting hat as evidence. When Neville stands up to Draco, he uses Harry's exact words (*SS*, p. 223). The characters convince Neville to enact the Gryffindor habitus so well that he stands up to them at the end of *SS*; he illustrates bravery, nerve, and daring, the virtues that typify the house's habitus. Within *SS*, Neville transforms from a scared, disorganized boy to a brave youth enacting and contributing to his house's habitus. At the end of *SS*, and the series, Neville truly comes into his own and embodies the essence of Gryffindor. The storyline's power derives from Neville's successful transformation, which relied upon him internalizing his house's habitus.

The main characters also practice the house habitus. Because the series focuses on the Gryffindor students, Rowling emphasizes acts of bravery, nobility, and chivalry. Harry's defining characteristic at the end of *SS* is bravery. Similarly, Ron supports his friend's quest by letting a stone knight beat him up, making a chivalric sacrifice. Ron and Harry together save Hermione from a troll, at a time when they do not care for her. Despite fearing the troll, they conclude, "what choice did they have?" (*SS*, p. 175). By following the habitus, despite their contrary desires, they internalize the bravery, nobility, and chivalry expected from Gryffindors. Hermione also employs this habitus. For example, she sneaks out of the castle with Harry to help save Hagrid's dragon—and later Buckbeak, as well. In short, the characters enact and reinforce the existing scripts that define the Gryffindor habitus.

Actively and Purposefully Create the Binary

Most prominently, Harry Potter and Draco Malfoy represent Gryffindor and Slytherin. Antipathy directed at the Other is incorporated as a major part of every students' habitus, whatever the house, and is modeled for the readers by these characters. The two students create and maintain an antagonistic relationship, constructing a binary between the houses. For example, they set up a wizard's duel, taunt and chase one another on brooms (in class and in Quidditch), get the other in trouble with teachers, and jealously goad one another. Draco derives joy from Harry's troubles with Professor Snape and tries to get Harry expelled. Similarly, Harry and Ron are delighted when Madam Hooch corrects Malfoy's flying technique and brainstorm ways to get Draco expelled (even Hermione rejoices when Draco earns detention). Harry feels ill when Malfoy celebrates a Slytherin Quidditch win; Draco feels shock and horror when Slytherin loses the house competition at the last minute in *SS*. Their actions, and emotions, are similar. Both Harry and Draco can be cruel. Draco taunts Harry about his parents' death and mocks the Weasleys' poverty (*SS*, pp. 109, 195, 223). Harry hates Draco and rejoices at his panic in the woods during detention. Although Draco's barbs derive from snobbery and his lack of bravery ultimately leads to his downfall, all of these children act petulantly. Rowling uses Draco as a foil for Harry, showing how Harry might have turned out had he joined Slytherin and internalized cunning instead of bravery. Either way, deriding the Other animates the habitus for Hogwarts' houses. The institution, with its inter-house competitions, bolsters this antipathy; the rivalry reinforces each house's identity via contrast with the Other.

Rule-Breaking/Rule-Following Binary

Identity binaries are not the only structuring binaries, however. Indeed, in the wizarding world, rules abound. Wizards may not keep dragons as pets. Underage wizards are not to practice magic away from school grounds, nor may they cast spells between class periods. Students may not visit the Forbidden Forest. Unsupervised wizard dueling is right out. Although many of the rules focus on the school, others extend to adults, like not doing magic in front of Muggles. In a world peppered with prohibitions, some wizards are bound to break rules on occasion. However, for some, rule-breaking is not an exception to the rule but a complete habitus. This happens frequently enough in the series that it has already garnered scholarly attention (Cooley, 2005). Some characters embrace breaking rules, some unconsciously enact this habitus, and others convert to this habitus to forge identification.

Embrace the Habitus

The masters of this habitus, Fred and George Weasley, revel in mischief. In *SS*, they try to steal a toilet seat for Harry, sneak food from the kitchens, and perform pranks (*SS*, pp. 297, 227). The Weasley twins actively embrace the rule-breaking habitus and open a shop to extend it once they leave Hogwarts. They pass on the marauder's map to bring Harry into the rule-breaking habitus. Their glee makes the main characters' rule-breaking appear less severe.

The Weasley twins are punished, but officials endorse Harry's rule-breaking. When Harry disobeys Madam Hooch, Professor McGonagall does not punish him; she recruits him for the house Quidditch team. Harry becomes the only first-year allowed a broom at school, establishing the official endorsement of his rule-breaking from his first year. Dumbledore frequently forgives Harry's transgressions and shares that Harry's father sneaked around at night. When he catches Harry out of bed in the middle of the night, gazing into the mirror of Erised, Harry receives a lesson but no punishment (*SS*, p. 214). Dumbledore—or at least Rowling—uses the opportunity to equip Harry to confront Voldemort. In later books, as the stakes rise, Harry gets away with breaking the law numerous times, as well. He is punished on occasion, but readers are taught to approve of this rule-breaking habitus—at least when Harry employs it.

(Mostly) Unintentionally Enact the Habitus

The main characters break a lot of rules. They do not consciously intend to create trouble as the Weasley twins do, however. This habitus (and the consequent criticisms about the books teaching children to misbehave) has drawn scholarly attention (Hallett, 2005). The main characters may not celebrate the rule-breaking habitus, but they embody, support, and help craft it through their actions. For example, although they realize they are breaking rules, Harry flies over the Forbidden Forest to spy on Professor Snape, and Ron, Hermione, and Harry trespass into the school's—and the Ministry's—restricted areas. They blatantly and frequently violate curfew. Harry's invisibility cloak enables them to break rules but avoid detection or punishment. Although their rule-breaking may not aim to break rules, they participate actively in this habitus.

After they are caught breaking curfew and their entire house suffers, Harry swears he will stop breaking rules. His declaration is motivated not by a change of beliefs but due to a fear of exile. Harry's resolve does not endure. Turn a couple of pages, and he is once again enacting the rule-breaking habitus (*SS*, p. 245). Indeed, despite life-threatening danger, possible expulsion, and the risk of being ostracized by their house and later their society, the main characters disobey the rules and the law repeatedly to save the world. Rule-breaking is an omnipresent conscious *and* unconscious habitus.

Employ a Different Habitus to Join "Us"

Hermione begins the series righteously following the rules, even policing others' rule-breaking. In *SS*, she overhears Ron tell Harry no one likes her because of her prissy attitude. His mean-spirited comment, issued right after she bests him in class, sends her crying to the girls' lavatory, putting her at the mercy of a troll. Immediately after Ron and Harry defeat the troll, Hermione drastically alters her habitus. She rejects the habitus of the quintessential good student. To identify with the boys, she begins to bend and break rules, starting by lying to Professor McGonagall (*SS*, p. 177).

The boys are delighted by this conversion. Harry notes, "Hermione had become a bit more relaxed about breaking rules … and she was much nicer for it" (*SS*, p. 181). She still refuses to let the boys cheat by copying her homework and respects the professors. Hermione changes, though. She starts to question the motives of authority figures (even setting Professor Snape on fire), creates dangerous potions in secret, and helps the boys to break rules. Hermione has adopted the habitus enough by the end of *SS*, that, although she worries about the practicality of keeping a dragon, she does not voice any concern about Hagrid illegally raising one and helps him to avoid punishment.

Mischief is associated more with boys than girls. Hermione's willingness to break rules, to act like a boy by employing this habitus, was crucial for her to become one of the guys. Although she never fully internalizes it, Hermione's conversion reinforces this habitus. Like each of the others, this habitus shapes what it means to be part of "us" in the wizarding world.

In Conclusion

These habiti illustrate how the characters in the Harry Potter series negotiate the binaries structuring their world. To navigate the Muggle/wizard binary, characters use four strategies in *SS*: (1) avoiding and abjecting the Other (e.g., the Dursleys), (2) being near the group with whom they identify (e.g., Hagrid), (3) relying on inborn talent to embody identification (e.g., Harry), and (4) working hard to identify with the desired group (e.g., Hermione). To navigate the Gryffindor/Slytherin binary, characters use two strategies: (1) follow the scripts provided (e.g., Neville), and (2) actively and purposefully create the binary (e.g., Harry and Draco). Finally, to navigate the rule-breaking/rule-following binary, characters use three strategies: (1) embrace it (e.g., Fred and George Weasley), (2) (mostly) unconsciously enact it (e.g., Harry and Ron), and (3) convert to this habitus to forge identification (e.g., Hermione). In sum, I have shown that the Harry Potter characters strategically construct, change, and navigate identifications in *SS* by employing a wide range of habiti.

The ways each of the characters negotiates these structuring binaries reveal ideological and identity scripts. All of these habiti are employed so an individual character can identify with one group or way-of-being instead of another. They model myriad ways to form narrative identity for readers. Furthermore, they reinforce identification as a goal, with a number of different habiti offering ways to create connections with others. Although most readers probably do not face the choice between Muggle and wizard, they do face binaries. The various habiti modeled provide, as Kenneth Burke would put it, equipment for living that can be applied to readers' everyday lives. By looking at a widely consumed text like the Potter series, we gain a greater understanding of the Potter texts, of the rhetorical nature of fiction, and of the utility of using habitus and identification as tools for analyzing rhetorical fiction.

By considering how habitus and identification interact in *SS*, we can see some of the ways narrative intersects with identity. The various strategies sometimes seek identification; sometimes they seek to enact the habitus for other reasons. Identification and habitus interact closely in each strategy, however, providing evidence of the usefulness for considering these two theoretical tools together. Exploring how identity is crafted, how it functions through and against various habiti and identifications, deserves sustained scholarly analysis. I have but opened the door. Much yet remains to learn about how fiction, rhetoric, and identity work through identification and habitus in the Harry Potter universe.

References

Abanes, R. (2001). *Harry Potter and the Bible: The menace behind the magick*. Camp Hill, PA: Horizon.

Aristotle. (1999). *Nicomachean ethics* (T. Irwin, Trans.). (2nd edition). Indianapolis: Hackett.

Aristotle. (2000). *Metaphysics* (A. Madigan, Trans.). Oxford: Oxford University Press.

Aristotle. (2002). *The categories on interpretation* (H. P. Cooke, Trans.). Cambridge: Harvard University Press.

Bloom, H. (2001). Can 35 million book buyers be wrong? Yes. *The San Francisco Jung Institute Library Journal, 19*(4), p. 49–51. Doi: 10.1525/jung.1.2001.19.4.49.
Boffetti, J. (1999). Not quite Narnia: The Harry Potter books in review. *Crisis, 17*(11), 44–45.
Booth, W. C. (1974). *A rhetoric of irony* (Vol. 641). Chicago: University of Chicago Press.
Booth, W. C. (1983). *The rhetoric of fiction* (2nd edition). Chicago: University of Chicago Press.
Bourdieu, P. (1984). *Distinction: A social critique of the judgment of taste* (R. Nice, Trans.). Cambridge: Harvard University Press.
Bourdieu, P. (1990a). *In other words: Essays towards a reflexive sociology* (M. Adamson, Trans.). Cambridge, MA: Polity Press.
Bourdieu, P. (1990b). *The logic of practice* (R. Nice, Trans.). Cambridge, MA: Polity Press.
Bourdieu, P. (1992). *The rules of art: Genesis and structure of the literary field* (S. Emanuel, Trans.). Stanford: Stanford University Press.
Bouveresse, J. (1999). Rules, dispositions, and the *habitus*. In R. Shusterman (Ed.), *Bourdieu: A critical reader* (pp. 45–63). Malden, MA: Blackwell.
Burke, K. (1969a). *A grammar of motives*. Berkeley: University of California Press.
Burke, K. (1969b). *A rhetoric of motives*. Berkeley: University of California Press.
Byatt, A. S. (2003, July 7). Harry Potter and the childish adult. *New York Times*. Retrieved from http://www.nytimes.com/2003/07/07/opinion/harry-potter-and-the-childish-adult.html.
Celenza, C. S. (2004). *The lost Italian renaissance: Humanists, historians, and Latin's legacy*. Baltimore: Johns Hopkins University Press.
Chatman, S. B. (1990). Coming to terms: The rhetoric of narrative in fiction and film. Ithaca: Cornell University Press.
Cooley, R. W. (2005). Harry Potter and the temporal prime directive: Time travel, rule-breaking, and misapprehension in *Harry Potter and the prisoner of Azkaban*. In C. W. Hallett (Ed.), *Scholarly studies in Harry Potter: Applying academic methods to a popular text* (pp. 29–42). Lewiston, NY: Edwin Mellen Press.
Fisher, W. R. (1984). Narration as a human communication paradigm: The case of public moral argument. *Communications Monographs, 51*(1), 1–22.
Fisher, W. R. (1985). The narrative paradigm: An elaboration. *Communication Monographs, 52*(4), 347–367.
Fisher, W. R. (1988). The narrative paradigm and the interpretation and assessment of historical texts. *Argumentation and Advocacy, 25*(2), 49–53.
Fisher, W. R. (1989). Clarifying the narrative paradigm. *Communication Monographs, 56*(1), 55–58.
Gelder, K. (2004). *Popular fiction: The logics and practices of a literary field*. London: Routledge.
Hall, S., & Rutherford, J. (1990). *Identity: Community, culture, difference*. London: Lawrence and Wishart.
Hallett, C. W. (Ed.). (2005). *Scholarly studies in Harry Potter: Applying academic methods to a popular text*. Lewiston, NY: Edwin Mellen Press.
Jordan, D. (April 4, 2007). Time comes for Harry to fly to the rescue. *Times UK*.
Komschlies, J. (2000). The perils of Harry Potter: Literary device or not, witchcraft is real—and dangerous. *Christianity Today, 44*(12).
Lucaites, J. L., & Condit, C. M. (1985). Re-constructing narrative theory: A functional perspective. *Journal of Communication, 35*(4), 90–108.

Mac an Ghaill, M. (1994). *The making of men: Masculinities, sexualities, and schooling.* Buckingham: Open University Press.
Margolis, J. (1999). Pierre Bourdieu: *Habitus* and the logic of practice. In R. Shusterman (Ed.), *Bourdieu: A critical reader* (pp. 64–83). Malden, MA: Blackwell.
Mayes-Elma, R. (2006). *Females and Harry Potter: Not all that empowering.* Lanham, MD: Rowman & Littlefield.
Mendelsohn, F. (2008). *Rhetorics of fantasy.* Hanover, NH: Wesleyan University Press.
Pegis, A. C. (Ed.). (1948). *Introduction to St. Thomas Aquinas.* New York: Modern Library.
Pennington, J. (2002). From Elfland to Hogwarts, or the aesthetic trouble with Harry Potter. *The Lion and the Unicorn, 26*(1), 78–97.
Phelan, J. (2007). Experiencing fiction: Judgments, progressions, and the rhetorical theory of narrative. Columbus: Ohio State University Press.
Roberts, K. G. (2004). Texturing the narrative paradigm: Folklore and communication. *Communication Quarterly, 52*(2), 129–142.
Rosenberg, B. (1986). *Genreflecting: A guide to reading interests in genre fiction* (2nd edition). Littleton, CO: Libraries Unlimited.
Rowling, J. K. (1997). *Harry Potter and the sorcerer's stone.* New York: Arthur A. Levine Books.
Rushing, J. H. (1983). The rhetoric of the American western myth. *Communication Monographs, 50*(March), 14–32.
Rushing, J. H. (1985). *E.T.* as rhetorical transcendence. *Quarterly Journal of Speech, 71*(2), 188–203.
Rushing, J. H., & Frentz, T. S. (1980). "The deer hunter": Rhetoric of the warrior. *Quarterly Journal of Speech, 66*(December), 392–406.
Rushing, J. H., & Frentz, T. S. (1993). Integrating ideology and archetype in rhetorical criticism, part II: A case study of *Jaws. Quarterly Journal of Speech, 79*(February), 61–81.
Rushing, J. H., & Frentz, T. S. (2000). Singing over the bones: James Cameron's *Titanic. Critical Studies in Media Communication, 17*(March), 1–27.
Schoefer, C. (2000, January). Harry Potter's girl trouble: The world of everyone's favorite kid wizard is a place where boys come first. *Salon.* Retrieved from http://dir.salon.com/books/feature/2000/01/13/potter/index.html.
Stroud, S. R. (2001). Technology and mythic narrative: *The Matrix* as technological hero-quest. *Western Journal of Communication, 65*(4), 416–441.
Stroud, S. R. (2002). Multivalent narratives: Extending the narrative paradigm with insights from ancient Indian philosophical texts. *Western Journal of Communication, 66*(3), 369–393.
Thompson, J. B. (1991). Editor's introduction to *Language and symbolic power*, by Pierre Bourdieu (pp. 1–31). Cambridge: Harvard University Press.
Walkerdine, V. (1990). *Schoolgirl fictions.* London: Verso.
Wittgenstein, L. (1932). *Wittgenstein's lectures, Cambridge, 1932–1935.* Oxford: Basil Blackwell.

Gendered Heroism: Family Romance and Transformations of the Hero-Type

SHIRA WOLOSKY

The figure of the hero emerges with apparent clarity from the archive of myth, folk-tales, fairy-tales and narratives that invoke them. Vladimir Propp's list of 31 hero functions and motifs reduces the flesh of narrative heroism to skeletal form. Lord Raglan and Joseph Campbell similarly X-ray the hero to produce distilled heroic tables of elements. Otto Rank, Bruno Bettelheim and Northrop Frye in turn align mythic, folkloric and romance patterns with deep psychological structures identified and described by Freud, most vividly in his essay on "Family Romances." As outlined there, core narrative patterns and their heroes correspond to Oedipal conflicts and their resolutions, at once following and leading the reader along the courses of maturation embodied in the tales.

This hermeneutic of family romance is a powerful and persuasive one. But like all hermeneutical mirrors, the narratives tend to reflect what is put in front of them. In the case of family romance, this reflection is male. Early feminist psychologists and literary critics, and indeed Freud himself noticed a gender asymmetry in both his family romance structures and the Oedipal analysis on which it was based. In "Family Romances" itself Freud simply muses that "the imagination of girls is apt to show itself much weaker" than that of boys. Girls do not and cannot pursue and fulfill the romance structure. The fantasy of being adopted as the node of family romance unfolds as an Oedipal narrative of identification but also rivalry with the father over the mother; acted out through a series of heroic adventures of overcoming obstacles and defeating adversaries; which allows the hero to lay claim to the lady who substitutes for the mother, now possessed by the hero himself, taking the father's place. But the child in this narrative is a boy, as Freud himself eventually noticed. Girls in Freud do not identify with fathers, nor rival them, nor set out on adventures of challenge, test and conquest. What they do instead is wait for the Hero to rescue and claim them.

The *Harry Potter* series has on the whole been assimilated into and interpreted through just these heroic romance patterns. The result has been treatments of gender that are among the books' most controversial topics. The girls and women have been criticized as stereotypical, unfeminist, unheroic, secondary to the male figures. Hermione is said to weep and giggle and shriek. McGonagall is prissy and just a Professor and not Headmaster (although she is Head of House, vice–Headmaster, and there have been women headmasters and heads of major institutions such as St. Mungo's hospital). Molly is a traditional housewife. There are no women central figures for good or evil. The main character is male. At times the discussion seems to be a kind of gender score-keeping, with the focus centered on the social status of each fantasy character with little regard to narrative context (Zettel, 2005, p. 84). Hermione especially attracts skepticism, as approval-seeking, emotional, a stereotypically "helpless fairy tale damsel in distress" (Schoeffer, 2000).

These readings, however, impose the very stereotypes they claim to discover. They confirm the essentialized feminine traits they set out to protest, misreading as rigid oppositions what the books re-write as complex, multiple and shared qualities. The way certain qualities have been gendered masculine and feminine is something the books investigate, showing them to be historical categories and practices, not as necessary or essential human forms. Many of the negative judgments of *Harry Potter's* gendering themselves depend upon and reconfirm the traditional gendering of heroism and its hero-model, taken as the interpretive framework or paradigm in Thomas Kuhn's sense. The girls, according to these norms, are unheroic and secondary; and so that is what they find.

This, however, is not an adequate reading of *Harry Potter*. Instead of representing and reflecting what happens in the books, the books are seen to reflect and represent a heroic paradigm that is highly gendered. In fairness, most of these readings were published before the series was completed, based at most on the first four books. *SS*, in particular was quickly typed as a Cinderella story (with gender most fully discussed by Ximena Gallardo-C. & C. Jason Smith, 2002, who see Harry as a "boy caught in a girl's story," p. 196). As to the hero, Harry is consistently defined through the hero-model of fairy-tale family romance: the hero as solitary adventurer, sallying forth to confront and overcome obstacle and enemy, to claim a Lady who awaits his rescue in a state either of confinement or sleep, which represents (his) psychological maturity and resolution of the Oedipus complex. Helpers often do aid him on his way (Vladimir Propp [1968] Hero Functions 12 and 14, in which Hero is tested, interrogated, attacked, etc., preparing the way for his/her receiving magical agent or helper [donor], p. 31). But the hero story is the story of the hero. He is its center and focus, and indeed the more central and focal he is the more he fulfills himself and embodies heroism. For to be heroic is to be independent, autonomous, self-reliant. This is also what it is to be psychologically mature. As Freud writes in the opening of "Family Romances": "The liberation of an individual, as he grows up, from the authority of his parents is one of the most necessary though one of the most painful results brought about by the course of his development" (1909, p. 235).

But the Solitary Hero–type is not a good depiction of Harry or of *Harry Potter*. Harry is not a classical hero embodying autonomous action as the psychological or, indeed, moral ideal. It is rather Voldemort who represents autonomous action. Nor are girls or women figures in *Harry Potter* either simply object-goals or Helpers. Hermione, far from being a crybaby, is a co-hero, along with although to a greater extent than Ron. Friendship itself, as in Aristotle, emerges as central to defining and realizing the self as well as society, as against purely autonomous models. In *Harry Potter*, heroism itself is redefined not as the solitary adventurer proving prowess, but as joint commitment in a shared heroism that also recasts masculine and feminine typologies.

This transformation of the hero-model significantly revises the family romance structure and the developmental models based on it. The position, definition, and roles of fathers and especially of mothers shift, reconstituting processes of individuation and reconceiving maturity as incorporating not only assertion but also identification, attachment, and dependence. Exploring and acknowledging the importance of pre–Oedipal as well as Oedipal formations and distributions, the very definition of maturity, emerges in altered configurations. Strikingly, although Harry's development and identification is first closely associated with his father James, it gradually comes to center on his mother alongside and even more profoundly than his father. The books pursue a course from earlier father-centered identification to recognition and embrace of his mother, who emerges in the astonishing conclusion of Book 7 as the hidden figure around whom the entire narrative has revolved. Harry's likeness to her, beyond although not refuting his identification with James, comes to define his heroism, hence re-defining heroism itself. That this woman-authored narrative recasts gender representation and the whole figure of the hero suggests evidence of feminist claims that transformation in social structure can also transform psychological models and experience.

Family Romance

The opening of Book 1 of *Harry Potter* immediately places it in the family romance tradition (Doniger, 2000, p. 26). Like so very many heroes in fairy-tales, folklore, and narratives that echo them, Harry is an orphan, living with grotesque, cruel, abusive step-parents. But Harry really belongs to a far superior family, with parents who are powerful, elevated, indeed magical. In this he fulfills the core structure of family romance in Freud. As Freud writes, the child (i.e., the boy) begins with the "intense wish … to be like his parents (that is the parent of his own sex)" (1909, p. 235). However, he inevitably becomes disappointed in them, through comparison to other adults but above all through rivalry. This rivalry extends not only to the father in competition over the mother as in the core Oedipal structure, but also with his siblings. The child feels "he is not receiving the whole of his parents' love … which he feels regrets at having to share with brothers and sisters." Accordingly he conceives a fantasy "of being a step-child or an adopted child." In this wise he fulfills his wish of "getting free from the parents of whom he now has a low opinion and of replacing them by others, who, as a rule, are of higher social standing." This pattern is enumerated in Otto Rank's *The Myth of the Birth of the Hero* as Points (1) the hero's descent from noble, powerful parents; (3) his being raised by lowly parents; (4) his return to his first parents, ultimately followed by (6) acknowledgement of the hero by the father; and (7) the hero's being honored (pp. xx, 47). In Raglan, family romance runs through the twenty-two "common traits of god-heroes" which make up the "mythic hero archetype." The idealized parents appear as Points 1–2, where the hero's mother is a "royal virgin" and his father a "king." The rivalry with the father emerges in Point 6 where "at birth an attempt is made, usually by his father or his maternal grandfather, to kill him." Points 7–9 introduce the family romance proper in which the hero is "spirited away, and "reared by foster parents in a far country," "told nothing of his childhood." What follows is a series of adventures in which he achieves "victory over the king, and/or a giant, dragon, or wild beast," marries "a princess, often the daughter of his predecessor, and becomes king," and lastly receives a mysterious burial (1956, pp. 174–175).

Bruno Bettelheim elaborates and excavates this family romance structure specifically in fairy tales. There, it is not necessary that the hero be descended from an elite and powerful true family but rather that he joins one as the conclusion of the tale, when the (boy) child through his adventures earns the hand of the King's Daughter and thus himself becomes royal. In Bettelheim's reading, this conclusion represents maturity: the child becomes king of himself. In the case of a girl, she too is a despised step-daughter who is elevated into royal Princesshood only through marriage to an appropriate Prince. She then attains the high status, confirmation, and triumph over rivals for which the child yearns (1977, pp. 66–73).[1] In the case of the girl, however, there are no real adventures through which this status is attained. The only exploits ventured by Cinderella are going to the ball and trying on shoes, when she reverts to being the object of pursuit of the Prince. As Freud writes in both "Family Romances" (1909, p. 237) and "Creative Writers and Daydreaming" (1907, pp. 147), the boy's dreams are both "erotic and ambitious" each confirming the other. In the dreams of girls, however, "erotic wishes predominate almost exclusively," "their ambition is as a rule absorbed by erotic trends," since girls can never fulfill ambition on their own but only through a male partner.

Bettelheim incorporates into his Freudian analysis elements from object-relations psychology. Here, the two trends of identification/idealization and rivalry/aggression are split apart, into separate good and bad fathers and mothers. The child cannot bear the ambivalence he feels to his father, whom he needs for the protection and support without which no child can survive; and whom he admires and identifies with, or hopes and wishes to. Therefore he splits the father into a bad one who can safely be the object of the boy's anger, aggression, disappointment and rivalry, projected onto adversarial figures the boy can oppose rather than acknowledging them to be his own feelings. The other, good father, is idealized to remain the positive object of the boy's devotion, identification, and trust (1979, p. 68). As a narrative form, being an orphan releases the child to enact this split as well as initiating the "liberation" from parental authority that alone, in Freud as well as Erikson and Kohlberg, will allow him to grow into a mature adult (male).[2] The horrible, unworthy, abusive grown-ups the child lives with cannot be his true parents, who are instead elevated and marvelous (and if dead, even easier to idealize), who would properly value him and who confirm his own true, high worth as their son.

The relevance of family romance structure to *Harry Potter* is pretty much a given. Harry is the family romance orphan, living with those hideous step-parents, who, as in Raglan's Point 3, are "close relatives of the parents," the split off "bad" parents opposite to the ideal "good" parents they double. Harry discovers these true parents, and with them his own identity as magical, elevated, rich, and famous—that is, heroic beyond any dream. He himself has even defeated (although not finally or there would be no story) the evil figure who acts in family romance as the object of aggression and competition both within the hero and projected outside him, something *Harry Potter* underscores through the insistence that Voldemort is Harry's own double—"strange likenesses," as Tom Riddle tells Harry in Book 2 (*CoS*, p. 317). Book 1's opening chapter "The Boy Who Lived" recounts the traumatic threat at birth or soon thereafter often associated with heroes. Harry then leaves his false parental home, to engage in a series of confrontations with the evil enemy who is his rival antagonist, ultimately defeating him. Harry thus fulfills his nature as hero, achieves identification with and also replacement of his father, finally (in the epilogue) to marry a mother substitute.[3]

Many a summary of *Harry Potter* has hewn to this plot line, characterizing Harry's heroism in accordance with it. As Elizabeth Schafer sums it up, each (of the first few) *Harry Potter* books offers "a happy ending complete with a vanquished archenemy, restoration of the status quo, and recognition of Harry's prowess" (2000, p. 6). Jack Zipes, too, reads Harry in the first four books as "the hero" who has "supernatural gifts that enable him to perform heroic deeds and defeat the cynical forces of evil much like the knights of Arthurian legend" (2001, p. 174). But the series as it unfolds both further explores the terms of classical family romance and redefines its heroism. The figures of evil embody split off elements both within the self and represented by bad fathers. Maturity requires that these be re-integrated into a father-figure who is no longer either idealized or demonized. The child must come to terms with the ambivalence he harbors regarding his parents, must be able to accept that his parents are indeed imperfect and flawed beings, as all humans are.

Harry undergoes just such a process in regard to James and other father-figures. The first books entirely idealize James, with whom Harry strongly identifies. Harry's Patronus takes the form of a stag, his father's Animagus shape. Indeed, in Book 3 Harry mistakes himself for his father, actively taking the place and doing the saving action he had first thought his father to perform. Throughout the first books, Harry takes the many times he is told that he resembles James as the compliments they are intended to be. Snape is the exception. When Snape likens Harry to James he means it as an insult. But Harry dismisses Snape's snide snipes as insidious slurs.

This simple idealization and identification becomes complicated in Book 5. Harry steals into Snape's memory to witness a scene from the schooldays in which James humiliates Snape out of rivalry and spite. Harry is shaken. His idealization of his father has been punctured and his need for reassurance drives him to question his father's friends who are now his own substitute father figures. Lupin confirms the events Harry has witnessed, but indulgently. James had been wrong but he had grown up afterwards. Driven as he was over rivalry for Lily, James matured when he succeeded in winning her. Still, Harry is thrown. He must accept that his father was not perfect. Such a step towards acceptance of imperfection in his father is necessary to accept it in others, and in himself.

Indeed, the break in idealization and integration of the "good" and "bad" aspects of others must finally also include oneself. Each of us is a being of many elements, unconscious as well as conscious desires and aggressions, partly integrated but never completely, exerting diverse pressures on our behavior and interior lives with or without our knowledge and consent.

Acknowledging the humanity of one's parents allows the growing child to reintegrate what had been split apart figures. No mother, however well-intentioned and attentive, can provide the child with the total focus, milk, comfort, ease and approval the child desires. Sometimes she has to sleep. There are aches she cannot ease. Disappointment is inevitable. Accepting this heals the splitting of figures and allows the child to accept not only the parent, but ultimately him or herself. Only by forgiving one's parents can one forgive and accept oneself too, moving forward to a fuller self-integration and with it the ability to love actual, non-ideal, imperfect human beings.

This course of accepting and embracing the mixed nature of human selves is re-experienced again in Book 7, when Harry must confront Rita Skeeter's exposé of Dumbledore, another idealized father-figure. One plotline of the final book pursues Harry's attempt to uncover Dumbledore's history, which his headmaster had not shared with him; to recognize and ultimately accept Dumbledore's weaknesses, vulnerabilities, failures, and difficult, at times compromised, choices. When Harry in the end chooses to trust and follow the path Dumbledore has shown him and the tasks he has given him (*DH*, p. 563), the family romance split into bad and good fathers is healed into a more integrated, self-accepting self.

This embrace of partial motives, compromised actions, vulnerabilities and forgiveness of failure and disappointment is not part of the traditional hero-model's C.V. Harry in fact has not been the solitary self-defining autonomous individual hero in other ways, almost from the beginning. *The Sorcerer's Stone,* the closest to the fairy-tale format, presents Harry at his most heroic-typehood. He can fly better than anyone, born to it like and through his father, like James a fabulous Seeker. Hermione tells him he is "a great wizard" (*SS*, p. 367). But as things go along Harry's great wizardhood thins. He has his strengths, but he has his weaknesses. In terms of sheer magical ability and power, he is bested by Voldemort, Dumbledore, Snape, Lupin, indeed by Hermione herself. She is the better student, the more clever, able, powerful, resourceful, inventive wizard—or rather witch—than he is. When Snape complains to Dumbledore that Harry is "mediocre" in magic Dumbledore responds only that Harry is "reasonably talented"; and to Snape's accusation that Harry is "arrogant as his father," "his father all over again"; Dumbledore replies that although he resembles his father "in looks ... his deepest nature is much more like his mother's" (*DH*, pp. 679, 684).

Heroic Paradigms

That Freud's family romance and corresponding Oedipal structures were heavily masculine in norm and form was noticed by feminist criticism as soon as there was any. In literary theory, a major feminist interest has been in tracing how attention to the girl's experience rather than the boy's, as character, writer, and reader, may alter the paradigms of narrative. Can the girl character take on a role more active than imprisonment in towers like Rapunzel, or swooning into a coma like Sleeping Beauty and Snow White? Can she pursue, as Freud said she could not, both erotics and ambition? To see that girl's don't get to go on adventures all you need to do is read the classic stories: what Anne Sexton calls "the glass Snow White" and Sleeping Beauty "a catatonic stuck in a time machine" (1981, pp. 228, 292). What would happen to the whole structure and its values, not least heroism, if she ventured forth?

When family romance is enacted as narrative, the result has been called Quest Romance. Family romance appoints a constellation of characters: orphan, ideal parents, step-parents, villain adversaries who represent rivalries, the lady-prize figure. When put into action, the narrative takes shape as quest. The orphan (boy) departs from the step-parents, acts out his rivalries on antagonists whom he defeats, identifies with the ideal father by becoming one himself or achieving some other status showing maturity, self-possession, and elevation, signaled by marrying the ideal mother-substitute prize. The arc is from dispossessed orphan to possessive individual hero. In doing so, he is able to integrate his own opposing impulses and aspects, the aggressive drives expressed in rivalry but also, in sequence, the desire embodied in identification with the ideal. Aggression and idealization that split into the good and bad parents also represent a split in the self, the aggression projected from the self onto the father and onto all the other opponents he overcomes, the identification realized as he pursues his goal, the attainment of which also means admitting and accepting both impulses in the mature hero, healing his self-division.

As to female characters, in the Quest Romance they are figures for the mother who is the object of the Oedipal rivalry between father and son. In Quest Romance she is idealized in her good aspect as the Lady whom the prince rescues and marries, and, in her bad aspect, as the step-mother or other female monsters and dragons he encounters and defeats. Identification with the father is accomplished by attaining a Lady who substitutes for the mother (or some other goal such as the Grail which stands in for her), at once satisfying but also displacing his rivalrous desire in a socially and psychologically acceptable outcome.

The narrative Quest structure thus sets the family romance characters in motion towards resolving the conflict between aggression and desire, rivalry and identification, defeating the rivals who represent the first and expressing identification through claiming the Lady-prize and a status that represents the self as an integrated person. Northrop Frye succinctly schematizes the Quest narrative and correlates it with both myth and psychological romance. As he sums up, the romance quest

> has three main stages: the stage of the perilous journey and the preliminary minor adventures; the crucial struggle, usually some kind of battle in which either the hero or his foe, or both, must die; and the exaltation of the hero.

These foes, he continues,

> clearly have a parental origin; and yet redeemed and emancipated paternal figures are involved too, as they are in the psychological quests of both Freud and Jung. Translated into ritual terms, the quest-romance is the victory of fertility over the waste land [1971, pp. 186, 192].

But girls don't go on Quests. As in Sleeping Beauty, Snow White, Rapunzel et al., they either are imprisoned or asleep, awaiting recognition and rescue from those who do. Attempts on the part of the girl to become herself a Quester tend to conflict with her gender status and role. This is the case in social senses. Girls, as myriad etiquette books have instructed, are pure, submissive, obedient, silent (Welter, 1966, p. 152). They are not questers but their objects. The figure of the Lady, who in various guises serves as an image of the Quest's achievement, represents the hero's triumph and maturity, not her own. To embark on adventure conflicts with the historical norms of femininity. It is to risk social condemnation, ostracism, rejection, and internal anxiety (Gilligan, 1983, p. 15). And what would be her Quest's goal? As feminist literary critics have explored, if the goal of the Quest is figured as male, then on attaining him, she loses her initiative, becoming in normal gender hierarchy his wife or mistress rather than emerging as her own master (Gilbert & Gubar, 1979, pp. 47–51). To achieve the male is to lose herself, in subordination to the husband. Same-sex figuration of the goal might represent another option, resulting in a model of sisterhood rather than traditional marriage hierarchies. But rivalry is necessary in the Family and Quest Romance. The repression of rivalry that the sisterhood model may entail could sap the very energy and drive required to Quest at all. Identification with the father also remains problematic, whether to claim his authority for herself, take him as her model, or claim his inheritance, all forbidden in Freud (Benjamin, 1988, p. 109).

Feminist critics and psychologists have explored these and other configurations of family romance, considering how patterns may shift if women are seen as actors and not only as objects in the quests of men. Marianne Hirsch's *The Mother/Daughter Plot* (1989) traces variations in family romance structures. These move from "disidentification" with an absent mother in the 19th century (pp. 10–11), to "fraternal" relationships that evade motherhood in the early 20th (p. 44), to rebellion against mothers and renouncing love and marriage for work (p. 54), to more contemporary displacements of heterosexual romance to focus instead on female relationships which leave only a secondary role to men (pp. 96–97). These and other feminist reconsiderations of the family romance almost entirely approach it from the feminine viewpoint, of the woman writer and her female characters (Zagarell, 1988). But the reassessment of family romance should also be applied to male figures. Among the gender complaints that have been directed at Rowling is the fact that hers is a male main character. Most women writers of children's literature create girl characters in books which are in turn read mainly by girls (Clark, 1996, p. 22; Trites, 1997, p. 3).[4] Rowling's invention of a male main character ultimately registers not her selling-out (although commercial considerations have deeply penetrated discourses about children's literature and *Harry Potter*) but a recasting of heroism and the terms of its gendering.

There are two problems with the portrait of Harry as solitary hero. The first is that he isn't one. Harry is rarely solitary, except when miserably locked up at the Dursleys.' He undertakes few adventures alone. His heroic deeds are fully framed and mostly shared with his companions. Indeed he finds being alone distressing, a sign of being cut off, of depressive isolation from others in the aftermath of Sirius's death (*OotP*, p. 855). The character who IS solitary and independent is Voldemort.

Voldemort's case history is a demonstration of failed family romance, or, rather, the failure of classical family romance structure itself. It shows the vulnerability of invulnerability in the heroic models the classic Quest romance offers.

Voldemort is independent and autonomous. As Dumbledore observes to Harry about Voldemort in one of their tutorials, Tom Riddle is as a child "already highly self-sufficient, secretive, and apparently friendless.... He preferred to operate alone ... Lord Voldemort has never had a friend, nor do I believe that he has ever wanted one" (*HBP*, p. 277). Throughout the books he refuses all assistance. He thinks that trust of others is a betrayal of the self. Of James and Lily in their final moments he hisses to himself, "How stupid they were, and how trusting, thinking that their safety lay in friends" (*DH*, p. 344). In his panic to ensure that the Horcruxes safeguarding his soul are safe, he reflects that "it had been a grave mistake to trust Bellatrix and Malfoy: Didn't their stupidity and carelessness prove how unwise it was ever to trust?" (*DH*, p. 551). Book 7 is constructed of intercrossing and cross-purposive Quests. While Harry pursues the Horcruxes to defeat Voldemort (not the Hallows to empower himself), Voldemort pursues the Elder Wand (not knowing it is a Hallow). And Harry works only with others: Hermione and Ron, Dobby and Aberforth, Neville and Dumbledore's Army. Very striking is the fact that of the seven Horcruxes, Harry himself destroys only one: the Diary. The others are destroyed by Dumbledore (the Ring), Ron (the Locket), Hermione (the Cup), Malfoy and his cohorts (the Diadem, by the Fiendfyre they unleash); Neville (the Snake), and Voldemort himself (Harry). As to his own venture, Voldemort muses: "A job, like the quest for the Elder Wand, [is one] that he must undertake alone" (*DH*, p. 551).

That Voldemort is a parricide is a clear mark of failed family romance: killing your father is one sure way to tell. This is to be entrapped by the Oedipal rivalry instead of resolving it. But Voldemort experiences no identification, no attachment to offset or frame the rivalry that drives him. He repudiates both father and mother. His explanation to Harry of his name change from Tom Riddle sums up failed family romance and the fantasy of domination it breeds:

> I, keep the name of a foul, common Muggle, who abandoned me even before I was born, just because he found out his wife was a witch? No, Harry—I fashioned myself a new name, a name I knew wizards everywhere would one day fear to speak, when I had become the greatest sorcerer in the world! [*CoS*, p. 314].

As with Milton's Satan who also embodied certain heroic traits (as Blake saw), such utter assertion of the self is ultimately self-defeating. As in the first attack on Harry, and the last, Voldemort repeatedly destroys himself. Harry, in contrast, is unimaginable without his friends. As Harry steels his nerve after Sirus's death to challenge Voldemort, Dumbledore urges him not to do so alone. "You need your friends, Harry. As you so rightly said, Sirius would not have wanted you to shut yourself away" (*HBP*, p. 78).

The series of *Harry Potter* is bursting with variations on family romance. Malfoy both identifies with his father and is also in fierce rivalry in ways he displaces onto Harry. As is true fundamentally in the books, his most redemptive relationship is with his mother, who saves him and, in an act of powerful symbolism in the books, gives him her wand, the ultimate emblem of (masculine) assertive power (not to mention obvious phallic symbolism). The Weasleys offer a father who is loved and flawed, loved as flawed, evading pure idealization. Percy, who insists on idealization and is unconscious of his rivalries, comes closest to failed family romance among the Weasleys. Rivalry is likewise explored through Ron, against his brothers and Harry. But he contends with and integrates it through strong loyalties and attachments. Then there is Ginny. Ginny's crush on Harry is off-putting if plausible. But she from the first thirsts for independence, longing to go to Hogwarts with her brothers, scornfully rejecting her brothers' attempts to dictate her behavior, in striking contrast against poor Merope who is utterly cowed, abused, and despised by her brother and father. Once Ginny gets older she, as Hermione explains, gets over her infatuation with Harry to define herself with other relationships and interests.

Which brings us to Hermione. Discussions of *Harry Potter* seethe with pro- and con-gender assessments of its various female characters. These include Ginny, McGonagall, to a lesser extent Molly and Lily and Fleur, and above all Hermione, who often seems like a Quaffle ball knocked around in gender score-keeping. On one side, the female characters are seen as weak, passive, secondary, fulfilling and hence enforcing gender stereotypes (notably Schoefer 2000, Heilman, Gupta 2003). On the other the girls are defended as strong figures that subvert and not merely confirm gender stereotypes, emphasizing as well that the female characters grow as the series does. The novels are seen then not to show what should be but rather what is, the gender hierarchies that continue to govern the society we inhabit (notably Dresang, 2002, p. 220; Zettel, 2005; Fry, 2001). I will not enter these lists of debate over gender status character by character. At issue here are rather the paradigms which establish the terms of judgment to begin with. Attacks on Hermione and other *Harry Potter* women interestingly reproduce and enforce the very distributions and evaluations of gender they purport to protest. They assume (1) that specific characteristics are gendered male and female and (2) that the ones gendered male are superior and provide the measure for assessing both men and women. To protest that Hermione and other women weep and are emotional, that McGonagall is motherly, that Molly is devoted to her family, that the women are more caring than the men are, while praising the men as engaged in power struggles which make clear their various strengths, is to accept and embrace male gender definitions within a male gendered paradigm, and to disregard what is happening in *Harry Potter* (Heilman, 2003, pp. 223, 227, 225, 226, 231). Farah Mendelsohn, for example, complains that Harry is limited in his magic powers, relies on gifts, owes his success to aid from his companions; that he is in many ways "passive," and that he is thereby "inconsistent" with the hero-prince paradigm (2002, pp. 366–376, pp. 368–369).

But these are not inconsistencies; they are rather the point. Rowling is not failing properly to fulfill the hero-type. She is proposing a different one. Mendelsohn demonstrates how a given paradigm can force data into its interpretive patterns. Instead of seeing these anomalies as failures of her paradigm, what they point to is a different paradigm of heroism that embraces different values.

Companionate Heroism

Other readings of *Harry Potter* see in it not the mechanical reproduction of gender roles, but the subversion of gender stereotypes. Harry and Hermione then display neither standard gendered attributes nor mere role reversal, but a mix of characteristics classically assigned as gendered.[5] Both display both sorts of characteristics: courage, strength, coolness, logic—and also self-doubt and fear (Fry, 2001, p. 157). Hermione is both just and caring, incorporating into her character what have been seen as male and female moral tendencies. Both qualities are evident in her legal defense of the hippogryph in *Prisoner of Azkaban*. Many other of Hermione's actions are both bold and devoted, as when she and Harry rescue Sirius at the end of that book. Her social activism to liberate the house-elves (who suggest not only racial slavery but, since their enslavement is housework, also house-wifery) is a campaign both of justice and caring responsibility (Dresang 2002, pp. 222–224). Harry, too, has been distinguished from the classic hero. "Never the self-centered independent hero," he represents "not only self-reliance" but is "gender-transgressive," "associated with a feminine side" and "choosing feminine values" (Gallardo-C. & Smith, 2002, pp. 197–200).

Such challenges to gender typing can be further extended beyond characters to the broad narrative structures out of which they develop, and the psychological structures these both portray and open. The intersection of familial structures and plot that has been traced by Hirsch, "embedding the engenderment of narrative within the experience of family"; emerges in *Harry Potter* as transformation of core configurations of developmental structure, narrative course, and hero-type (Hirsch, 1989, p. 67). In the classic family romance, the mother, as anyone can notice, is inert. She does nothing. Her job is to stand for the object the hero desires and competes for. This desire grants the urgency that launches him on his quest, towards the Lady-prize who substitutes for the mother, signaling mature adulthood. Feminist psychology has exposed and explored this evasion of the maternal as both a mode of repression and an assignment of specific negative functions. Maturity here is defined as individuation and separation, that is, from the mother. But then what the mother represents is unseparation, as regression, absorption and engulfment that threatens individuation. This is the figure of the intrusive, overbearing mother which reappears in monsters that the hero must overcome. In order to separate, the child must identify with the father against the mother, which involves, as Nancy Chodorow has traced, an ideal of detachment. This defines masculinity: to be not attached to the mother, but also to claim her in rivalry with the father, deferred to a substitute that will be achieved through the boy's quest that enacts at once identification with the father, rivalry against him, separation from the mother, and then repossession of her in a substitute Lady.

This narrative of course grants the girl zero action; but also devalues the attachment to the mother represented by femininity. Such attachment, seen as psychological and also moral liability in the classic Oedipal charts of development, have now been recast by feminist psychologists such as Chodorow, Gilligan, and Jessica Benjamin, as a positive and not merely negative quality. Without degrading individuation, they argue for its balance with connection and the care and responsibility this fosters. The two need not be oppositional; and they need not be gendered in exclusionary ways. Both kinds of child, boy and girl, can each both identify with father and with mother, negotiating the various psychological formations each involves in ways that repudiate neither. This recovery, reconfiguration and reassessment of pre-Oedipal experience of bonding with the mother reformulates developmental charts, psychological maturity, and opens new narrative patterns that register these changes. Attachment becomes a positive psychological and moral attribute, not something to be repressed, feared, and fled from. Yet both identification and rivalry with the father as modeling and enforcing separation remains essential for both girls and boys in the process of individuation, which however now does not repudiate relationship or the maternal that represents the first experience of it. Only then can rivalry be balanced with identification, autonomy with attachment, independence with interdependence, which Benjamin calls mutual recognition as against repudiation and domination. (1988, pp. 125, 169).

Mutual recognition on one side guards against overbonding with the mother, as in sisterhood models—whose absence has been noted in *Harry Potter* (Dresang, p. 231)—which risk repressing the rivalry that expresses certain drives and is, with desire, necessary to the impetus towards questing. Idealization of the pre-Oedipal alone also risks, as in Lacanian models, re-associating womanhood with irrational inarticulation. To remain within the pre-Oedipal "semiotic" is to lose the possibility of rational language, thought, action, and psychological structure, which must be displaced by the "symbolic" paternal Oedipal model for these to be achieved (Kristeva, 1980). But mutual recognition guards on the other side against masculine models of detached autonomy which repress the conditions out of which humans emerge, which shape who they are, and which commits them to building a human social world without which no self can survive and on which all selves, despite denials of it, continue to depend, as much feminist psychological, moral, and political theory argues (Wolosky, 2013). It distorts and reduces who humans are, how they interact. It further denies creative resources which reside within the associative, affective, somatic pre-Oedipal experiences no less valuable than are the more directed, structured oedipal ones. Instead of either pure attachment models or pure detachment models, *Harry Potter* offers cross-gendered structures in which both masculine and feminine resources and modes are drawn upon. *Harry Potter* portrays mixed gender models for most activities and institutions, even if these remain within the recognizable privileging of men that reflects, after all, the world we still inhabit.

What marks the change is Lily. Each time Harry is told that he resembles his father, he is told in addition, in an apparent afterthought, "But you have your mother's eyes" (when Slughorn says this, Harry has "heard it so often he found it a bit wearing" [*HBP*, p. 59]). But this resemblance turns out to be his defining one. Lily is represented as James's equal. Both are members of the Order of the Phoenix (as are Molly, who defeats Bellatrix, good mother against bad, in defense of children [*DH*, p. 736] and Arthur, Tonks and Lupin). There is no indication that they did not oppose Voldemort together. Both are represented by the War Memorial at Godric's Hollow (*DH*, p. 332). Nor is Lily's death of a different order than James's. They both, along with many others, men and women, sacrifice themselves for the sake of others. These are not acts of self-denial, but of commitment to living values. As Lupin puts it about his own death, "I was trying to make a world in which [his own son] could live a happier life" (*DH*, p. 700). Lily is only exceptional in that she could have escaped death, she had a choice which she refused ("Stand aside, silly girl, stand aside," Voldemort tells her in a vision Harry glimpses [*DH*, p. 344]). This gives her act a special power of protection of Harry even after her death; while Harry, too, achieves such power of protection to those he defends in choosing to face his own death by Voldemort: "I've done what my mother did, they're protected from you, haven't you noticed none of the spells you put on them are binding?" (*DH*, p. 738). It is in fact the power to shield, to protect, to disarm that has been Harry's greatest strength, the power of attachment represented by the mother above all, with whom he identifies no less than with his father.

The *Harry Potter* books in fact present a steady series of events in which Harry has been drawn into contact with his mother and his pre–Oedipal experiences of attachment to her. Despite his terror of the Dementors, he also is attracted to them since they return him to a primal scene of his mother's voice at her death (*PoA*, 240–241). The Mirror of Erised shows how this can be regressive; how the desire to return to a lost past can engulf and absorb. But, rather than repudiating his longing for contact with his parents, who he lost when he was one, Hagrid gives him photographs that allow access without loss of boundary. Learning to control rather than either repress or be engulfed by these contacts is essential for Harry's own growth.

Rowling has said that her own mother's death deeply shaped her creative experience of writing *Harry Potter* (2001). Lily's centrality to *Harry Potter* is most dramatized in Snape's tale. Like Voldemort with whom he is allied, Snape's is a story of failed family romance, rejecting and rejected by both parents, whom he despises.

His drives toward rivalry, aggression and domination are not offset by positive identification with either father or mother. Yet his love for Lily is stunningly revealed as the secret heart of Snape's inner life, and thus also of the whole series' plot. Through her Snape has access to feelings of devotion, and of moral responsibility—although the balance in him of his opposite drives is so fine that it is impossible throughout to tell which is the mask of which. Snape's division focuses how painful and dangerous is the split between rivalry and attachment, domination and love. Harry's final access to Snape's memories, this time authorized by Snape himself (although made possible through Hermione's magical intervention) reveals his own mother to be both center and model of the course he has been following to love and protect not only on a personal level but towards his whole community, and his decision to follow it to its end.

Harry's greatest magical skill has been in his powerful shield charms and ability to disarm rather than attack, Disarming as his "signature" spell (*DH*, p.71). Just so his particular and legitimate Hallow is the Invisibility Cloak, "the true magic of which," as Dumbledore tells Harry, "is that it can be used to protect and shield others as well as its owner" (*DH*, p. 716). His repeated defeats of Voldemort have been not with direct attack but by disarming opponents and shielding others. Thus the final duel that fulfills the Quest Romance structure of masculine hero defeating villain is no less a structure in which the mother's strength of attachment, protection, and concern triumphs. Even to this final duel Harry does not walk alone. He is accompanied by father-figures and his mother, each of whom lost his/her life defending, protecting, and strengthening those and what they cherish. The Resurrection Stone has summoned them in its proper use: to return the self to the lost past not as regression but to draw strength of purpose. It is not even really right to refer to Harry as the one hero. Nor is he the only chosen one. Neville equally fulfilled the conditions of the prophecy, could have been in Harry's position, and ultimately emerges as leader and heroic in his own right, destroying the snake who is the last Horcrux harboring Voldemort's soul.

Harry is thus one among heroes, among whom Hermione stands out (Dresang, 2002, p. 224). She is not only "indispensable" (Milulan, p. 289) but is herself a heroine—for which perhaps her name is an anagram more than a genealogy. Harry and she together are co-heroes; or what may be called companionate heroes, which, just as companionate love involves companionship, care and commitment, redefines heroism in terms of commitment, responsibility, and devotion among co-heroes. James, Lily, and Sirius, too, are companionate heroes. Perhaps this helps explain Ginny's strange absence from the final book—puzzling within the standard family romance, since she is Harry's romance figure. But Harry invites not Ginny but Hermione and Ron to his final action in the narrative. This, far from asserting power, renounces the Invincible Wand of conquest, while retaining the Invisibility Cloak—a heritage from his father but protective like his mother. As to Hermione, she is not mere Helper to the hero nor Lady-prize. She is companionate adventurer, not romantic goal, at least not for Harry. Hermione is neither the "prize or temptation to regression" of classic family romance (Benjamin, 1988, p. 8; Fry, 2001, p. 162). She is also explicitly removed from the triangle in which women are terms of exchange between men, when Harry denies any romantic relation to her. As to Ron, her relationship to him is far from subordinate. No one, least of all Ron himself, mistakes her for anything but an agent creative self. Ron's own role in the heroic companionship is one of deflation. His humor puts a check on the idealization classical heroism dangerously projects, towards a different heroism where attachment and initiative both remain values despite the tensions between them, towards a more integrated selfhood. Their relationship will be far less gender-traditional than was Molly's and Arthur's, a mark of change in social options that characters and narrative patterns in *Harry Potter* represent.

It is Ron as well who urges Harry to enlist the rebellious students in the search for the last Horcrux. Voldemort, when offered Bellatrix's hand, says coldly: "I do not require assistance" (*DH*, p. 715) (Wolosky, 2010, pp. 153–155). That's severe autonomy, repressing all attachment as weakness and threat. Harry's heroism is not invested in autonomy. As Ron tells him, "They can help ... you don't have to do everything alone" (*DH*, p. 383). Friends will not weaken but rather strengthen him. Teachers and students, the wider community, the centaurs and elves, now voluntarily, join together. If Harry is leader, this is more as democratic delegate (as he is voted, at Hermione's urging, to lead Dumbledore's Army [*OotP*, p. 301]) than incorporative and authoritative King's body.

The building of community, so central to feminist discourses, has been discussed as a feminist commitment in children's literature as well. Roberta Trites claims that "almost every feminist children's text shows some sort of community being built" but in ways that allow value to community without sacrificing individual selfhood. The either/or opposition between masculine assertion and feminine self-sacrifice both assume a discrete individuality measured through terms of its own gain or loss. Trites suggests instead that feminist novels "demonstrate people interacting, gaining strength from each other, and being strong in their relationships" in ways that do not oppose self against relationship, but that "rely on their own unique voices to foster their relationships ... within this community they are still free to explore subjectivity, agency, and voices" (Trites, 1997, pp. 99, 84, 98; cf. Dresang, 2002, p. 230). This vision of community frames Harry's heroism. Against a Freudian reading of Harry as the hero-center, Harry's heroism relies on others, engages and awakens others, and is engaged and awakened by them (Noel-Smith, 2001, p. 204). What emerges is not lone venture and antagonistic daring, but courage in commitment and a vision beyond, although including the self.

Does redefining heroic venture, redefining heroes, redefining the gendering of heroism, redefine gender itself? If *Harry Potter*'s heroes cross gender characteristics, does this transcend or undo gender status and roles? In its representation of gender hierarchies, the novels are not utopian. They register gender as it continues to structure social life (Zettel, pp. 92, 97; Dresang,

2002, pp. 225, 238). But even as antidote, the novels do not propose an androgynous erasure of gender, which has too often meant adopting male models in any case (Zettel, 2005, p. 93; Milulan, 2009, pp. 290, 294). Yet it does re-distribute gender roles and characteristics. Instead of assigning male and female characteristics, Harry and Hermione display both; although perhaps the most cross-gendered character is Hagrid, a giant hairy bearded male who is mommy to creatures and monsters, wears a frilly apron and whose wand is a pink umbrella. Rather than erasing gender, the books move towards opening gender so that iron-clad assignments are questioned and redistributed. This is to undo their antithesis, but not eliminate difference in a fantasy of what Jessica Benjamin calls a "neuter gender free universal" that, in its repudiation of particularity is still basically a masculine model. Benjamin instead speaks of tension between acceptance of difference and recognition of likeness, something the "change in social relations make possible [through] greater value to pre-Oedipal and more flexible acceptance of difference," and not its abolition (1988, pp. 184, 169–172). How each individual distributes gender options is a matter of his and her own unique intercalations. These distributions are not rigid, nor are they polarized as mutually negating; but neither are they radically abolished, rendering everyone the same.

Harry Potter registers just such changes in social relations as they open new representation of characters and narrative structure. The books point avenues to identifying with both mothers and fathers, allowing both attachment and individuation—individuation that includes attachment, then seen not as erasure of identity but its basis. Indeed, the books across their seven years trace development not only in Harry but also the other characters. Time in the books is a positive dimension. If girls in the beginning appear closer to standard gender roles, as the first critics complained, they grow and change (Zettel, 2005, p. 84), the possibility of which is a fundamental principle of the book. This possibility is directly related to its core imagery of rebirth. Change is also generational. The older women are much more caught in the mutual exclusion of love and work, erotics and ambition. McGonagall and Professor Sprout (like the male dons at Hogwarts) are not married. For Molly and Narcissa (and Petunia), wifery precludes work. But Hermione, married and a mother, is "high up" in the Ministry's Department of Law Enforcement. Different arrangements emerge. Luna is off on her own as a "naturalist," Neville is a bachelor don, while Malfoy one presumes is in a traditional marriage. Ginny first played professional Quidditch, but then became a sports journalist while raising her three children. As to Harry, he is neither Minister of Magic nor Headmaster, but the Auror he had wanted to be (although head of the Auror department) (Rowling, 2007). Interestingly, the epilogue focuses attention on the Sorting Hat, a troubling image in its apparently deterministic assignments and divisions into group categories. In the books, however, it is a salvific and cross-gendered figure. Out of its containing space it delivers Gryffindor's sword to both Harry and Neville. And the epilogue emphasizes that each person can influence how he or she is Sorted, as Harry did in his own Sorting (*DH*, p. 758). It is Voldemort who desires to abolish the Houses and with them all difference. The books thus conclude with the question of how to retain difference, but not through domination and determinism. In such way gender may remain, not in rigid ways, but as an organizational principle within which a variety of attributes can find place, often in changing priority and emphasis across time and events. Current discussions of less rigid gender identities tend to argue for multiple subject positions whose complete fluidity dissolves all identity boundaries.[6] Perhaps instead it is possible to speak not only of companionate hero-friends, but also of companionate selves, each of whom negotiates among options and attributes without abrogating difference or dissolving selfhood. These options are opened by new social circumstances *Harry Potter* reflects, as these draw on new psychic territories and combinations among them in a narrative whose winding ways affirm the mother figure who the hero reclaims and embraces.

Notes

1. Bettelheim denies that gender matters in the characters and narrative of fairy tales, claiming that the "two together symbolize the two ways in which one has to gain selfhood" (p. 226).

2. Carole Gilligan reviews and critiques these developmental charts as masculine (pp. 12–13).

3. Kelly Noel-Smith (2001) offers a classic Freudian reading of Harry as trapped in Oedipal conflict. M. Katherine Grimes (2002) follows Bettelheim, reading Harry's as an Oedipal emphasis on autonomy and separation (p. 110).

4. Clark's literary history of school stories includes some written by women, but admits these are "few."

5. As Fry notes: "Rowling challenges the stereotypical 20th century hero myth through these two characters" (p. 157). Roni Natov (2001) identifies Harry with hero-types such as Campbell's, who "like other questing heroes must prove himself through a series of tests" (pp. 315–316). Yet Natov also recognizes Harry as "one among others," with Hermione smarter and more sensitive, and observes that Rowling "blends the male quester with the feminized hero of tales of school and home; these stories are relational, psychologically nuanced, and in that sense realistic" (p. 317).

6. The difficulties of this argument can be seen in M. Cherland (2008), where she proposes against the oppressive "male/female binary" of *Harry Potter* (p. 275) the possibility of "refusing to take up subject positions" altogether (p. 279). But then she inconsistently claims Hermione's multiple positions make her incoherent: "Granger takes up so many different subject positions in the Harry Potter novels, I find her one of the least credible characters in this series" (p. 278).

References

Benjamin, J. (1988). *The bonds of love: Psychoanalysis, feminism, and the problem of domination.* New York: Pantheon.

Bettelheim, B. (1977). *The uses of enchantment*. New York: Vintage.

Cherland, M. (2008) Harry's girls: Harry Potter and discourse of gender. *Journal of Adolescent and Adult Literacy*, 52(4), 273–282.

Chodorow, N. (1999). *The reproduction of mothering* (2nd edition). Berkeley: University of California Press.

Clark, B.L. (1996). *Regendering the school story: Sassy sissies and tattling tomboys*. New York: Garland.

Doniger, W. (2000). Can you spot the source? *London Review of Books, 22*(4).

Dresang, E.T. (2002). Hermione Granger and the heritage of gender. In L. A. Whited (Ed.), *The ivory tower and Harry Potter* (pp. 211–242). Columbia: University of Missouri Press.

Freud, S. (1908). Creative Writers and Daydreaming, In J. Stachey (Ed.), *The standard edition of the complete psychological Works of Sigmund Freud, Volume IX (1906–1908)* (pp. 141–154). London: Hogarth Press.

Freud, S. (1909). Family Romances. In J. Stachey (Ed.), *The standard edition of the complete psychological Works of Sigmund Freud, Volume IX (1906–1908)* (pp. 235–242). Retrieved from http://www.arch.mcgill.ca/prof/bressani/arch653/winter 2010/Freud_FamilyRomance.pdf.

Fry, M. (2001). Heroes and heroines: Myth and gender roles in the Harry Potter books. *The New Review of Children's Literature and Librarianship, 7*(1), 157–167.

Frye, N. (1971). *The anatomy of criticism*. Princeton: Princeton University Press.

Gallardo-C., X., and Smith, C. J. (2003). Cinderfella: J.K. Rowling's wily web of gender. In G. L. Anatol (Ed.), *Reading Harry Potter: Critical essays* (191–207). Westport, CT: Greenwood Press.

Gilbert, S., & Gubar, S. (1979). *The madwoman in the attic*. New Haven: Yale University Press.

Gilligan, C. (1982). *In a different voice: Psychological theory and women's development*. Cambridge: Harvard University Press.

Grimes, M.K. (2002). Harry Potter: Fairy tale prince, real boy, and archetypal hero. In L.A. Whited (Ed.), *The ivory tower and Harry Potter: Perspectives on a literary phenomenon* (pp. 89–122). Columbia: University of Missouri Press.

Gupta, S. (2003). *Re-Reading Harry Potter*. New York: Palgrave Macmillan.

Heilman, E. (2003). Blue wizards and pink witches: Representations of gender identity and power. In E. Heilman (Ed.), *Harry Potter's World: Multidisciplinary perspectives* (pp. 221–239). New York: Routledge.

Hirsch, M. (1989). *The mother/daughter plot: Narrative, psychoanalysis, feminism*. Bloomington: Indiana University Press.

Hourihan, M. (1997) *Deconstructing the Hero: Literary Theory and Children's Literature*. New York: Routledge.

Kristeva, J. (1980). *Desire in language*. Oxford: Blackwell.

Kuhn, T. (1970). *The structure of scientific revolutions*. Chicago: University of Chicago Press.

Mendelsohn, F. (2002). Crowning the king: Harry Potter and the construction of authority. In L. A. Whited (Ed.), *The ivory tower and Harry Potter: Perspectives on a literary phenomenon*. Columbia: University of Missouri Press.

Milulan, K. (2009). Harry Potter through the focus of feminist literary theory: Examples of (un)founded criticism. *The Journal of International Social Research, 2*(9), 288–298.

Natov, R. (2001). Harry Potter and the extraordinariness of the ordinary. *The Lion and the Unicorn, 25*, 310–327.

Noel-Smith, K. (2001). Harry Potter's oedipal issues. *Psychoanalytic Studies, 3*, 199–207.
Propp, V. (1968). *Morphology of the Folk Tale* (2nd edition). Austin: University of Texas Press.
Raglan, L. (1956), *The hero: A study in tradition, myth and drama*. New York: Vintage.
Rank, O. (2004). *The myth of the birth of the hero*. Baltimore: Johns Hopkins University Press.
Rowling, J.K. (2001). Harry and me. BBC 28 December. Retrieved from https://www.youtube.com/watch?v=SrJiAG8GmnQ.
Rowling, J.K. (2007). Beyond Hogwarts: Interviews with the Today show on NBC. July 26. Retrieved from http://www.beyondhogwarts.com/harry potter/articles/jk-rowling-goes-beyond-the-epilogue.html.
Schoeffer, C. (2000). Harry Potter's Girl Trouble. *San Francisco Chronicle*, Jan. 12. Retrieved from www.salon.com.
Sexton, A. (1981). *The complete poems*. Boston: Houghton, Mifflin.
Shafer, E. (2000). *Exploring Harry Potter* (pp. 148–149). Osprey, FL: Beacham.
Trites, R. (1997). *Waking sleeping beauty*. Iowa City: University of Iowa Press.
Welter, B. (1966). The cult of true womanhood: 1820–1860. *American Quarterly, 18*(2), 151–174.
Wolosky, S. (2010) *The riddles of Harry Potter*. New York: Macmillan Palgrave.
Wolosky, S. (2013). *Feminist theory across disciplines*. New York: Routledge.
Zagarell, S. (1988). Narratives of community: The identification of a genre. *Signs, 13*(3), 498–527.
Zettel, S. (2005). Hermione Granger and the charge of sexism. In M. Lackey & L. Wilson (Eds.), *Mapping the world of Harry Potter* (pp. 83–99). Dallas: BenBella.
Zipes, J. (2001). *Sticks and stones*. New York: Routledge.

Muggle Studies: Muggle Identity

Quenching the Quill: How Fan Art Builds Meaning, Creates Bonds and Triggers Imagination

JELENA BOROJEVIĆ

Fandom is a story of outcasts, existing on shaky, unstable ground that is losing all boundaries of borders, language and cultures, and becoming one massive field where everyone is allowed to play. The fandom is comprised of a large number of people who are often referred to as "the adoring public," and yet who are not nearly as passive and controlling as they allow themselves to be viewed. "Fans are characterized as 'kooks' (p. 68) obsessed with trivia, celebrity, and collectibles; as social inepts, cultural misfits, and crazies" (Jenkins, 2006, p. 39).

Fan fiction, fan art, fan clubs, and forums that were once kept in the underground scene have now become the media's biggest target for exploitation, ridicule, and an opportunity for further profits to be made by attempting to break into these previously secluded communities. However, what the media thinks of as a simple-minded group of people, who will easily follow the latest trends, is in fact a huge net of very private and personal communities who care a lot more about the current state of the world than shiny objects on a supermarket's shelf. Fandom is playtime for some and a way of life for others.

The 21st century media and social networking boom has created a worldwide platform for fan art to be created and shared with a global audience. The world of fandom is not new in its existence, but it is one that has gone through a sudden peak of interest in the last decade. What was once a world in hiding, uninteresting to many and unexplored by outsiders, is now receiving an overwhelming amount of attention, not necessarily from people who wish to understand it, but from those who wish to exploit it—mainly for purposes of profit and entertainment.

In the words of Jenkins (2006), "Fandom has provided a powerful lens for understanding important intellectual questions" (p. 3). It unites heterogeneous groups of people with similar ideals, beliefs, and aspirations at a particular point in time, and leads them toward a path where they will feel accepted, and have the freedom to express themselves in a group of other likeminded individuals. Unlike high culture, its membership is not chosen on the basis of education or social class, but instead uses symbols of art, culture and fantasy to identify the boundaries between one group and another. It is at all times unstable in its existence and is both formed and broken apart by the people.

The story of *Harry Potter* alone, despite its enormous fantasy world, is not enough to solely represent a culture or its existential problems, because "texts are activated, or made meaningful, only in social relations and in intertextual relations" (Fiske, 1989, p. 3). Therefore the meaning of a text can only be projected fully in an environment that understands it in the social, emotional and cultural setting that it is placed in. *Harry Potter* will not be received the same way by everyone, because not everyone belongs to the same social group, or holds the same beliefs about life.

Although fandoms certainly exist for works that are hugely popular, as is the case with *Harry Potter*, they also exist for many other works no matter how well known they are. Fandoms do not form because of the popularity of a work, but because there was a need to become part of that world and to be heard and understood through it. The world of *Harry Potter* provides an abundance of very versatile characters that many can relate to, and in turn choose the character that they either closely associate themselves with, admire, fall in love with, or aspire to be like.

Fans are not treated equally by society because the reactions from the public are so often based on *who* they happen to be a fan of, endorsing the constant need to categorize things into high and low culture, as if someone could at all times be an exclusive member of either one or the other, and nothing in between. Many fans are ridiculed for having a crush on Harry Potter, and yet falling in love with someone like Mr. Darcy from *Pride and Prejudice* is not frowned upon because it is part of classic literature. This categorization of fictional characters into those who "deserve" to be loved more than others is a reflection of how society treats people in general, and is one of the first evident changes that fans hope to make toward an atmosphere of greater equality and support than currently exist. Fictional characters are not frequently categorized into such high and low culture, and in fandom, it is a character's inner traits that are admired and that inspire fan art, rather than their physical appearance. The imaginative world of fandom experiments with the lives of its characters on an emotional level, and not on one that is based on the character's social status or professional achievements.

Kundu's (2006) description of consumers as "robotic morons who may be easily controlled or coerced" (p. 180) is a harsh account of people who are lost in the whirlwind of information that they are exposed to on a daily basis, and who have a hard time understanding their own purpose and place in society. Blindly following trends is a behavior that requires much more complex explanations and understanding, rather than just dismissing it as a simple-minded reflex. People, especially young people and those belonging to the poorer class, will spend what little money they have if it means becoming part of a group and being accepted as equals to others. Owning a copy of the book is a pleasure that only fully comes alive when the person is allowed to spend time with its pages away from the gaze of others. It is a symbol of a community which they belong to. Having it in the presence of other fans brings one sense of pleasure and belonging, but once all the doors close, and all the other fans have gone, the true, personal meaning of this symbol reveals itself.

Although the audience does not have any control over production, when it comes to consumerism, they have the power to choose which products they will pay money for, and which they will have the satisfaction of rejecting (Fiske, 1989). It's ridiculous to call fans "obsessed" for wanting to buy symbols of their devotion when they are the ones that are encouraged by the media to do so. The majority of fans are completely unaware of just how much power they have in the success of a project, and often absorb the shame that is thrown upon them without fighting back with the most powerful tool that they have—the power to ignore.

In a crumbling economy and a world where the young and those who have been shunned by society see little bright future ahead, something that has the power to bring people together and form a new, international, non-judgmental community will quickly be accepted and used to forge new meaning and bring out the voices of those who are left in the shadows of society. The more a work satisfies our internal desires, the more attention will be given to it in order to ensure that the fans are given the chance to live their own dreams and ambitions through it.

"Childhood has become a new cultural idiom" (Roberts, 2014), a concept where the idea of a "teenager" created a completely new area of cultural production. This new transition period between a child and an adult now has a specific marketing category called "youth culture," which communicates through TV, books, music, movies, games and comic books. Young people have now been given their own culture to work on and develop, separate from that which belongs to the artists of the past, and one that will in many ways shape our future.

> The world honors the man who is eager to plant new seeds of study today so he may harvest a fresh crop tomorrow. The world is sick of the man who is always harking back to the past and thinks everything worth knowing has already been learned. Respect the past, take what it offers, but don't live in it [Mangan, 1934, p. 107].

In recent years, literature has gained in popularity among teenagers through the young adult genre and its representation of worlds where it is specifically the teenagers who are needed to save the world and bring peace. Young adult fiction does not lean on the adults of the past because it does not even do so with adults from the present. Children are expected to stand up for themselves and to choose who they want to be at a very early age, but at a time when they don't yet know *who* they are. Authors like J.K. Rowling create worlds where teenagers, the oppressed, gain in strength and confidence, and bring down the rule of adults to create a new world where adults are no longer "right," but are instead rejected for being stuck in the past, controlled by old laws that are no longer accepted in the world of young adult fiction. These are books that don't look toward the past but instead seek a revolution, something new.

Despite its worldwide popularity, it is not popular culture that has brought the world of *Harry Potter* so many followers. Although popular culture is often related to fandom, the fan base does not create art based on the instructions of consumerism. Fans have gained the power to criticize the same society that has labeled them as outsiders and the lower class. Fandom is not a passing phase or primitive obsession, but a window to people's deepest thoughts and desires that they cannot freely express in their current place in society. It is not an act of escapism but a description of what members of such groups think of as resistance and an act to produce a change in the world and be heard and recognized for their own voice. Re-creating the world and characters of *Harry Potter* outside the ones that have been set in the original text is a way for fans to bond with the world of Hogwarts on a much deeper level, and to share these ideas and enthusiasm with other people all over the world.

Cooley (1909) suggests four characteristics of symbols that facilitate social action:

> Expressiveness, or the range of ideas and feelings it is competent to carry; permanence of record, or the overcoming of time; swiftness, or the overcoming of space; diffusion, or access to all classes of men [p. 80].

A story is never really finished. It is also impossible to note down every single character's thoughts, ambitions, and unraveling future once the book, movie or series is over. The original creators are limited on the space they have to tell a story, but the story will still continue to develop and transform once the original creator "leaves" it. If we understand stories as complex worlds that exist in parallel to our own, then we can also understand that characters continue to exist and to "live" in the background of a story when the spotlight of the narrative is not on them. Characters are not puppets that are pushed on and off the stage, so if authors really are emotionally connected to their work, they must give them the freedom to continue their journey, and not simply be filed away when the creator decides that their job and purpose of storytelling is now over.

In Jenkins' (2006) words, "Fandom is not about Bourdieu's notion of holding art at a distance, it's not that high art discourse at all; it's about having control and mastery over art by pulling it close and integrating it into your sense of self" (p. 23). Fans use and re-use texts in order to create stories that will show their own life and position in society through the characters; lives that are so rarely honestly represented in books, and even less so on the big screen.

Original stories often create characters that are based on stereotypes, or at the very least are reinforced with characteristics that hope to attract the biggest possible audience. Fans have the ability to use their writing and their art to show how the characters could behave if they are set completely free and allowed to interact with different characters, in different times, and in different social settings. "This ability to transform personal reaction into social interaction, spectatorial culture into participatory culture, is one of the central characteristics of fandom" (Jenkins, 2006, p. 41).

The most important element of any story or character is the symbolism that they bring with them, things that many other people can relate to and make their own. Works that are not relatable in any way, or that do not question our society or support those who are in the minority, will not be supported by a fandom, and instead will be left in solitude; because authors of such works have chosen to play it safe and try to create a product that will be easily commercialized toward the audience demographic with the greatest financial stability. To sell out quickly before anyone realizes that it is empty.

Our social experience and the environment we live in constantly produce meaning that builds up our social identity (Fiske, 1989). What develops from this continuity is an understanding that there are other people in the world who feel the same, and who help us form a group to belong to.

Jaeger and Selznick (1964) define culture as "everything that is produced by and is capable of, sustaining shared symbolic experience" (pp. 653–659). The key to the existence of any culture is for it to have enough symbols that can be understood and shared among its members. So in this view, not only is fan art the symbol of what represents that particular fandom, but also the symbol of the very private world inside the fan art creator's mind, which can reveal many things about the current state of our world. More importantly, what emerges from the many similarities found between different fan art is the realization that perhaps the reason why the same symbols have been used and referred to over the years is because society hasn't done much to change them. Lives have improved for those who society deems as important and most influential (usually from a financial standpoint), but not in any way equally for all its people. The issues of sexuality, professional ambition and gender roles that women face and write about today are very similar to those that were expressed by women in the 19th century.

Langer (1951) believed that "a philosophy is characterized more by the formulation of its problems than by its solution to them" (p. 4). What we need to try and understand is the nature of the questions formed by fandom and why there was a need for such a community to evolve in the first place. People understand issues, current and past events in accordance to their own framework of the world. Additionally, the position which a person holds in society will affect their understanding of the question, and will also accordingly have an effect on how they eventually form an answer.

Not all people in this world are allowed to express their opinion, because while some more developed countries are aiming for equality for all, other nations restrict many of their people from having their voices heard.

Holzner (1968) recognized these moments of realization when a person feels misunderstood and excluded and refers to them as "reality shocks," when "reality may collapse, and it must then be reconstructed in a sometimes frantic search for an appropriate new perspective" (p. 12). Fan art stands on its own ground as a work of expression, separating the fictitious world from our current reality, and operates under its own rules. Outsiders find this uniqueness very difficult to comprehend, and when they try to enter this world without grasping its purpose and the people in it, their behavior completely clashes with the world of fandom and creates embarrassing situations caused by ignorance.

Jaeger and Selznick (1964) developed a concept for the shared symbolic meaning of new experiences as the "culture-creating act" (p. 659). They describe culture-creation as "the transformation of an impersonal setting into a personal one" (Jaeger & Selznick, 1964, p. 659). Characters who initially seem so distant from our current world can become meaningful to the reader if they embody any trait that can be empathized with. The hierarchical divisions based on social class and stereotypical beliefs that are so frequent in our society, and which place certain people in subordinate positions, are nowhere near as pronounced or as destructive in the world of fandom.

There are no such limits in the world of fan art, because essentially, the only thing that is required is an Internet connection. It is only here that it does not matter how pretty your home is, how great your costume, or how expensive your laptop looks next to your Starbucks coffee, because fan art is welcoming in its existence and focuses on the final art piece, and not the tools or the environment that preceded its creation. A museum-like sculpture with no price tag, that remains still and serene, and can be marveled upon by anyone. Fan art is a free invitation to another world, and a place where social status is not a requirement for entry.

Coined by Appadurai (1990, p. 6), the current "mediascapes" play an even bigger role in how people see themselves, and what kind of future they can hope for. Appadurai (1996) discovered significant shifts in the role of imagination on the current global scale. Most importantly, that imagination is no longer produced only on an individual level, but on a global one, enabling "conditions of collective reading, criticism, and pleasure" (p. 8) with very few obstacles in the way.

Fan art has the ability to mix universes, cultures, ethnicities and religions without insult and without care that they have been mixed. "It's not an exclusive relationship" (Jenkins, 2006, p. 18) and fandom does not create boundaries between different fandoms. They are all welcome to exist simultaneously and fans can jump from one ship to another without being pried on by sharks from the deep waters below. Fans have, for a long time, been followed by much scrutiny and negativity, especially from those who are "committed to the interest of textual producers" (Jenkins, 2006, p. 39). They have only recently come under the spotlight in their full power, and are now squinted at by those who are trying very hard to understand what makes them tick—and failing miserably to do so, because admiration and understanding that comes from the viewpoint of a fan is difficult both to explain and to identify with by those who refuse to accept it as anything more complex than day-dreaming.

According to Rama Kundu (2006):

> One of the important contributions of Postmodernism has been the erasure of boundaries between high and popular culture and directing of attentions towards popular cultural forms like cinema, television shows, games and advertising, as an authentic signifier of the hopes, desires and anxieties of a nation, a race or simply a social group [p. 178].

Although Kundu here only refers to forms of popular culture that are backed by producers and production companies, what we can now easily add to this list is fan art, which has its own special way of directing attention to the wishes of the "consumers," who use popular culture to express themselves.

While some condemn the power of popular culture for what they believe is controlling the minds of its followers, Rushdie believes that it denotes "liberation, joy and subversion" (Kundu, 2006, p. 179).

According to Karl Marx and Friedrich Engels (1998):

> The ideas of the ruling class are in every epoch the ruling ideas: i.e., the class which is the ruling material force of society is at the same time its ruling intellectual force. The class which has the means of material production at its disposal has control at the same time over the means of mental production, so that thereby, generally speaking, the ideas of those who lack the means of mental production are subject to it. The ruling ideas are nothing more than the ideal expression of the dominant material relationships grasped as ideas; hence of the relationships which make the one class the ruling one, therefore the ideas of dominance [p. 62].

Music, television, fashion, language, video games, and other elements of popular culture create an atmosphere that projects what the ruling power at the time deems to be popular, and hopes to entice the same feelings in the viewers. A well-controlled media wave places certain people, objects and trends into the spotlight, and uses every opportunity to spread the need for that which is in the spotlight among the masses. If the hook is caught, the trend will continue until all sources have been dried out, and enough profit has been made to allow the audience a moment to breathe before moving on to something else. But whether or not the projected symbols of entertainment catch the attention of viewers and turn them into consumers depends on a number of different advertising elements, something that fan art does not rely on to become popular or understood as an individual piece. Fans create their own symbols, which are then circulated throughout the fandom by other fans and often do not correlate with what is popular in the outside world. "Media does have influence but media is most powerful when it reinforces our existing beliefs and behaviors, least powerful when it seeks to change them" (Jenkins, 2006, p. 206).

The media representation of a culture can, if unchallenged, create stereotypical images that become rooted into society which are very difficult to get rid of. Apart from creating new stories about already loved worlds and characters, fan art has the even more important ability to show how these original works have been viewed, accepted and interpreted across the world. Some of the most frequent issues of identity and sexuality are tested and discussed by placing already existing characters from a story into new situations that portray how the fans would want the characters to behave in ways that would perhaps be more realistic than the ones used in the original work.

In a discussion entitled *Reality, Hyperreality and Public Relations*, Alan Rycroft (2007) argues that postmodernism has

> taken us beyond reality, to a place … where "reality" has been drowned in an ocean of media, messages and symbols, spun out by legions of PR professionals and elites manipulating "reality" through the all-pervasive mediascape.

Fans and their art are often called "delusional," and yet there is nothing *less* delusional about advertisements in our world; images that have been so altered that they no longer have any connection to reality whatsoever, and instead build a very shallow fantasy whose sole purpose is to exploit those who are already struggling.

"It ... is only by defying existing realities, by dreaming 'Otherwise' that one can remake and remold the world" (Kundu, 2006, p. 186). Culture itself has become an industry controlled by the ruling class to "suppress the true needs and create false ones among the masses" (Kundu, 2006, p. 180). Herein lies the source for the entire debate on body image, self-love and individualism, because if people are happy with who they are and what body they call home, how can they be convinced to purchase something that they do not need?

What fan art has the ability to do is challenge the ruling class and share thoughts and opinions with people from all over the world, bringing them all together for one single purpose, and yet in an environment that is much more welcoming than any forcibly created group, however organized, could ever dream to be.

In the traditional sense of an audience, people are squished in crowds with others, marveling at the celebrity and sharing this one moment where they too belong to the mayhem, the popularity, and the trend, before continuing with their own lives off screen and back to reality. The presence of a fan in a mass of other people is a safe haven for never having to worry about being placed in the same category as those who are in the spotlight, and yet still feeling as if they share the same thoughts and popularity. But fandom challenges such notions of being left behind in a big crowd, and instead allows the fans a much more active participation, and more importantly, a way for their voice to be heard and distinguished from those of others.

But equality does not fully exist even among fans, because the majority of what they are allowed to witness and participate in is based on their own financial situation. Concert tickets, celebrity merchandise, fashion, music and even entry to the famous Comic-Con must be purchased before they are allowed to enter the "popular group." Once again those who cannot afford to visually show that they are members of the same fan base, with the same beliefs and aspirations, often feel like they are missing out and being discriminated against.

> The relationship of fantasy to reality, and that of the representation to the real are, to all intents and purposes, the same. Understanding their similarity requires us to reverse and deny the differences that are often set up between them in our patriarchal culture. Fantasy is often seen as feminine, whereas representation is associated with the masculine. In this view fantasy is constructed as "mere escapism," a sign of feminine weakness resulting from women's inability to come to terms with (masculine) reality. It is a sort of daydreaming that allows women to achieve their desires in a way that they are never capable of in the "real" world, a compensatory domain that results from and disguises their "real" lack of power [Fiske, 1989, p. 184].

Although it may be true that the majority of fan art is often created by women, the idea that fan art is "a sign of feminine weakness" and that women are unable "to come to terms with (masculine) reality" is one that has changed greatly since Fiske's claim in 1989. Women are very much aware of the reality that they are currently living in, and the 'masculine' rule is no longer impressive in its solitude, but has sparked dialogues on how equality could be achieved once and for all. The reason why fandoms are often ridiculed for their creations is because they are private worlds that do not have to prove themselves to anyone in order to exist. However, imagination and creativity are certainly not restricted to younger generations, but the reason why most creators of fan art are thought to be young people is because adults will likely be ridiculed, even more, for such creative hobbies that are wrongly generalized as being "childish."

What Hermione represents for adolescent girls is their struggle between acting in ways that society deems as acceptable, and allowing themselves the freedom to express their ideas, visions, sexuality and heritage, and the strength to showcase these features of their lives without being affected by the outside world, regardless of how many times society decides to become a bully. The rules that the patriarchy has made for women, and the rules that society has made for men and the minority among the characters in *Harry Potter*, reflects their actions in the wizarding world both in times of peace and in times of war. Their complexity and relevance found in almost all the characters (particularly Harry, Ron, Hermione, Neville, Luna and Hagrid) are what makes them so easy to be recreated in other situations through fan art. This is where fan art stands out as different. *Harry Potter* and its characters are a very realistic portrayal of the struggles that young people face while growing up, but in a fantasy setting.

> We mostly conform, we pretend to be motivated by loyalties and solidarities we do not really feel, we hide our secret identities beneath the false skins of those identities which bear the belonger's seal of approval. But the truth leaks out in our dreams; alone in our beds, we soar, we fly, we flee [Rushdie, 1999, p. 73].

Because what young girls are trying to fight are not their internal wishes; it is not a question of pushing these thoughts back, but instead of finding the right moment, place and group of people to let these feelings run loose. Young women know exactly what they want and feel. They are not confused or unsure in their existence, but the fear of what others will think of them if these thoughts were to come to light. Adults are made to feel as if they have the only right to an opinion while the young must succumb to the wishes of those in power.

Without any regard for their own feelings, their fan art, which they spend so much time and effort on, has been shunned for blurring the boundary between not only our distinction of fantasy and reality but also that of the original work. However, a fandom's creations are not simply an act of escapism, but a description of what members of such groups think of as resistance and an act to create a change in our world and be heard and recognized for their own art. Fans struggle for control and understanding of their art, while at the same time including members of all ages, cultures and social classes, and enforcing intercultural communication and global acceptance and understanding. In Rushdie's (1999) words, "What we forbid ourselves we pay good money to watch, in a playhouse, a movie theatre, or to read about between the secret covers of a book" (p. 73).

One of the hardest things to do in life is to allow the mind to run free, to let go of *itself*. Not only because this is a difficult accomplishment because of the way that the brain is designed to work, but also because there are so many social and environmental factors that cause barriers and prevent a mind from being free and reaching its full creative potential. A tantalizing burden is placed on young people, who have become very aware of the social pressures that are placed on them on a daily basis, and who are expected to be successful at a much earlier age than their predecessors.

We have created a world that stigmatizes mistakes, and this has a destructive impact on how creative people will allow themselves to be. People who are afraid of making mistakes will always think of society and their position in it first, and how they will be viewed by such a society, before allowing themselves to be creative or to make any decisions.

People have an extraordinary ability for creativity, and their innovation is what helps our world develop and hopefully change for the better. However, not all people allow themselves this freedom, because there are many who shy away from it and believe that they have no talents. What they do not understand is that the longer they hide who they truly are and what they truly love about life, the harder it will be to share these feelings with the world and to reveal their true self and live a life of prosperity and without fear.

Children are forgiven for their creativity and their playtime, and yet they are gradually discouraged from doing so as soon as they grow up. It is no wonder that young people are running away from our current world and trying to change it. It hasn't exactly been the most welcoming place for a very long time. Parents drag their children away from computers and hobbies and encourage them to study for a school curriculum, and yet they have no idea if their children are being correctly educated for the future, because we have no way of actually knowing what the future will look like, or whether our predictions about it are correct. So when people are dragged away and humiliated for something they love, they are being imposed by great restrictions on their freedom as human beings.

There is no logic to supporting the idea of placing young people into categories and forcing them to be something that they are not if such actions will only create unfulfilled people who hate their job, and who will also hate the society that prevented them from achieving their dreams. What good will bitter doctors, lawyers or engineers make to the world apart from make it more dangerous?

In an environment that allows them to express themselves, people will easily show that they have amazing abilities for innovation and creativity. Although certain people are selectively picked out of the crowd and allowed to show their talent as if they are the only ones capable of such a feat, the truth is that everyone most certainly has something that they are talented at, but they are squandered and ridiculed, unless their talent can potentially produce a large income. Being talented in debating and mathematics is often thought of as the grounds for, financially, great careers, but a talent for drawing, storytelling and craft is "cute."

So much importance is placed on how an individual is perceived and accepted in the outside world that very little time, if any, is spent on focusing on what goes on in the world inside their mind; a world that is private, and a much better representation of the person than the "reality" that they are continuously being forced to fit into.

Sir Ken Robinson (2006) described the different levels that construct our intelligence:

> We know three things about intelligence: One, it's diverse, we think about the world in all the ways we experience it. We think visually, we think in sound, we think kinesthetically. We think in abstract terms, we think in movement. Secondly, intelligence is dynamic. If you look at the interactions of a human brain ... intelligence is wonderfully interactive. The brain isn't divided into compartments. In fact, creativity, which I define as the process of having original ideas that have value, more often than not comes about through the interaction of different disciplinary ways of seeing things.

The core of fan art is not to impress with artistic ability, but to spread imagination and provide emotional support for those who have finally found a place where they feel like they belong. Spontaneous creativity found in the stories and the art of fans reveals a lot about a person's mind and what troubles they are currently going through than the conscious behavior that likes to mold itself to fit the opinions and approval of others. People will express the most accurate image of their thoughts when they are left alone to work under non-stressful conditions. Silence, and the absence of the outside world can awaken innovation in ways that constructed and monitored thought never could.

The aim of fan fiction is not to plagiarize the original, but to build a community, free the mind, and allow freedom of speech and expression. Fan art allows people to cross all boundaries set by society and to experiment in a new, more welcoming space than the one that they are used to in their daily lives. These creations develop both language and artistic skills and bring new meaning out of something that is usually only considered a hobby. There is no telling what such creative works could do for the development of the individual's life, and for the global development of equality and free speech.

Online communities and the vast number of people in them are showing the world just how powerful this era of globalization is, and how much communication can be achieved through it. They create new social structures where people are able to understand each other on a global scale and to look past the cultural differences that are so often reinforced by the media, so that we can understand each other better, rather than drift further and further apart.

Fan art may be primarily present in the online world, but it has a very strong connection with the offline world as well because of the emotions that go into the creation of this type of art. Social and political issues from countries and cultures all over the world come together to encourage discussions on various existential problems, as well as to marvel on someone else's imagination. Its creative nature allows people to hope for a better world, and to then work together to make that thought a reality.

Although a number of scholarly studies have attempted to understand the world of fandom, a problem occurs when you try to collect objective data about fans, through say, interviews, because you take away their "privacy." And while this is true for the behavior of almost everyone who has ever been interviewed, it has a specific negative effect on fan culture because many people still feel ashamed to admit that they are fans, since they will likely be ridiculed for simply calling themselves by that name. Both fans and academics have a profound understanding of popular culture, and yet it is almost always the academics who are given the right of way with their opinions, while the fans are huddled together and pushed to the side without much thought for the value of their opinion. The goal of fan art is not to *lecture*, but to show and experience. A story is read in solitude, and its message doesn't need to be chanted among others in order to be real or to have an effect on the person's development as a human being.

Jenkins (2006) believes that fans are "undaunted by traditional conceptions of literary and intellectual property," who "raid mass culture, claiming its materials for their own use, reworking them as the basis for their own cultural creations and social interactions" (p. 18). Fans are challenging their traditional role as a consumer in a way that now forms a collective imagination of online fan communities across the world.

Some authors greatly dislike the idea of any kind of fan art developing from their original work because they view it as a theft of their own story.

However, people cannot be expected to purchase books in silence, without having the freedom to share and contribute to those worlds with others. Blocking all possible fan creativity is a ridiculous way of asking people to stay quiet and to spend time and money on something that will treat them purely as consumers and a source of income.

Remakes are constantly being made for movies, fairy tales, books and autobiographies, so how is re-creation within a fandom any different? Once again the answer boils down to money and profit. Because fans rarely have titles like "director" and "producer" next to their name they are thought of as "ordinary" people who sit in a dark room and fantasize. Ironically, this process of creativity is the same for any creator, regardless of their social status or profession.

Harry Potter continues to inspire people long after the last book in the series was published. Not only because of the characters in the book but because of what they stand for, their virtues, the world they wish to see develop in the future, and the specific evil that they want to get rid of.

Fans hold a close bond with the stories that have inspired them and they take them with them wherever they go. Their journey isn't about high art, but about mutual understanding and belonging. This is what allows members of any fandom so much freedom of creativity, because members of one fandom do not feel a need to shun others that are part of different communities, since in their essence, they are all going through similar emotional conflicts in their lives, but through the expression and use of different characters and invented worlds.

Jenkins (2006) feels that

> fandom is a vehicle for marginalized sub-cultural groups (women, the young, gays, and so on) to pry open space for their cultural concerns within dominant representations; fandom is a way of appropriating media texts and rereading them in a fashion that serves different interests, a way of transforming mass culture into popular culture [p. 40].

The world of *Harry Potter* would not be so enchanting and worldly popular if it were not for the fans. Taking a story apart and putting it back together is very different from simply re-reading the whole text over and over again. Fan art allows thoughts to go from "What if?" to the creation of new circumstances by simply rearranging the story to fit another reality, to envision different endings, different depictions of their culture, religion, sexuality, gender, and to make their voices heard on these issues.

> In this polarized climate, it becomes impossible for young people to explain to us what their popular culture means to them. We're pushing this culture further and further underground and thus further and further from our understanding [Jenkins, 2006, p. 197].

If people continue to fail in their comprehension and support of fandom, then they continue to create an even bigger distance between themselves and that world. "Fans" aren't mythical creatures. They are the children, friends, partners and colleagues of those who continuously fail to understand them, and who in turn are in no way helping to make their lives better.

> Banning games doesn't put a stop to domestic violence, doesn't ensure that mentally unstable kids get the help they need, doesn't stop bullying in the hallways, and doesn't deal with the economic inequalities and racial tensions that are the real source of violence in American culture [Jenkins, 2006, p. 201].

The more we push young people away because we cannot empathize with them and because we are scared of what they do on a computer, the less we will understand them and the bigger the gap between us will form.

Everyone must be given the freedom to be creative because it broadens their minds and helps them question the world around them. People are, from a very young age, brought up to live in fear of asking questions, in fear of not understanding something, in fear of dressing how they don't want to dress, listen to music that they don't love and speak words that do not reflect who they are. It certainly is a lot easier to rule over people who have become numb to the media, the politics, and the constant bombardment of what is "right." Those who have been trained to nod along to the latest trends and to follow them blindly. "Fan culture is dialogic rather than disruptive, affective more than ideological, and collaborative rather than confrontational" (Jenkins, 2006, p. 150).

The creators of fan art are not obsessed with money or prosperity, but are guided by the need to become visible to others and to allow others to be visible to them. To use what current resources they have and to develop them in ways that will encourage others to do the same and to step away from the shadowy thoughts of thinking that they are lesser than those in power. Stories and art continue to live on and to evoke feelings from people even when the creators are long gone and their faces forgotten. When we do things that diminish a fandom and all of its creativity, we are also diminishing potentially brilliant ideas and exceptional talent.

References

Cooley, C. (1909). *Social organization: A study of the larger mind.* New York: Charles Scribner's Sons.

Fiske, J. (1989). *Understanding popular culture.* Boston: Unwin Hyman.

Holzner, B. (1968). *Reality construction in society.* Cambridge, MA: Schenkman.

Jeger, G., & Selznick, P. (1964). A normative theory of culture. *American Sociological Review, 29*(5), 653–669.

Jenkins, H. (2006). *Fans, bloggers, and gamers: Exploring participatory culture.* New York: New York University Press.

Kundu, R. (2006). *Salman Rushdie: Critical essays (Vol. 2).* New Delhi: Atlantic & Distributors.

Langer, S. (1951). *Philosophy in a new key.* Cambridge: Harvard University Press.
Mangan, J. (1934). *You can do anything!* New York: Dartnell Corporation.
Marx, K., & Engels, F. (1998). *The german ideology.* Prometheus.
Roberts, A. (2014). In praise of Sci-Fi. *iai news.* Retrieved from http://iainews.iai.tv/articles/in-defence-of-sci-fi-auid-385.
Robinson, K. (2006). Do schools kill creativity? TED. Retrieved from http://www.ted.com/talks/ken_robinson_says_schools_kill_creativity/transcript?language=en.
Rushdie, S. (1999). *The ground beneath her feet: A novel.* London: Jonathan Cape.
Rycroft, A. (2007). *Reality, hyperreality and public relations.* Peace, Earth & Justice News. Retrieved from http://pej.org/html/print.php?sid=6693.

Transcending Hogwarts: Pedagogical Practices Engendering Discourses of Aggression and Bullying

Kristen L. Cole

> "As it is, contemporary social issues do not exist in Potter books. Harry's fellow-pupils live in a world where drugs, alcohol, divorce, or sexual activity of any kind is simply not a problem. Difficulties instead arise from more remote, less instantly recognizable sources such as old-fashioned malicious teachers with dangerous sounding names like Severus Snape, scheming young bullies from moneyed backgrounds, and the odd villain pushed on by a terrifying wraith with murderous intent"
>
> —Tucker, 1999

Claims of wholesomeness, morality, and progressive values as represented in *Harry Potter*—through a narrative of triumph of good over evil (Ionoaia, 2009; Morris, 2009) positive representations of relationships and role models (Panos, 2009), and experiential based education (Dickinson, 2006; Elster, 2003)—are fairly consistent among popular and academic critiques. In contrast to fundamentalist religious condemnations of the series' encouragement of witchcraft and wizardry, many critiques suggests that *Harry Potter* is "deeply humane, with real warmth towards all people; one that is based on the most conventional morality" (Eccleshare, 2002, p. 73). A recent, and highly popularized, article in the *Journal of Applied Social Psychology* even reveals a positive relationship between reading *Harry Potter* novels and reducing prejudices against stigmatized groups (Vezzali, Stathi,

Giovannini, Capozza & Trifiletti, 2014). Critiques and studies such as these reflect a wide spread and long standing interest in the role that children's literature, and especially the *Harry Potter* series, plays in learning and socialization processes. As researchers of popular culture suggest:

> Children are not the bastions of wholesome innocence that is often purported, but they are impressionable and can be physically, emotionally, and intellectually vulnerable to the ideological constructs underlying all texts, from picture books to history textbooks to television commercials [Anatol, 2003, p. xiv].

Therefore, popular literature series such as *Harry Potter* can be "a powerful tool for inculcating social roles and behaviors, moral guides, desires, and fears" (Anatol, 2003, p. xv). Long standing fascination with the positive moral influence of *Harry Potter* and researcher's increasing interest in the role that *Harry Potter* plays in the teaching and socialization of children leads me to question the possibility of more covert, deeply imbedded ideological constructs in the series and how these have transcended representation.

In terms of representation and ideology, many research projects have sought to reveal what we can learn from *Harry Potter*, including cultivating critical pedagogies (Dickinson, 2006), working against racism (Ostry, 2003), fighting class oppression (Park, 2003), and constructing gender identity (Heilman & Donaldson, 2009). Separately, these critiques have generated interesting and important conversation regarding the ways character interactions and narrative developments reflect larger cultural issues in the real world. However, what these essays leave unexplored are the systemic issues that are reflected in and emerge from the intersection of race, gender, class, and pedagogy. Therefore, I am interested in exploring ideologies related to gender, race, and class as they are embedded within the pedagogy—methods and practices related to teaching and disciplining—developed at Hogwarts.

Hogwarts' pedagogy is not only a common focus among scholars interested in the ways that children learn from *Harry Potter* but it has also transcended representation and become a model of teaching for many real world schools and extra-curricular learning spaces. For example, while presenting an earlier version of this essay at the Southwest Popular Culture Association in Albuquerque, NM, a fellow panelist informed me about her son's *Harry Potter* themed middle school in Morgantown, WV. She explained that, similar to Hogwarts, students are separated into houses and compete for the house cup by earning points for academic and athletic achievement, good behavior, and school spirit. Many *Harry Potter*–themed day and summer camps have also been established across the United States, designed to increase children's literacy. These camps separate children into four competing houses, host regular Quidditch tournaments, and award houses points based on "costumes, good behavior, and participation" (Associated Press, 2005). In discussing my research on this topic with students and colleagues I have come across many stories regarding the use of houses or teams in schools—some *Harry Potter* themed and some not—as a model for motivating students to learn and feel engaged with their academic institution. Although I cannot argue that the non-*Harry Potter* themed schools are designed after or are in any way inspired by *Harry Potter*, all of the aforementioned examples suggest that the prevalence of pedagogy modeled from or similar to Hogwarts warrants further investigation. Exploring the relationship between ideology and pedagogy at Hogwarts reveals new possibilities for understanding what is at stake in how we learn from and are socialized through *Harry Potter*, both literally and figuratively.

In order to uncover the ideologies embedded within the pedagogy of Hogwarts and the implications of these for learning and socialization, I focus my analysis on two levels: (1) the larger, systemic, organizing principles of Hogwarts as an academic institution and (2) the relationship between these principles and communicated instances of disciplining, conflict, aggression, and bullying among various characters. To sustain an in depth analysis at these two levels, I employ a critical feminist lens to analyze specific moments of interaction in the first book of the *Harry Potter* series, *SS*. However, in order to acknowledge and assess the implications of pedagogical and character development throughout the series, I also conclude my analysis by briefly turning my lens to examples from *DH*.

Through an analysis of Hogwarts' pedagogical foundations and practices of disciplining, this essay reveals the Eurocentric and androcentric ideologies that are embedded within the pedagogy of Hogwarts and how these discursively facilitate and foster bullying and aggression. Specifically, I argue that organizing learning around separation and competition, and privileging physical forms of competition through sport, facilitates the disciplining and rewarding of physical aggression and bullying while neglecting the impact of verbal aggression and bullying, which implicitly condones and encourages physical acts of retaliation, revenge, and violence. These ideologies reflect a privileging of particular raced, gendered, and classed norms and embodiments of identity; those who are represented as ideal pupils and narrative heroes are those who engage in and react to conflict, aggression, and bullying within Eurocentric and androcentric standards. In doing so, those who do not fit within these parameters are subjected to continuous practices of policing that manifest in these discourses of conflict, aggression, and bullying. Focusing on the ways pedagogy intersects with ideological paradigms and manifest in represented moments of communication at Hogwarts reveals implications for contemporary understandings of and interventions into bullying in real world schools and classrooms.

In the following sections, I first present an overview of existing literature on *Harry Potter* related to pedagogy; race, class, and gender; and conflict, bullying, and aggression in order to situate this present analysis. Then, I turn to an explanation of Eurocentrism and androcentrism as theoretical and analytical lenses. Finally, I present a summary of findings from my textual analysis, discuss implications of this analysis, and offer recommendations for future action in light of this research.

Critiques of Pedagogy in Harry Potter

Scholarly discussions and analyses of pedagogy at Hogwarts range from praise to speculation. What all of these studies consistently agree upon, however, is that learning at Hogwarts is not primarily found in the classroom. For example, Dickinson (2006) suggests that "teaching ends up having very little to do with the instructors of record" (p. 240). In fact, the culture of learning at Hogwarts "favors the annihilation of direct instruction in preference of practical life experience" (p. 240). Dickinson ultimately praises this representation of pedagogy, suggesting it constructs "an environment of discovery," which should become a model for real world schools and teachers (p. 244).

Other scholars, such as Elster (2003) and Birch (2009), agree with the idea that, at Hogwarts, "learning occurs through progressive 'hands-on' experiences and mostly outside of the classroom" (Birch, 2009, p. 104). Elster (2003) argues that this complex representation of knowledge and learning (occurring both inside and outside the classroom) is a factor in what makes the books appealing to audiences. Birch (2009), however, is more skeptical of this pedagogical approach, suggesting that it teaches readers "the most important aspects of school do not occur during class instruction" (p. 115) and that "real learning occurs outside the classroom and with little influence from a teacher's instructional style and ability or their knowledge" (pp. 116–117). In teaching this, the *Harry Potter* series suggests that characteristics such as "bravery" and "physical prowess on the broom" are more valuable than "intellectual and academic achievement" (p. 117). Overall, Birch argues that the series creates a mockery of schools and teachers.

What these research studies all suggest is that engaging with the topic of pedagogy in *Harry Potter* requires analysis of the elements of Hogwarts and interpersonal interaction that go beyond the representations of teachers and classroom instruction. Additionally, although these research studies provide important insight on the pedagogical structures and practices of Hogwarts, they do not fully consider the relationship between education and race, class, and gender, systemically or otherwise. As will become evident in the next section, studies of *Harry Potter* that do engage with race, class, and gender offer significant discussions of ideology and identity and, as such, should be expanded to include discussions of pedagogy.

Critiques of Race, Class and Gender in Harry Potter

Many scholarly analyses engage with issues of gender, race, and class from critical and feminist standpoints. For example, in analyzing representations of race in the *Harry Potter* series, Ostry (2003) argues that the overall plot to end Lord Voldemort's terror "enacts a great 'race war,' in which the heroes fight against those wizards who possess a vision of racial purity" (p. 89). He goes on to suggest that this particular battle of good versus evil "intends to teach children that what matters is one's character, not color, pedigree, or wealth" (p. 89). Although representations of race, as we would normally think of them, are lacking in the books, Rowling creates new racial distinctions between muggles or mudbloods and pureblood witches and wizards. In doing so she blurs other, arguably real world, racial distinctions and creates an antiracist crusade that is "foiled" by "reliance on 'color blindness'" (Ostry, 2003, p. 90).

In addition to this blurring of racial issues, Rowling also uses the middle class to obfuscate class issues. In a critique of Rowling's representation of the middle class, Park (2003) argues that the *Harry Potter* books "repeat the same Eurocentric, hetero/patriarchal, class biases of conventional classical fairy tales" (p. 188). The setting of the series in a public boarding school with amenities that more realistically mirror those of a very high priced private boarding school evokes connotations of the protestant work ethic narrative that if a person works hard enough at being a good person they can have access to educational opportunities that are otherwise not afforded to them. In addition, Rowling's representation of Potter as a white boy from the suburbs suggests that Harry is not actually that different from any other white, suburban British kid, which does little to disrupt class boundaries. Rowling's representation of rich (Malfoy) as evil and lower income (Potter, Weasley, and Granger) as good also privileges a particular socioeconomic representation.

Many feminist critiques, such as that of Heilman (2003) and Heilman and Donaldson (2009), discuss the gender stereotypes present in the *Harry Potter* books. Such stereotypes include the numerical dominance and overall prominence of male characters in the books, and the representation of female characters as emotional and hysterical, helpers and sidekicks, or concerned with their body and appearance. For example, the main female character in *Harry Potter*, Hermione Granger, is represented as the smart one who always manages to posses the intellectual resources to successful assist Harry in any danger he encounters. Additionally, Hermione is often represented as panicking irrationally when faced with danger, where Harry is represented as brave and heroic.

In exploring the intersection of race, class, and gender, Heilman and Gregory (2003) argue that Rowling "reinscribes and normalizes the marginalized status" of many identities by constructing several representations of in-groups versus out-groups (p. 245). In particular, these group distinctions are made based on the separation of students into different houses, socioeconomic status, racial or biological "blood" lines, nationality, and language. They claim that these representations give "credence to the erroneous view positing that oppressed people can and should be satisfied with their lot" (p. 245). Out groups are also often represented as not being able to speak for themselves and needing assistance from someone in a dominant group (in-group) to help them move out of their marginalized status.

Contrary to claims that *Harry Potter* represents wholesomeness, morality, and progressive values and does not engage with recognizable problems, these studies reveal many underlying ideologies embedded within representations and narratives in *Harry Potter*. In an effort to engage with and extend these ideological projects, this study seeks to not only examine the ways that narratives and characters reflect race, class, and gender but also how marginalization based on race, class, and gender is systemically reproduced through pedagogical structures and practices. An analysis of the systemic manifestation of oppression allows for a more comprehensive engagement with and understanding of discourses of conflict, aggression, and bullying.

Critiques of Conflict, Aggression and Bullying in Harry Potter

Many sources acknowledge the existence of bullying at Hogwarts, and often highlight Draco as the series' central bully and Neville as the series' most popular victim of that bullying. However, these are often presented as background information or thematic descriptions rather than sustained critiques. For example, Heilman and Gregory (2003) suggest, "most of the comments made by the Malfoys throughout the *Harry Potter* series are offered in an effort to bully and remind others of their inferior position in relation to them" (Heilman & Gregory, 2003, p. 244). Similarly, Smith (2003) claims that Draco Malfoy's bullying is "motivated by jealousy and snobbery," which are mechanisms for maintaining class exclusivity. Smith also suggests that, similar to other boarding school novels, "schoolboy and schoolgirl heroes find themselves defending their weaker comrades from school bullies" (p.

77). Neville Longbottom, Colin Creevy, and Ginny Weasley all need "protection from themselves and from Draco Malfoy, and, sometimes from Professor Snape" (p. 77). Consistent acknowledgement of bullying as a theme, perpetrated and received by varying characters, suggests that it warrants more in-depth exploration. Some scholars even allude to systemic ideologies hidden within instances of bullying and aggression in Hogwarts, further emphasizing the need for critique.

For example, in favor of viewing *Harry Potter* as a model of morality and ethics, Ionoaia (2009) states,

> Challenging problems, looming menaces, frightening spells, dangerous creatures lurking in the dark are all present in this world of wizards and witches, yet they are not countered simply by magic. Instead, intelligence and reason, courage and determination are the qualities required to overcome them [Ionoaia, 2009, p. 49].

Additionally, Morris (2009) claims that conflict and violence in *Harry Potter* are important elements in character development. Specially, Morris argues that fighting Voldemort "creates men from mice" in the series' narrative (Morris, 2009, p. 145). Both of these authors, without acknowledging it, evoke, reinforce, and even condone Eurocentric and androcentric ideologies as a product of conflict and as ways of dealing with conflict. Although seemingly separate spheres of interest; pedagogy, race, class, gender, conflict, bullying, and aggression are all interconnected in *Harry Potter*. Utilizing Eurocentricity and androcentricity as theoretical and analytical lenses to explore these dimensions within *Harry Potter* reveals their interwoven, ideological complexity and implications.

Theoretical and Analytical Lenses: Eurocentrism and Androcentrism

At its most basic level, Eurocentricity translates to European-centeredness and androcentricity translates to male-centeredness; meaning, ideologies, world-views, and ways of knowing that center the European and male experience as the norm. These concepts are derived from the idea that those in historically dominant groups and positions of power, such as European (read: white) men, have developed and determined our values, beliefs, evaluative standards, and paradigms of thought in ways that privilege and benefit their own positionality and lived experiences. The notion of Eurocentricity includes "those beliefs, actions, and human behaviors that promote White privilege and European hegemony" (Jackson, 2010, p. 268). Meaning, Eurocentricity encompasses ideologies that reflect and maintain the interests of whiteness and Western perspectives.

Similarly, Androcentrism encompasses the paradigms of thought that reflect and maintain the interests of patriarchy. As Bem (1993) indicates, androcentrism is a useful concept because "it goes beyond telling *who* is in power to tell *how* that power is culturally and psychologically reproduced" (p. 41). In other words, Eurocentricity and androcentricity refer to systems of power, not categorizations of identity. They are normalized, deeply embedded ideological structures that are "pursued at the expense of others" while being justified as "paradigms of ethical norms that proclaim universal benefits for all" (Ozay, 2002, p. 10). Therefore, identifying Eurocentric and androcentric ideologies that are embedded within Hogwarts as an institution lend insight into the ways systems, discourses, and patterns of communication in *Harry Potter* perpetuate power and oppression.

Defining Characteristics of Eurocentric Ideology

White privilege, the dominant position of whiteness, and the power of the West all developed from histories of European conquest and colonization and are sustained by neocolonialism and imperialism. As such, Eurocentrism is characterized by control and power over the "other." This control and power manifest in concepts such as (1) competition and meritocracy; (2) valuing the scientific method over other ways of knowing; (3) relying on binary ways of thinking; and (4) using language as a tool of oppression.

Discourses of meritocracy and competition are premised on the assumption that, no matter what your circumstances, if you work hard enough and try hard enough you have an equal chance at achievement as everyone else. However, as Allen (2004) points out, these are "powerful myths that cast people of color as fundamentally inept participants in an allegedly just, fair, and meritocratic society based on individual competition and reward" (p. 127). In reality, these myths obscure the systemic privileging of whiteness in not only determining material access to various achievements but also in constructing what counts as success and achievement.

What counts as objective and legitimate knowledge is also a result of Eurocentrism. As Jackson (2010) indicates, the scientific method is a Western way of thinking that is often touted as objective and "universal," thus marginalizing other ways of knowing. The scientific method is rooted in the perspective that reality is "observable, measurable, and verifiable" (p. 268). This material view of reality produces a linear model of thinking, which is "the foundation for the development of dichotomous thinking, that is, right/wrong, black/white, good/bad, and the creation of categories" (p. 268). These dichotomies serve to reinscribe hierarchies of power. This reinscription occurs most insidiously through language and communication.

Language and communication have been used as tools of oppression in two primary ways: (1) to maintain control over the "other" through naming and labeling and (2) to normalize Eurocentrism by constructing it as neutral and universal, thus veiling its dominance. According to Jackson (2010), "Europeans recognized that if you take away the ability of the other to define self, you can then replace self-definition with a language of your own making" (p. 269). For example, "words such as savages, heathens, minority, riots, natives, and mainstream become markers of Eurocentric identity" (p. 269). Furthermore, "these labels and the naming process have their greatest effect when they have been internalized and acted out by the oppressed" (p. 269). In other words, Eurocentrism operates through the construction of ideologically weighted and value-laden terms and labels, which are used to police and normalize identity.

More broadly, communication becomes a mechanism whereby competition, meritocracy, objectivity, and duality become unchallenged ways of perceiving and interacting with the world. As Allen (2004) argues, "oppression creates a communicative illusion where it appears as though the oppressor is using common sense and the oppressed is irrational" (Allen, 2004, p. 132). Eurocentric ideologies, then, operate under the guise of common and universal standards, thus constructing those who do not meet these standards as inept and illogical due to their own personal inadequacies. Unchecked, these ideologies further "material and political" objectives that benefit those in dominant positions and keep the marginalized from realizing the conditions of their oppression.

Defining Characteristics of Androcentric Ideology

Androcentrism overlaps with Eurocentrism in many respects. The defining characteristics of androcentrism include preference for and valuing of (1) competition and assertiveness; (2) objectivity and rationality; and (3) polarization and essentialism. As Rooks (2000) describes, androcentrism "accepts male dominance and assertiveness as the norm" (para. 7). In doing so, achievement is defined by and emphasizes "mastery and competitiveness, especially in such areas as sports, school, and occupations" (Basow, 2002, p. 126). In an androcentric paradigm, characteristics and orientations to the world that are constructed as opposite to competition and assertiveness, such as cooperation and passiveness, are feminized and deemed inferior.

Other binary, and hierarchical, distinctions that emerge from an androcentric paradigm, include "the explicit over the implicit; the straight forward and highly directional over the tentative ... the cognitive over the emotional; the objective over the subjective or intersubjective; and the logical, scientific, and highly measurable over the artistic and non-numeric" (Burstow, 1994, pp. 6–7). Burstow (1994) also suggests that the establishment of the aforementioned traits as superior/subordinate is maintained in higher education through an emphasis on individual responsibility, freedom, and self-direction. In other words, the ideal pupil is not only one who is explicit, rational, objective, and logical but also one who internalizes these characteristics and holds themselves personally responsible for their achievements based on these standards, thus directing attention away from the constructed and hegemonic nature of these ideologies.

The use of male experience and embodiment as norms and standards are also tied to histories of biological essentialism and identity polarization. Bem (1993) and Basow (2002) both point out that scientific research has historically been used to benefit men by categorizing women as naturally, or innately, different from men. For example, claiming that women are naturally more passive and nurturing suggests that they are more suitable for domestic work and caring for children. This way of thinking justifies separating people into groups, or separate spheres, based on presumed innate qualities and differences, which is an ideological paradigm that is evoked prevalently to justify social problems and inequalities as natural.

These various, overlapping Eurocentric and androcentric paradigms are embedded in Hogwarts as an institution, which manifest in practices of reward and discipline. They also emerge in interpersonal interactions among students and faculty and become particularly problematic in instances of conflict. As the following analysis reveals, systems of competition set the stage for divisive and aggressive discourses that model oppressive and marginalizing patters of behavior.

Harry Potter *Pedagogy*

One of the defining features of Hogwarts is that students are separated into four different houses, which determine their sleeping quarters, their class cohort, and ultimately pits them against one another in an annual point-based competition to win the "house cup." Points are earned, or taken away, based on student achievement, behavior, and a reoccurring sports competition called Quidditch. Overall, "the entire structure of the institution, through the awarding of House points, is built of reward and coercive power" (Birch, 2009, p. 118). Furthermore, the organization of Hogwarts around competition is "imbued with a legacy of conflicts" (Birch, 2009, p. 114). In particular, for students at Hogwarts "team loyalty and competition is serious business" (Elster, 2003, p. 211). The culture of competition leads to favoritism and alliance building among students and faculty, which often "results in bullying" and inconsistent awarding or deduction of points (Elster, 2003, p. 211). The practice of separating students into houses and the utilization of a competitive point-based system for motivating and disciplining students reflects a privileging of Eurocentric and androcentric ideologies of competition, meritocracy, assertiveness, polarization and essentialism. In doing so, Hogwarts fosters an environment of aggression and bullying and privileges modes of disciplining and response to conflict that reinforce hegemonic embodiments of identity. This is evident through an analysis of Hogwarts' sorting process and institutionalized obsession with Quidditch.

Houses and Sorting

The four houses at Hogwarts include Gryffindor, Slytherin, Hufflepuff, and Ravenclaw. Students are sorted into houses by a magical sorting hat, which accounts for family legacy and individual characteristics when making determinations. Gryffindors are said to be "brave of heart," with "daring, nerve, and chivalry" (*SS*, p. 118). Those in Hufflepuff are characterized as "just," "loyal," "true," and "unafraid of toil" (*SS*, p. 118). Students in Ravenclaw are said to have a "ready mind" and maintain a disposition "of wit and learning" (*SS*, p. 118). Finally, the Slytherins are described as "cunning folk" who often turn out to be dark (evil) wizards (*SS*, p. 118). The division of houses is significant to the identities and interactions of the students at Hogwarts and, ideologically, it works to separate and polarize them based on seemingly inherited or predetermined characteristics. According to Birch (2009), this division "affects student experiences in and out of classrooms, and it affects the social order and the learning at school" (p. 114). The division of students also affects which houses are positioned as most competitive and, therefore, which houses win the cup most frequently (Slytherin and Gryffindor). Although determining a winner of the house cup wanes in significance throughout the *Harry Potter* series, because many real world interpretations of Hogwarts pedagogy depend upon house distinctions, competitions, and the awarding of a house cup, it is still important to understand its meaning and implications.

Elster (2003) suggests that the sorting of students into "instructional and social groups" using a magical hat is "evidence of an inherited-trait view of aptitude" (p. 212). Furthermore, this process "seems to equal recognition of certain natural traits" (p. 212). Evocative of androcentric ideologies, this separation process suggests that some students are just naturally predisposed toward certain qualities and characteristics, which make them more or less competitive. Because competition is institutionally valued, this pedagogical practice separates students into different roles and spheres while obscuring their hierarchical differences. For example, the competitive, point-based culture of Hogwarts seems to imply that everyone has an equal chance of earning and losing points. However, the androcentric characteristics that define

Slytherin and Gryffindor—such as being brave, daring, and cunning—are consistently praised, valued, and rewarded more than the characteristics that define the other houses. This discrepancy can be seen in the alternating pattern of Slytherin/Gryffindor as house cup winners and the awarding and deduction of points based on courage and physical prowess, which is especially noticeable in competitions of Quidditch.

Quidditch

Nowhere is competition more fully embodied and idealized at Hogwarts than through the game of Qudditch; a high contact wizarding sport played high in the air on broomsticks. Quidditch is played in teams, selected and dictated by the various houses. Students try to earn points for either throwing balls through differently positioned rings or being the first to spot and catch the snitch, which is a small gold ball that flies quickly, dodges players, and hides. Both of these tasks occur while players avoid being hit by bludgers, which are bewitched balls that try to knock players off of their broomsticks. In addition to the bludgers, other players consistently try to knock into one another and push each other off their broomsticks, which is usually accompanied by physical or verbal provocations that result in conflict.

Although Quidditch is a co-ed sport, many feminist scholars highlight the androcentric foundations of competitive sports, which "have become, for boys and men, as players and as spectators, a way of constructing a masculine identity, a legitimated outlet for violence and aggression, and an avenue for upward mobility" (Lorber, 1993, p. 571). In other words, sports such as Quidditch emphasize and legitimize aggression as a key factor in achievement and success, especially within a framework of competition. In *Harry Potter* those who possess the assertiveness, aggressiveness, and competitiveness required to be a valuable Quidditch player are often afforded special privileges, while those who do not are often ridiculed and bullied.

For example, in *SS*, Madam Hooch must take Neville to the infirmary after a flying accident and tells the students to remain on the ground while she is gone. Once out of Madam Hooch's supervision, however, Malfoy steals Neville's dropped remembrall and takes off on his broomstick while taunting the others on the ground. In a moment of anger and frustration, Harry jumps on his broom and chases Malfoy. Their aerial feud ends abruptly when Professor McGonagall catches them breaking the rules and the following exchange occurs:

> "Never—in all my time at Hogwarts—"
> Professor McGonagall was almost speechless with shock, and her glasses flashed furiously, "—how dare you—might have broken your neck—"
> "It wasn't his fault, Professor—"

"Be quiet, Miss Patil—"
"But Malfoy—"
"That's enough, Mr. Weasley. Potter, follow me, now" [*SS*, pp. 149–150].

Harry is then taken to meet Oliver Wood, where Professor McGonagall recommends Harry as the new seeker for Gryffindor's Quidditch team. She follows her introduction of Harry to Oliver by stating: "I want to hear you're training hard, Potter, or I may change my mind about punishing you" (*SS*, p. 152). In this instance, competition and the manifestation of that competition in the androcentric sport of Quidditch are made more important than following school rules. In other words, disciplining at Hogwarts serves to maintain competition and, by proxy, aggression as the most fundamental ideological interests of the institution.

There are many implications that emerge from the establishment of competition and aggression as foundational, pedagogical ideologies. As Heilman and Gregory (2003) observe "according privilege to certain sports players reinforces inequalities based on race, class, and gender and serves to create a large group of outsider children" (p. 247). Eurocentricity and androcentricity, then, become the standards for how insiders and outsiders are determined. In particular, multi-dimensional character classifications in *Harry Potter*, such as the title hero, are tied to one's ability to navigate and conform to these standards. Eurocentricity and androcentricity also become standards for disciplining conflict among students at Hogwarts, which greatly influences how bullying and aggression take form and are managed.

Disciplining and Bullying at Hogwarts

Beyond valuing physical forms of competition through sport, Hogwarts also places higher importance on physical manifestations of aggression and bullying. This is made clear in the ways that physical bullying is disciplined in comparison to verbal bullying; the ways that physical prowess and bravery are rewarded in comparison to verbal assertiveness and courage; and the ways that physical retaliation is favored as a response to aggression and bullying over verbal and intellectual willpower. The following examples of these various instances of disciplining, aggression, and bullying are embedded within Eurocentric and androcentric ideologies of objectivity and rationality, which privilege the observable (read: physical) and the rational (read: non-emotional).

Disciplining: Privileging the Physical Over the Verbal

Although physically aggressive instances of bullying are almost always reprimanded (when caught) by figures of authority at Hogwarts, verbal bullying is almost never reprimanded. Taken from *SS*, the following dialogue is an example of the disciplining practices at Hogwarts:

> "Would you mind moving out of the way?" came Malfoy's cold drawl from behind them. "Are you trying to earn some extra money, Weasley? Hoping to be gamekeeper yourself when you leave Hogwarts, I suppose—that hut of Hagrid's must seem like a palace compared to what your family's used to."
>
> Ron dived at Malfoy just as Snape came up the stairs.
>
> "WEASLEY!"
>
> Ron let go of the front of Malfoy's robes.
>
> "He was provoked, Professor Snape," said Hagrid, sticking his huge hairy face out from behind the tree. "Malfoy was insultin' his family."
>
> "Be that as it may, fighting is against Hogwarts rules, Hagrid," said Snape silkily. "Five points from Gryffindor, Weasley, and be grateful it isn't more" [*SS*, p. 196].

In this instance, Snape uses school policy and, subsequently, point deduction to articulate and systemically construct physical aggression as a more significant action than verbal teasing and bullying. As Serbin (1983) suggests, "loud reprimands" of behavior such as that presented in the dialogue above, often "reinforce aggression and other forms of disruptive behavior" (p. 29). In a qualitative study of gendered practices in preschools, Martin (1998) also reveals that this type of disciplining reflects androcentric assumptions and binaries that men/boys are socialized to be aggressive (often through physicality) where women/girls are taught to be sensitive (often through communication). Therefore, physical acts are read and reprimanded as legitimate aggression whereas verbal teasing and bullying are not. Although all bodies are restricted in educational institutions through discipline and reprimand, physical violence is privileged as most detrimental, thus delegitimizing the impact of verbal bullying and those who experience its consequences.

In a discussion of feminist epistemology, Jaggar (1996) also sheds light on how valuing the impact of physical aggression over verbal resonates with Westernized and androcentric paradigms of thought. She suggests that verbal and communicative responses are often characterized as emotional and hysterical, thus irrational, unintentional, and more easily dismissed. In contrast, because the act and consequences of physically aggressive responses are more readily observable, their consequences are often interpreted as intentional and their reprimand is deemed more rational. The institutionalization of these Eurocentric and androcentric approaches to disciplining students at Hogwarts are seen in the students' acknowledgement, internalization, and embodiment of these policies.

For example, while in the great hall preparing to have dinner, Draco Malfoy approaches Harry and the two begin exchanging verbal insults. As their exchange escalates they acknowledge that "as the high table was full of teachers, neither of them could do more than crack their knuckles as scowl"

(*SS*, p. 153). In this instance, it is made clear that the policies of Hogwarts do very little to minimize verbal threats among students because students are fully aware that physicality is the only line that, if crossed, will lose their house points.

The awarding of points at Hogwarts is also a strong motivating factor for students. At the end of *SS*, Dumbledore awards Gryffindor final points for a series of student accomplishments, which inevitably leads to Gryffindor winning the house cup. The characteristics, and the quantifiable values attached to the characteristics that are rewarded, point to the deep entrenchment of Hogwarts in Eurocentric and androcentric ideologies. Ron is awarded 50 points for a good game of chess, which is another reward for competition; Hermione is awarded 50 points for the use of "cool logic in the face of fire," which is a reward for conquering her emotional irrationality in favor of what is considered more rational behavior (*SS*, p. 305); Harry is awarded 60 points for "pure nerve and outstanding courage" after his effort involved in keeping the sorcerer's stone from Voldemort nearly killed him (*SS*, p. 306); and Neville is awarded a mere 10 points for his bravery in standing up to his friends. Harry's physical, and death defying efforts against Voldemort are awarded six times the number of points as Neville's verbal attempts to urge his friends not to leave their dormitory late at night—advice geared toward insuring the security of Gryffindor's house points and the safety of his friends. Both rewards reflect the hierarchical valuing of bravery at Hogwarts but what counts as bravery and what counts as the highest form of bravery are defined in very specific terms. These terms are further constructed and reinforced in how bullying is managed and overcome at Hogwarts.

Bullying: Condoning Acts of Retaliation and Revenge

Another category of interaction that functions to reinforce Eurocentric and androcentric ideologies at Hogwarts is the management of bullying. Effective and appropriate forms of management are almost always represented as forms of retaliation and revenge. Not only is retaliation represented as an appropriate and powerful response to instances of bullying, but physical retaliation is also represented as the most consistently successful response to bullying. In fact, those who do not retaliate physically are represented as feminine and weak. The following is an example of these representations of retaliation:

> At that moment Neville toppled into the common room. How he had managed to climb through the portrait hole was anyone's guess, because his legs had been stuck together with what they recognized at one as the Leg-Locker Curse. He must have had to bunny hop all the way up to Gryffindor tower.
>
> Everyone fell over laughing except Hermione, who leapt up and performed the courtercurse. Neville's legs sprang apart and he got to his feet, trembling.

> "What happened?" Hermione asked him, leading him over to sit with Harry and Ron.
>
> "Malfoy," said Neville shakily. "I met him outside the library. He said he'd been looking for someone to practice that on."
>
> "Go to Professor McGonagall!" Hermione urged Neville. "Report him!"
>
> Neville shook his head.
>
> "I don't want more trouble," he mumbled.
>
> "You've got to stand up to him, Neville!" said Ron, "He's used to walking all over people, but that's no reason to lie down in front of him and make it easier."
>
> "There's no need to tell me I'm not brave enough to be in Gryffindor, Malfoy's already done that," Neville choked out [*SS*, pp. 217–218].

The discussion of this conflict ends here. As you can see, Neville's fear of retaliation in this instance of bullying is challenged as cowardly, which reinforces the brave and appropriate management of the situation as one of retaliation. However, it must be physical retaliation. The dismissal of Hermione's suggestion of what is represented as tattle telling to a professor is replaced with a braver response of sticking up for oneself. Contrasting this discourse of sticking-up-for-oneself with Ron Weasley's description of Neville lying down in front of Draco Malfoy and taking his bullying suggests that legitimately advocating for one's own behalf can only occur though physical retaliation.

Neville's unwillingness to physically retaliate against instances of bullying results in his representation as weak, foolish, and often times feminine throughout the series. In *SS*, reference is made to "poor, blundering Neville" (*SS*, p. 243). Additionally, Hermione and Neville are often characteristically hierarchicalized in similar ways. For example, when Harry, Ron, Hermione, and Neville all cause the Gryffindor house to lose a significant number of points for being caught sneaking out of their dormitories late at night, they are resented by fellow members of the Gryffindor house and experience a lot of persecution. However, the narrative suggests that Hermione and Neville "didn't have as bad a time as Harry, because they weren't as well-known" (*SS*, p. 245). Indeed, because of Harry's position on the Quidditch team and his brave persona, he is canonized as the hegemonic masculine hero, whereas persons, who cannot or choose not to physically stick up for themselves, such as Hermione and Neville, are of a lesser status.

Throughout the *Harry Potter* series, Neville manages to overcome his marginalized status but only by embracing and embodying these Eurocentric and androcentric standards of bravery and masculinity. In *DH*, Neville becomes a co-leader of Dumbledore's Army and leads a group of students in opposition to the Death Eater's control of Hogwarts. Towards the end of the book, Neville sees Harry, Ron, and Hermione after being separated from them for a while and they notice that he has physical injuries. He says he received them from standing up to the Carrows at Hogwarts and then states:

"you wouldn't have stood it either. The thing is, it helps when people stand up to them, it gives everyone hope. I used to notice that when you did it, Harry" (*DH*, p. 574). Here, it becomes clear that Neville learns to emulate the hegemonic ideologies that characterize Harry as brave: physical aggression and endangerment as legitimate forms of resistance. The penultimate moments of Neville's transformation are when he risks his life by standing up to Voldemort and when he aggressively wields a sword to behead Voldemort's snake, Nagini, the final Horcrux, which inevitably leads to the destruction of Voldemort himself. The following statements made by Voldemort during Neville's last stand against him are representative of this transformation and, more implicitly, the dark implications that accompany such a transformation. Voldemort asks: "who has volunteered to demonstrate what happens to those who continue to fight when the battle is lost" (*DH*, p. 731). After Neville responds, Voldemort replies with: "You show spirit and bravery, and you come of noble stock. You will make a very valuable Death Eater. We need your kind, Neville Longbottom" (*DH*, p. 731).

Implications for Real World Pedagogy

Overall, the foundations of competition, practices of disciplining and idealizing physical conflict, and the discourses of retaliation present within the walls of Hogwarts all function to reinforce Eurocentrism and androcentrism in an educational context. These Eurocentric and androcentric ideologies suggest that there are innate characteristics and differences between people, which are the basis of marginalization and differential achievement; competition is constructed as a positive motivator and a model of equal education for all; physical aggression is categorized as more detrimental and effective than verbal aggression; and hegemonic embodiments of identity are provided as tools for combating bullies.

In looking at the *Harry Potter* series as a socializing tool, these narratives suggest that the only way to be powerful, successful and defeat bullies is by being brave and using the resources presented to Harry: be white, be a man, be competitive, be physically aggressive, and be rational. However, this message is detrimental in understanding and promoting non-competitive learning environments; educational spaces free of verbal and physical aggression and bullying; and safe and practical tools for dealing with verbal and physical bullying and aggression. These issues present in the *Harry Potter* series are real, they affect contemporary society, and, as of yet, there is no magical solution.

Cases of cyber bullying, LGBTQ bullying, and violence against people of color continue to increase in number and severity in schools across the

United States. For example, the case of Seth Walsh in Tehachapi, CA—a 13-year-old boy who hung himself after enduring bullying at school because he was perceived as being gay—resulted in legal precedent for K–12 school in California (Barrios, 2012). Schools across the state are now being held more accountable for their policies and prevention programs in relation to bullying. Institutional role models for inclusive pedagogy and appropriate management of verbal and physical aggression are particularly important now and the popularity of *Harry Potter*, as well as the convincing claims that *Harry Potter* provides children with messages of ethics and morality, suggest that it has the power to serve this role. However, this analysis aims to prove otherwise and, in contrast, I suggest that rather than use *Harry Potter* as a model of pedagogy and conflict management we learn how to begin addressing and changing systemic structures and ideologies that mirror Hogwarts, which continue to facilitate aggression and oppression.

References

Allen, R. L. (2004). Whiteness and critical pedagogy. *Educational Philosophy and Theory, 36*(2), 121–136.

Anatol, G. L. (2003). *Reading Harry Potter: Critical essays*. Westport, CT: Praeger.

Associated Press. (2005, July). Children discover magic at Harry Potter camps. Today. Retrieved from http://www.today.com/id/8660078/ns/today-today_books/t/children-discover-magic-harry-potter-camps/.

Barrios, H. A. (2012, February). Seth's legacy: Tehachapi teen's suicide launches national, local anti-bullying fights. *The Bakersfield Californian*. Retrieved from http://www.bakersfieldcalifornian.com/local/x1997183419/SETHS-LEGACY-Tehachapi-teens-suicide-launches-national-local-anti-bullying-fight.

Basow, S. A. (2002). Androcentrism. In J. Worell (Ed.), *Encyclopedia of women and gender: Sex similarities and differences and the impact of society on gender* (pp. 125–135). San Diego: Academic Press.

Bem, S. L. (1993). *The lenses of gender: Transforming the debate on sexual inequality*. New Have: Yale University Press.

Birch, M. L. (2009). Schooling Harry Potter: Teachers and learning, power and knowledge. In E. E. Heilman (Ed.), *Critical perspectives on Harry Potter* (2nd edition) (pp. 103–120). New York: Routledge.

Burstow, B. (1994). Problematizing adult education: A feminist perspective. *CJSAE/RCÉÉA, 8*(1), 1–14.

Dickinson, R. (2006). What we learn about teaching and learning from J.K. Rowling. *The Clearing House, 79*(6), 240–244.

Eccleshare, J. (2002). *Contemporary classics of children's literature: A guide to the Harry Potter novels*. London: Continuum.

Elster, C. (2003). The seeker of secrets: Images of learning, knowing, and schooling. In E. E. Heilman (Ed.), Harry Potter's world: Multidisciplinary critical perspectives (pp. 203–220). New York: Routledge.

Heilman, E. E. (2003). Blue wizards and pink witches: Representations of gender identity and power. In E. E. Heilman (Ed.), *Harry Potter's world: Multidisciplinary critical perspectives* (pp. 221–240). New York: Routledge.

Heilman, E. E. (Ed.). (2009). *Critical perspective on Harry Potter*. New York: Routledge.

Heilman, E. E., & Donaldson, T. (2009). From sexist to (sort-of) feminist representations of gender in the Harry Potter series. In E. E. Heilman (Ed.), *Critical perspectives on Harry Potter* (139–161). New York: Routledge.

Heilman, E. E. & Gregory, A. E. (2003). Images of the privileged insider and outcast outsider. In E. E. Heilman (Ed.), *Harry Potter's world: Multidisciplinary critical perspectives* (pp. 241–260). New York: Routledge.

Ionoaia, E. (2009). Moral fibre and outstanding courage: Harry Potter's ethics of courage as a paradigm for the muggle world. In D. Patterson (Ed.), *Harry Potter's world wide influence* (pp. 49–76). Newcastle upon Tyne: Cambridge Scholars.

Jackson, R. L. (2010). *Encyclopedia of identity*. Thousand Oaks: Sage.

Jaggar, A. (1996). Love and knowledge: Emotion in feminist epistemology. In A. Garry & M. Pearsall (Eds.), *Women, knowledge, and reality: Explorations in feminist philosophy* (166–190). New York: Routledge.

Lorber, J. (1993). Believing is seeing: Biology as ideology. *Gender & Society, 7*(4), 568–581.

Martin, K. A. (1998). Becoming a gendered body: Practices of preschools. *American Sociological Review, 63*(4), 494–511.

Morris, P. (2009). From Gred to Forge to Fred and George: Character transformation in Harry Potter. In D. Patterson (Ed.), *Harry Potter's world wide influence* (pp. 145–168). Newcastle upon Tyne: Cambridge Scholars.

Ostry, E. (2003). Accepting mudbloods: The ambivalent social vision of J.K. Rowling's fairy tales. In G. L. Anatol (Ed.), *Reading Harry Potter: Critical essays* (pp. 89–101). Westport, CT: Praeger.

Ozay, M. (2002). *Westernizing the third world: The Eurocentricity of economic development theories*. New York: Routledge.

Panos, A. (2009). Harry Potter and friends: Models for Psychological Resiliency. In D. Patterson (Ed.), *Harry Potter's world wide influence* (pp. 169–180). Newcastle upon Tyne: Cambridge Scholars.

Park, J. (2003). Class and socioeconomic Identity in Harry Potter's England. In G. L. Anatol (Ed.), *Reading Harry Potter: Critical essays* (pp. 179–189). Westport, CT: Praeger.

Rooks, S. C. (2000). Looking at G.I. Jane through lenses of gender. *American Communication Journal, 2*(1). Retrieved from http://www1.appstate.edu/orgs/acjournal/holdings/vol2/Iss1/essays/rooks.html.

Rowling, J. K. (1997). *Harry Potter and the sorcerer's stone*. New York: Scholastic.

Rowling, J. K. (2007). *Harry Potter and the deathly hallows*. New York: Scholastic.

Serbin, L. (1983). The hidden curriculum: Academic consequences of teacher expectations. In M. Marland (Ed.), *Sex differentiation and schooling* (pp. 18–41). London: Heinemann Educational.

Tucker, N. (1999). The rise and rise of Harry Potter. *Children's Literature in Education, 30*(4), 221–234.

Vezzali, L., Stathi, S., Giovannini, D., Capozza, D., & Trifiletti, E. (2014). The greatest magic of Harry Potter: Reducing prejudice. *Journal of Applied Social Psychology*. Doi: 10.1111/jasp.12279.

Culpability for Curses in Jewish Law and Mystical Lore[1]

LEVI COOPER

Would a court of law judging according to Jewish Law find Voldemort guilty for the murders of James and Lily Potter? Clearly Voldemort had the intention to kill. The legal question is: Would Jewish Law consider the Killing Curse to be an act of murder?

This study explores legal aspects of three magical phenomena—incantations that kill, automatic writing, and every flavor food—as they are discussed in the tomes of Jewish Law. My contention is that these discussions are indicative of the legal system, they may be key for legal history and especially for judicial biography, and they may be useful in contemporary legal education.

Jewish Law is rooted in the Bible. The texts and traditions of the Jewish legal system have been religiously studied and debated from time immemorial. Jewish Law has accompanied Jews on their wanderings across the globe. It has evolved over the ages, addressing new realities and pressing questions. Even communities that did not see Jewish Law as binding often defined themselves by their relationship to the legal system. To this day, Jewish Law remains part of the fabric of Jewish life.

Jewish esoteric lore has a rich tradition that has conventionally been the province of the mystically adept. *Inter alia*, it recognizes various magical phenomena.[2] Though laypeople may not have been proficient in magic, the mystical tradition was part of the vernacular: its footprints can be found in texts that were widely accessible and it impacted everyday practices. This created a well-informed laity that turned to a professional class of mystics for guidance and assistance. A by-product of this situation was that jurists—who may or may not have been mystics—considered legal implications of magic. Legal opinions on magical phenomena can therefore be found in the treasure trove of Jewish legal literature, making this corpus fertile ground for legal analysis of magic.

This study draws on the scholarly fields of Comparative Law, Law and Literature, and Legal History, considering how a particular legal system has dealt with magical phenomena. We will trek through the swampy region of *nomos* and narrative: the area where law and lore are not clearly delineated as different literary, intellectual, and cultural enterprises (Bialik, 2000; Cover, 1983). This paper chooses a methodological approach ground in legal history: I will not consider hypothetical questions that *could* come before jurists; I will not ask: How *might* Jewish Law adjudge a particular spell? Rather, I will focus on the actual: How *did* Jewish Law jurists adjudicate specific magical phenomena?

Jewish legal literature is almost entirely in Hebrew, written for those familiar with the assumptions of the tradition and legal vernacular. It is, however, eclectic: Law is expressed in a variety of genres, and jurists are not cut of one cloth. For the sake of accessibility, I have translated and elucidated the texts presented herein; my additions within citations are indicated by brackets.

I begin with the Killing Curse, demonstrating how Jewish Law jurists analyzed lethal incantations. This exploration will indicate the common legal ground of different worlds. I will then explore legal discussions of parallels in Jewish mystical tradition to Tom Riddle's Diary and Bertie Bott's Every Flavor Beans.[3] I conclude by ruminating on the broader implications of this peregrination through the bountiful expanse of law and lore.

Murder: Avada Kedavra and the Divine Name

A foundational concept in Common Law jurisdictions is that a criminal act consists of two elements: a mental element and a physical element. The mental element, known in Latin as *mens rea* (guilty mind), refers to the perpetrator's intent to commit a crime. The physical element, known in Latin as *actus reus* (guilty act), refers to the criminality of the act itself, without consideration for the perpetrator's mental state. While criminal law differs from one jurisdiction to another, for the present discussion I will borrow these Common Law terms. To be sure, Jewish Law has detailed terminology and an extensive framework for the criminal elements of homicide (Enker, 2014, p. 282; Habba, 1999), but for the present purposes the familiar terms suffice.[4]

There can be no doubt regarding the mental element in the standard Killing Curse case: there is an intention to end life. The question is whether a verbal incantation qualifies as the *actus reus* of murder? A guilty act may consist of a result, conduct, omission, or state of affairs. Murder, as a result crime, focuses on the death of the victim; the guilty act causes death. In result crimes, an important element that must be proved is causation. Causation means that the act was sufficiently proximate to the result, such that the perpetrator can be deemed to bear criminal responsibility.

Jewish esoteric tradition recognized the efficacy of *a* Killing Curse; though not with the words "Avada Kedavra."[5] While the precise formula is a matter of oral tradition, it is described as the annunciation of a secret name of God by the mystically adroit. This is known in Jewish literature as "killing with a Name"; that is, the Divine Name.

Since murder is a result crime, the use of a Killing Curse should constitute a guilty act. In Jewish Law, however, criminal homicide requires an act of killing, not just the resultant death (Habba, 1999, pp. 115–163). Jewish jurists intuited that a lethal incantation must be considered murder, but grappled with finding a precedent indicating that a lethal verbal attack was indeed an act of killing. Of course, a wand could be considered a weapon that causes death, and precedents for murder with a weapon abound. Jewish tradition recognizes wand-like tools such as Moses' staff, but such vessels do not play a central role in the mystical tradition and are not mentioned in relation to lethal incantations. Hence the legal question before jurists focused on wandless magic: Is there a precedent for considering a lethal verbal attack an unlawful act that was a significant cause of death? Since we are discussing a result crime, a second question is also pertinent: Is a verbal lethal attack sufficiently proximate to the death of the victim in order to satisfy the causation requirement?

Two Jewish jurists in different places, eras, and cultural milieux, sought a precedent for culpability for killing with a Name. Their intellectual toiling bore fruit, as they identified sources from biblical traditions and from rabbinic literature that indicated that one who caused death by words could be liable for murder.

Rabbi Yaakov Hagiz (1620–1674) was born in Fez, Morocco, lived in Italy and then Jerusalem, and died in Constantinople. In the realm of Jewish Law, Hagiz is known for his inimitable collection of pithy responsa published posthumously in 1704.

A responsum is a specific answer to a legal question posed to a jurist. Despite the adverse circumstances of the Jewish community—being scattered across the globe without a central legal authority but with a collective identity—the Jewish legal system continued to operate, evolve, and adapt. When legal questions could not be answered locally, they were sent to jurists who responded in writing. A copy of each responsum might be saved and later published. The process of copying, preserving, collating, and finally publishing the collection reflects the perception that the opinions were worth bequeathing to future generations.

No formal rules governed the identity of respondents. "Election" to positions of authority was not institutionalized or subject to a predetermined process; rather, it was a popular decision. Thus, ultimate legal authority in Jewish Law was invested in the hands of the anonymous People.

Given that each responsum is embedded in a specific set of facts, responsa rulings are often limited in scope and application. The responsum may still be used by other jurists as a persuasive precedent, though Jewish Law does not have a strict principle of *stare decisis*; that is, legally binding precedent. The persuasive weight of a responsum is determined by a number of factors; principally the respondent's stature.

Responsa literature is often seen as a unique genre of legal writing, though the term is taken from Roman Law and there have been attempts to identify comparisons in other legal systems (Ceccarelli Morolli, 2012, p. 19; Freehof, 1955, pp. 16, 18, 21–23). The genre can be traced back to the seventh century Jewish community in Babylon, and the practice continues unabated today. As such, the responsa literature is the richest repository of Jewish Law.

As opposed to codes of law, responsa are generally not presented as apodictic statements. The narrative elements of a case are splendid: backstory, realia, legal reasoning, sources considered, extenuating circumstances taken into account, etc. In the responsa literature, the law is part of a story. Alas, the responsa analyzed here are exceptions to this rule: the narrative element is absent.

Hagiz's collection of responsa, entitled *Halakhot Ketanot* (Short Laws), includes succinct questions and cryptically curt answers. Hagiz (1704) recorded the following question: "One who kills someone by using a Name or by magic—what is [the law]?" (p. 34b, vol. 2, para. 98). There is no indication what precipitated the question. Hagiz responded:

> It is possible [that he is culpable], for since he performed an act with his speech, it is comparable to the law of commuting [one gift promised to the Temple with another], and it is like shooting an arrow to kill someone, and about such cases it says "Their tongue is a deadly arrow" [Jeremiah 9:7].

Hagiz cited two precedents: the first suggests that speech may be considered a guilty act; the second suggests that lethal words fulfill the causation requirement.

Hagiz explained that speech might be considered like a deed; hence it could be classified as a guilty act. As a precedent, Hagiz referred to the commuting prohibition; that is, substituting Temple gifts by verbally declaring that an unconsecrated animal should stand in the stead of a ritually pure consecrated animal. One who commutes is liable for the punishment of lashes.

Jewish Law does not mandate corporal punishment for crimes without action, but the crime of commuting is deemed an exception—though the crime is committed with speech, it is still subject to corporal punishment (Leviticus 27:9–10; *Babylonian Talmud, Makkot*, 16a; Maimonides, Laws of Substituted Offerings, 1:1; 2:1). Hagiz highlighted that in this case speech sufficed as a guilty act; thus there is a precedent for speech as *actus reus* in Jewish Law.

In result crimes, causation must be established. Though speech might be considered the *actus reus* of murder, there is still a question of linking the perpetrator's speech to the victim's death. Regarding this element, Hagiz offered his second comparison, likening a verbal attack to shooting an arrow—it flies through the air and eventually hits its target, all from the power of the one who released it. The person who fired the volley—whether it is an incantation or an arrow—has caused the victim's death.

My contention here is not to rank different legal systems according to parameters such as originality, effectiveness, morality, utilitarianism, etc. Nor do I seek to score points for one legal system over another. It is nonetheless worth noting that the Killing Curse was not declared "unforgiveable" by the Ministry of Magic until 1717 (Rowling, 2008). It seems that Hagiz had already recognized it as a criminal offence in the previous century, though his legal writing only became widely available upon publication in 1704.

Hagiz was not the only Jewish Law jurist who considered the criminality of a Killing Curse. A similar question arose in an entirely different setting. Rabbi Asher Anshil Yehuda Miller (1880–1959) served as rabbi in Petroşani, Romania for some fifty years. At the end of his life he moved to Israel where he spent his final two years. (P. Miller, 1984). Miller's responsa were published posthumously.

In early 1909 Transylvania, Miller (1991) wrote to his brother-in-law "regarding the analysis of one who kills a person by means of a Name—is he liable for this murder?" (p. 186, para. 164). Once again the backstory is missing, though it appears that the correspondents had previously discussed the matter. Miller was quick to state that the perpetrator was culpable. Miller, however, saw the challenge as identifying a precedent in Jewish legal literature. He began with the talmudic account of a dream interpreter known as Bar Hedya (*Babylonian Talmud, Berakhot* 56a).

Bar Hedya's escapades are recounted in the context of the maxim that the outcome of a dream depends upon the interpretation it is accorded (ibid., 55a). This rule is derived from the biblical story of Joseph, where the chief cupbearer reported to Pharaoh how adept Joseph was at interpreting dreams: "And as he interpreted for us, so it came to pass" (Genesis 41:13)—that is, it came to pass *as per* the interpretation Joseph provided.

Bar Hedya was aware of this maxim, and the Talmud relates that he utilized the rule for his financial benefit. When someone would come to him with a dream, Bar Hedya would tailor the interpretation according to the remuneration he received. If he was paid for his services, Bar Hedya would offer an auspicious interpretation; if he was not paid, he would portend calamity. This was a nasty business plan, since his clientele were apparently unaware of his policy.

The Talmud recounts that two fourth century Babylonian sages—Abbaye and Rava—each dreamed the same dream and they approached Bar Hedya separately. Abbaye paid Bar Hedya for his services and consequently received a promising interpretation. Rava did not pay Bar Hedya, and the interpretation he received was inauspicious. Thus the two sages both dreamed that a particular biblical verse was read to them: "Your ox will be slaughtered before your eyes but you will not eat from it" (Deuteronomy 28:31). For Rava, Bar Hedya interpreted: "Your business will fail and on account of your heart's sorrow, you will have no interest in eating." For his paying customer who had the same dream, Bar Hedya interpreted: "Your business will profit and on account of your heart's joy, you will have no interest in eating." As per the maxim, the fortunes of the two dreamers followed Bar Hedya's interpretation.

The Talmud relates that this charade continued—Abbaye's dreams were interpreted as auguring fortune, while Rava's identical dreams were interpreted as ominous harbingers. Financially ruined by Bar Hedya's adverse dream interpretations, Rava still brought his dreams to the interpreter unsuspecting that his ill-fortune was a result of Bar Hedya's financially-driven yardstick of dream interpretation:

- "I saw that the outer door [of my house] has fallen," recounted Rava.
- "Your wife will die," interpreted Bar Hedya.
- "I saw that my molars and front teeth have fallen out."
- "Your sons and daughters will die."

Given that the outcome of a dream is contingent on its interpretation, Rava sadly lost his wife and children. The Talmud recounts that later Rava started paying Bar Hedya for his services and consequently received auspicious interpretations. But Rava would not cotton on to Bar Hedya's method until they were once traveling in a boat together. As Bar Hedya disembarked, he dropped a book. Rava found it and saw what was written in the book: "All dreams follow the mouth," meaning that the outcome of a dream is dependent on its interpretation.

Rava understood what had happened and was enraged: "Wicked person! Because of you it happened and you caused me so much pain!" Despite the failure of Rava's business ventures and despite his financial losses, he only harbored a grudge for the deaths of his loved ones. For these calamities, Rava cursed his adversary: "May it be the will [of God] that this man,"—

referring to Bar Hedya—"Be handed over to a regime that will have no pity on him."

Bar Hedya's response to Rava's curse is germane to the question of speech as *actus reus*: "What shall I do? We have a tradition that the damning pronouncement of a sage, even one without cause, will be fulfilled. And certainly Rava—for he has justly cursed." Bar Hedya acknowledged that his own speech had killed Rava's wife and children, and for this he was culpable. The Talmud uses a word indicating that Bar Hedya felt that his responsibility was not just a moral accountability, but that Rava's condemnation was legally justified: Rava had cursed "*be-dina*," translatable as "according to law."

Returning to culpability for a Killing Curse: Miller reasoned that if Bar Hedya was culpable for his lethal dream interpretations, then other lethal uses of speech are also legally culpable. Presumably, this would include using a Divine Name to kill.

Despite the creative suggestion to see Bar Hedya as a precedent, Miller himself raised an objection. Perhaps Rava was only responding in kind—a verbal curse as retribution for lethal verbal dream interpretations—and Bar Hedya was acknowledging this symmetry rather than commenting on speech as *actus reus* of murder. I might add that the merit of comparing a Divine Name curse to negative dream interpretations is debatable. While both use speech, presumably they require different skills to bring about their desired outcome.

Whatever the strength of the Bar Hedya analogy, Miller sought a source that more clearly identified use of a Divine Name as an act of killing. To this end, he turned to rabbinic readings of the biblical encounter between Moses and the Egyptian (Exodus 2:11–12). When Moses went out of the Egyptian palace to his kinsfolk and witnessed their suffering, he encountered an Egyptian beating a Hebrew. Moses looked around and seeing no one about, he struck the Egyptian and hid the body in the sand.

No weapon is mentioned in the Bible, and the rabbis considered how Moses killed the Egyptian. According to one account, Moses took a trowel of clay that probably was available at the building site where the Hebrew slaves were working, and smashed the Egyptian's skull. According to an alternative account, Moses used his own fist. A third possibility relates to our discussion: Moses invoked the Divine Name and slayed the Egyptian. This approach is buttressed by the continuation of the biblical account. The next day, Moses encountered two Hebrews fighting. Moses chastised one of them saying, "Why do you strike your fellow?" The assailant retorted: "Who made you chief and ruler over us? Do you *say* to kill me, as you killed the Egyptian?" (Exodus 2:13–14). The rabbis noted the strange use of the word *say*; the assailant should have asked: "Do you *mean* to kill me?" The rabbi explained: the assailant was asking whether Moses would kill him by speech; namely, with the Divine Name (*Midrash Rabba*, 1512, Exodus, para. 1:29; *Midrash Tanhuma*, 1522, Exodus, para. 9–10[6]).

If a verbal attack can be considered murder, why did Moses kill the Egyptian? In fact, one rabbinic source has God chastising Moses: "Did I ever say to you to kill the Egyptian: wouldn't he be liable for murder?" (Jellinek, 1938, p. 119). Miller pointed to a passage in the Talmud that justified the death penalty for a Gentile who caused even minor harm to a Jew (*Babylonian Talmud, Avoda Zara*, 71b–72a). But such a position should be understood as an explanation born of the casuistic and theoretical nature of the talmudic discussion. It should not be read as a ruling in an actual courtroom, nor as a legislative guideline.

It is possible to parse Moses action in terms of the self-defense justification that is recognized in Criminal Law. This justification extends to prevention of injury to others, and means that the action is not considered a crime. Miller did not discuss why Moses fled Egypt after his exchange with the assailant. If Moses was acting under the justification of self-defense, why did he need to flee? Perhaps Moses feared that the self-defense justification may not hold up in Pharaoh's court of law. It not difficult to imagine that Pharaoh might deem killing with a Divine Name disproportionate and unreasonable force when used against an overseer assaulting a slave; particularly if the assault was considered part of his government sanctioned job. The question of reasonable force in self-defense was discussed in a famous Australian case on appeal to the Privy Council (*Palmer v. The Queen*, 1971). Certainly a British court might be less sympathetic than an American court to Moses' use of lethal methods for self-defense (*R v. Lindsay*, 2005; cf. *Runyan v. State*, 1877). Moses presumably did not want to be the test case for Pharaoh's court.[7]

Whatever Moses' considerations were, for Miller this source indicated that under normal circumstances—that is, had Moses not had the benefit of a justification—lethal use of a Divine Name is to be considered murder.

Still bereft of a clear precedent for murder charges brought for a lethal verbal attack, Miller cited a third case. At the behest of Balak king of Moab, the non-Jewish diviner Balaam, sought to curse the Israelites. When his repeated attempts were unsuccessful, Balak and Balaam parted ways. The following episode in the narrative describes how the Israelites were led astray by whoring Moabite women. This depraved conduct precipitated a plague that killed twenty-four thousand Israelites. Later Balaam is killed during the war against Midian, and the Bible suggests that Balaam bears responsibility for the Moabite women. That is, when Balaam's curse attempts did not succeed, he hatched an alternative plan to bring about Israel's downfall (Numbers 22–24; 25:1–9; 31:8, 16).

Miller picked up on this and noted that Balaam had committed two speech crimes. The first crime was when he attempted to curse the Israelites;

the second was when he suggested that Moabite women lead the Israelites astray with licentious behavior—a crime which resulted in numerous deaths. Balaam was held accountable for those deaths; an indication that causing death through speech—in this case wicked counsel—may be considered a guilty act.

Again the applicability of the Balaam precedent to killing with a Divine Name is debatable. Certainly the element of causation needs to be examined when discussing counsel to a king—to send women—to lead men astray—to precipitate a divine plague.

The weakness of the precedents did not cloud Miller's contention: when homicide is committed by using a Divine Name, the perpetrator is guilty. Before discussing Balaam, Miller stated unequivocally:

> To kill using a Name is certainly culpable like any other murder, because what is it to me if he killed him by his hand or by his mouth? At the end of the day the one who was killed, died and lost his life because of [the perpetrator]. Did not the holy Bible simply write "Do not murder" [Exodus 10:12; Deuteronomy 5:16], without making a distinction between hand and mouth!

Miller focused on the result-oriented nature of murder; as such he considered the weapon of secondary importance. Miller noted that according to Jewish Law, the murder weapon must be capable of inflicting death (*Babylonian Talmud, Bava Kama* 91a; Maimonides, Laws of Murder and Preservation of Life, 3:1–3). A Divine Name, in the mouth of someone proficient in its use, is such a weapon and the perpetrator is culpable.

It is worthwhile considering the sum of Miller's attempts. As opposed to the sources martialed by Hagiz, the sources that Miller pressed into service are not *prima facie* legal texts. Miller's sources belong to the genre of *aggada*—a term that is difficult to translate, but is best captured by the notion of narrative as opposed to *nomos*. *Aggada* is the flip side of law in that it does not require specific performance. Jewish legal writing beginning with the Bible is multi-layered, melding *nomos* and narrative, law and *aggada*. This spotlights an aspect of Jewish Law that is the source of much legal creativity. Law and *aggada* are inseparable siblings: they are independent entities, though systemically they work in tandem (Cooper, 2012, pp. 107–111). As Miller searched for a precedent, he had no hesitation in drawing from the corpus of *aggada* to answer the legal question.

Miller added a postscript to his analysis, indicating that he was aware that his discussion had veered from the distinct categories of law and narrative:

> And note that all this I have written by way of spicy study ["*pilpul*"] and sharpening [the mind] and by way of [intellectual] give and take, for the Holy One, blessed be He, enjoys spicy study. And in particular our Sages of blessed memory said that all idle chatter is bad, except for idle chatter of Torah for it is good [*Jerusalem Talmud, Berakhot* 9:5].

The distinction between *nomos* and narrative is blurred; narrative is conscripted in the service of law.

Lest the Killing Curse be seen as an idiosyncratic case of a foray by Jewish Law jurists into the world of magic: Two further examples will serve to further demonstrate Jewish Law's interest in the legal implications of magic.

Writing on Sabbath: Tom Riddle's Diary and Enchanted Quills

The magic writing in T. M. Riddle's Diary has an interesting, albeit tenuous, parallel in Jewish mystical tradition: the magical procedure termed *hashba'at kulmus*—"swearing in a quill" to write automatically without need of a human hand. One source attests to a Hebrew oath formula written in rhyming couplets:

> I swear in, by the name ___ and by the name ___, that this here quill will proceed with politeness, the ink will not end, and the nib will not become blunt; let it write with ease, cursive[8] letters. And while on my bed, my work will continue, it will write on its own, with no person with it. It will taste from its food and it will spew out slowly. I sleep and my pen is awake.[9] Let it write with hast without the candle, and at the time that I will wake, I will take the poetry. Etc. [Bar-Ilan, 2010[10]].

The idea of writing with an enchanted quill appears in Jewish literature in three senses. First, the notion has been used metaphorically to describe impressive literary output or a writer's talent to freely put pen to paper and write without pause. This capacity does not draw on magic. Second, the notion has been used to describe writing while in a mystically inspired state.[11] Third, the bewitched quill can be said to write on its own, dancing across the paper and leaving words of wisdom in its wake. As might be expected, the public might perceive writing prowess as an enchanted quill (Brodt, 2010, pp. 67–69; Brodt, 2014; Zevin, 1957, para. 209). An anonymous 15th century mystical work written in Spain distinguished between two types of magical writing: The lower level is when an angel dictates to the mystic, who transcribes the revelation. The higher level is when the angel transcribes the text without a human medium (Benayahu, 1959, pp. 291–292; Scholem, 1978, pp. 82–93; Tishby, 1985, 55–56 n. 160). It is this lofty level which is relevant to the present discussion.

The legal issue of the enchanted quill arises on Sabbath, when Jewish Law forbids writing (*Mishna, Shabbat* 7:2). We are not interested in theoretically exploring the question of culpability for bewitched quills that write on Sabbath; this study focuses on jurists who actually related to the case. Indeed, one of the most influential jurists of the early 19th century, Rabbi Moshe

Sofer (1762–1839), cited the notion of an enchanted quill in the context of a perplexing Jewish tradition.

Sofer's multi-volume responsa includes an 1830 letter, written to a student by the name of Noah Gavriel. Not much is known about Noah Gavriel, though he had corresponded with Sofer fifteen years earlier. By 1830, Noah Gavriel was described as a "dispenser of justice to his community," indicating that he filled an official rabbinic position. Noah Gavriel's original letter has not survived, but from Sofer's words we can reconstruct the correspondence (Kinstlikher, 1993, p. 310; Sofer, 1841, vol. 4, para. 155; vol. 6, para. 29).

Noah Gavriel referred to two rabbinic traditions regarding the day Moses died. When read together, these two narratives present a perplexing legal scenario. The first narrative relates to the day of the week that Moses died, the second to Moses' deeds on that day.

The Bible does not mention on which day of the week Moses passed away.[12] According to one tradition, Moses died on Sabbath afternoon. The seminal Jewish mystical text, Zohar, states this clearly: "Moses departed from the world at the time of the afternoon prayer on Sabbath" (*Zohar*, 2:156a). This statement concurs with ninth century texts from Jewish jurists in Babylon, such as Amram bar Sheshna (ca.810–ca.875). In response to an enquiry from Spain, Amram authored a prayer book with legal annotations. The influence of Amram's treatise cannot be overstated: his work shaped Jewish prayer books through to contemporary times. Amram recounted three customs that developed from the tradition that Moses died on Sabbath afternoon (Amram bar Sheshna, 1971, pp. 79–80).

First, a short prayer comprising three verses was added to the Sabbath afternoon service.[13] The verses recall divine justice, and the prayer was instituted in commemoration of the death of Moses, and perhaps of other biblical characters who passed away at the same time of the week.

Second, Amram mentioned a custom to sit silently and cease study of Jewish texts for a short interval each week. This was done in commemoration of Moses' death and was therefore instituted at the time he died; namely, late on Sabbath between the afternoon prayer and the evening prayer. Jewish Law mandates a one-time suspension of study upon the death of a *nasi*—literally a prince, but referring to any supreme leader (*Babylonian Talmud, Moed Katan* 22b; Maimonides, Laws of Mourning, 9:16). The weekly reenactment of mourning over Moses' death is an expansion of this custom, in consideration of the paragon of Jewish leadership.

Study is a central Jewish value, and cancelling learning is an unusual move. Instituting a weekly cessation of study has no parallel in Jewish tradition. On this backdrop, Amram reported that his predecessor Sar Shalom had explicitly stated that Talmud may be studied on Sabbath afternoon. Moreover, Sar Shalom reported a practice—and this is the third custom Amram recorded—whereby the community would study the tractate known as "Ethics of the Fathers" on Sabbath afternoon. Later medieval sources noted that this tractate opens with the words: "Moses received the Torah at Sinai," therefore studying this text was particularly appropriate as a weekly commemoration of Moses' demise (Ehrenreich, 1924, pp. 313–314; Yehuda ben Barzilai of Barcelona, 1903, p. 290)

Unrelated to this tradition and it attendant practices, another rabbinic source described Moses' conduct on the last day of his life. According to this source, Moses spent his final day writing Torah scrolls in a bid to stay his death. On that very day Moses transcribed thirteen scrolls: one scroll for each of the twelve tribes, and one scroll to be archived in the Tabernacle as the authoritative text (*Midrash Rabba*, 1512, Deuteronomy, para. 9:9).

Reading the two narratives together presents a legal problem: Moses wrote Torah scrolls on Sabbath. Could it be that Moses transgressed the injunction against writing on Sabbath?!

The conundrum presented by the juxtaposition of these two narratives was already noted by medieval jurists (*Rosh, Pesahim* 10:13). They solved the puzzle by simply preferring an alternative tradition according to which Moses died on Friday. Scrolls written on Moses' final day, therefore, were written on Friday, not Sabbath.

For readers it may have been difficult to embrace the dismissal of earlier sources of high repute that were unswerving in their assertion that Moses died on Sabbath. Moreover, those sources recorded customs commemorating the event; at least two of which—the three verse prayer and studying Ethics of the Fathers—continued to be practiced in traditional Jewish circles. Such discomfort may have been what drove Noah Gavriel in his desire to extricate Moses from the legally problematic position at the confluence of the two narratives.

Noah Gavriel wrote to Sofer, suggesting that Moses had employed an enchanted quill to do his bidding and write thirteen Torah scrolls. A bewitched quill—opined Noah Gavriel—would not constitute a transgression of the injunction against writing on Sabbath.

It is worth pausing to contrast killing with a Divine Name and writing with a bewitched quill on Sabbath. In both cases there can be no question of *mens rea*: Moses intended to kill the Egyptian with the Divine Name and he intended to write on Sabbath when he cast a spell on his quill. In both cases, the *actus reus* involves speech, and causation is comparable. Why then is swearing in a quill to write on Sabbath permitted?

It appears that the distinction between the cases is best explained by reference to an issue known in Hebrew parlance as *shevitat keilim*, meaning the requirement of vessels to rest on Sabbath. The Bible sets aside Sabbath as a day of rest, though the parameters of this directive are not fully explicated

(Genesis 2:2–3; Exodus 20:8–11). In the first century BCE, Jerusalem rabbis disagreed regarding the application of this directive to a person's property. The legal question is: Does the Sabbath rest requirement include a requirement that a person's property also does no work? (*Mishna, Shabbat* 1:5; *Babylonian Talmud, Shabbat* 18a). Jewish Law adopted the position that the obligation to rest is incumbent on Jews, non-Jewish employees of Jews, and animals owned by Jews. Other property owned by Jews was not subject to the Sabbath rest requirement (Maimonides, Laws of Sabbath, 6:16).[14] An enchanted quill writing on Sabbath is, therefore, not a guilty act.

Noah Gavriel was not satisfied with his creative suggestion. In the ancient dispute regarding Sabbath rest for property, one opinion held that property must rest. How would that opinion explain Moses' enchanted quill that wrote scrolls on Sabbath? This was the question that Noah Gavriel asked Sofer.

Sofer responded that the *actus reus* of Sabbath transgressions is defined by the standard method of committing the crime. Apparent Sabbath transgressors are not culpable for crimes committed in unusual ways. As a proof text, Sofer noted that a right handed person who writes with the left hand would not be considered culpable for writing on Sabbath (*Babylonian Talmud, Shabbat* 103a). Similarly, spinning thread is forbidden on Sabbath, but if one spins directly from a woolen fleece without first shearing the sheep there is no culpability (*Babylonian Talmud, Shabbat* 74b). Sofer cited this unusual case because according to rabbinic tradition, skillful women did just that during the Tabernacle's construction (*Rashi*, Exodus 35:26). Sofer explained that this textile art required rare wisdom and dexterity; it was certainly not standard spinning procedure. Hence such spinning would be permitted on Sabbath. Returning to the enchanted quill: there is nothing standard about bewitched writing implements. Thus, even according to the opinion that property must rest, a mystic would not be culpable for enchanting a quill to write on Sabbath.[15]

Regarding Noah Gavriel's creative suggestion that begot his query—Moses wrote on Sabbath with an enchanted quill—Sofer informed his student that the suggestion had already appeared in a well-known earlier work by Rabbi Yeshaya Horowitz (1558–1630). Horowitz's work was audaciously entitled *Shenei Luhot Ha-Berit*, "The Two Tablets of the Covenant," and published in Amsterdam in 1648–1649. Extant editions of Horowitz's work do not contain this passage, so we are fortunate that Sofer took the trouble to preserve his correspondence; without it, we may not have been privy to Noah Gavriel's suggestion. Whatever the source, Sofer accepted the position that writing with an enchanted quill is not considered a Sabbath transgression.

In this case, the magical narrative served the jurist in his attempt to save the lawgiver who had been complicated by rabbinic narratives. In other words:

the bewitched quill explained Moses' conduct that in light of two different accounts of his final day suddenly appeared precariously antinomian. Narratives created a legal problem that was magically solved.

Theft: Bertie Bott's Beans and Biblical Manna

The biblical manna that the Israelites ate while wandering in the desert is comparable to Bertie Bott's Every Flavor Beans. When the manna is first mentioned, its taste is described as "*tsapihit* in honey" (Exodus 16:31). Alas the word "*tsapihit*"—often translated as "wafer"—is a *hapax legomenon*; it appears once in the Bible and its meaning is a mystery. The Bible later describes manna, its appearance, and its preparation for consumption:

> Now the manna was like coriander seed, and in color it was like bdellium. The people would go about and gather, grind it between millstones or pound it in a mortar, boil it in a pot, make it into cakes. It tasted like cream of oil. And when the dew fell on the camp at night, the manna would fall upon it [Numbers 11:7–8].

The hazy description makes identification of this source of sustenance a mission impossible.[16] *Wisdom of Solomon*—a work not included in the Hebrew Bible, but probably written by a Jew during the second or first century BCE—described manna in the following terms: "Instead of these things Thou didst give Thy people food of angels, and without their toil Thou didst supply them from heaven with bread ready to eat, providing every pleasure and suited to every taste" (Wis. 16:20). Perhaps unwilling to identify the manna as a particular food that could be found in nature, perhaps unable to do so—the rabbis ascribed magical properties to this source of sustenance, echoing the notion that manna was adept at "providing every pleasure and suited to every taste."

In the verses that immediately precede the description of manna, the Israelites complained:

> If only we had meat to eat! We remember the fish that we used to eat free in Egypt; the cucumbers, the melons, the leeks, the onions, and the garlic. Now our gullets are shriveled. There is nothing at all! Nothing but this manna to look to! [Numbers, 11:4–6].

The rabbis wondered why these five vegetables were specifically mentioned. Two explanations were offered, both of them highlighting the magic of manna. According to the first explanation, manna could taste like any flavor except for these five items. According to the second explanation, not only could the manna taste like any substance, but it also had the texture of the desired food; that is, except for the five listed items—their flavor could be tasted, but their texture could not be sensed (*Babylonian Talmud*, *Yoma*, 75a).

For the rabbis, the magical properties of manna could not be denied; though there was a debate as to the extent of the magic. Jewish tradition remembers the manna as having an unlimited spectrum of tastes; truly "every flavor," including chocolate, peppermint, marmalade, spinach, liver, tripe, and presumably even earwax. While there may have been five items that the manna could not replicate, this divinely provided food had one clear advantage over Bertie Bott's Every Flavor Beans: the taste was selected by the person eating it. People who ate bogey-flavored or vomit-flavored manna only had themselves to blame!

The existence of every flavor manna raised a legal question: What is the appropriate benediction that should be recited over this magical food? It should be emphasized that as a pre-modern legal system, Jewish Law viewed the recital of a ritual benedictions before eating as a legal obligation. Such obligations were part of the same legal system that included civil obligations, the very obligations recognized by modern legal systems. This is apparent in the rabbis' exhortations to recite blessings: "It is forbidden for a person to derive benefit from this world without [first reciting] a benediction; and whoever derives benefit from this world without [first reciting] a benediction has committed an act of *me'ilah*," that is, unauthorized use of consecrated Temple property (*Babylonian Talmud, Berakhot* 35a–b). Since the world and all that is in it belongs to the Almighty (Psalms 24:1), eating food that is God's property without a blessing is akin to embezzlement.

Significantly, the rabbis compare one who eats without reciting a benediction to theft. To be sure, there are differences between theft and eating without a blessing: transfer of property requires the agreement of the previous owner, while partaking of food perceived as belonging to God requires a benediction. Moreover, the sanctions for the two criminal tortfeasors are dissimilar. Nonetheless, in the eyes of Jewish Law the crimes are comparable to an extent: property is taken without first gaining the requisite license.

Returning to the legal question: What benediction is to be recited before consuming manna? Five possibilities have been suggested. The earliest recorded answer appears in a text from medieval Germany. The matter was then addressed in early 17th century Italy. From there we can trace the question to late 18th century Galicia. Then in the 20th century the question was addressed in Baghdad and in Poland.

The first recorded suggestion appears in an early 14th century German manuscript of *Sefer Hasidim* (Book of the Pious). *Sefer Hasidim* was largely written by Yehuda of Regensburg (ca.1146–1217), and is linked to the Jewish pietists who flourished in Germany in the twelfth and thirteenth centuries. It is a work that is notoriously difficult to describe historically and categorize literarily. The different recensions, manuscripts, and printings have made authentication, dating, and attribution the subject of much scholarly discussion.[17] The goal and audience of the work is also questionable, and jurists have debated its standing as a legal text. Notwithstanding, *Sefer Hasidim* has generated norms. One manuscript includes the following: "On manna they would pronounce the benediction '[Blessed are You, O Lord, king of the universe] who gives bread from the heaven'" (MS Parma H 3280; Wistinetzki, 1891, para. 1640).

Benedictions before eating follow a standard formula. They open with the words "Blessed are You, O Lord, king of the universe," and continue with a reference to the type of food about to be ingested. Thus, if the food is bread then the blessing ends "who brings forth bread from the earth"; or fruit: "who creates the fruit of the tree"; or vegetables: "who creates the fruit of the soil." For food that is not grown and hence is not covered by the delineated categories, the blessing ends: "that everything came into being through His word" (*Mishna, Berakhot* 6:1, 3). The second phrase of the blessing is generally borrowed from the Bible (Genesis 4:3; Deuteronomy 26:2; Psalms 104:14). Following this format the blessing over manna begins with the standard opening, and then refers to manna by its biblical moniker—"bread from heaven" (Exodus 16:4; see also Psalms 78:24; 105:40; Nehemiah 9:15).

The next scholar who addressed this question was Rabbi Menahem Azarya da Fano (1548–1620), a prolific Italian writer and a patron of learning. Menahem Azarya made notable literary contributions in the fields of Kabbalah, theology, liturgy, and law. Many of his writings remain in manuscript, including sections of a work entitled *'Asara Ma'amarot* (Ten Essays). One of the essays that comprise the work was published in 1863, and includes a vivid description of the celebratory meal at the End of Days.

According to Menahem Azarya, the Leviathan and the Behemoth—the primal monsters of the sea and of the land—will be served as the main course. Angels will be on hand to wait on the righteous, repaying the kindness of Abraham who waited on them (Genesis 18:2–8). Gabriel will be the ritual slaughterer, Raphael will prepare the food, and Michael will serve as beverage butler. Wine, prepared from grapes from the Garden of Eden and aged since the beginning of time, will be served.

What about bread? Menahem Azarya felt that wheat products would not be served, since according to one opinion in the Talmud the forbidden fruit in the Garden of Eden was wheat (*Babylonian Talmud, Berakhot* 40a; *Sanhedrin* 70a): The food that brought about Adam and Eve's downfall would not be featured at the End of Days! Menahem Azarya explained that a jar of desert manna had been preserved specifically for this festive meal (Exodus 16:33–34). Which benediction will be recited over the manna? Menahem Azarya (1863) opined: "Blessed [are You, O Lord, king of the universe] who brings forth bread from the heaven" (pp. 9–10).

Presumably, Menahem Azarya did not have access to a manuscript of

Sefer Hasidim, thus his suggestion is an independent response. He followed the classic formula, and like *Sefer Hasidim* he referred to manna as "bread from heaven." Instead of saying "who gives," Menahem Azarya used the language of the regular bread blessing: "who brings forth."

The question arose again in late 18th century Galicia—the area of Poland that was annexed to the Austrian Empire. Rabbi Tsevi Elimelekh Shapira (1783–1841) began his rabbinic career as a judge in the religious court of Dynów. He then served in six other communities, before a four year sojourn as rabbi of the Hungarian town of Munkács. In 1829 he returned to serve as rabbi of Dynów. In addition to his rabbinic duties, Shapira was a leader of the hasidic movement—a religious revivalist movement that began in late 18th century Eastern Europe and flourished throughout 19th century. Shapira was a prolific writer, primarily bequeathing works in hasidic thought.

In his most famous work, Shapira recounted how during his youth, he had spent time with Rabbi Tsevi Hirsh Eichenstein of Żydaczów (1763–1831). Eichenstein was Shapira's older contemporary, and in addition to be related by marriage, Shapira went on to write a commentary on Eichenstein's mystical work. Shapira recounted that one day Eichenstein asked about the blessing before consuming manna. Shapira cited Menahem Azarya's opinion and those present debated the issue. One respected figure—Yisrael Dov—suggested that no blessing was recited on manna!

Shapira referred to this character as "Yisrael Dov," and in all likelihood this was Rabbi Yisrael Dov of Drohobycz (d. 1847), a student of Eichenstein. Yisrael Dov pointed to the verse that described manna as food of mighty heroes, meaning angel food (Psalms 78:25).[18] Playing on the Hebrew word for heroes—"*abirim*"—one opinion in the Talmud suggested that the manna was totally absorbed by limbs, in Hebrew "*eivarim*." In Hebrew *b* and *v* use the same grapheme; *v* with a diacritical mark is pronounced as *b*. Thus the two Hebrew words—*eivarim* (איברים) meaning limbs and *abirim* (אבירים) meaning heroes—have the same consonants with different vowels. Orthographically the two words appear almost identical, particularly since the Bible is traditionally written as graphemes without vowels or diacritical marks (*Babylonian Talmud, Yoma* 75b). One opinion in the Talmud seems to suggest that because of its divine composition, manna did not produce human waste; it left nothing to excrete for it was entirely absorbed by the body. Yisrael Dov translated this comment about digestion into a statement about mystical valence.

According to Jewish mystical tradition, every physical item has an element of the Divine. Without this divine component, the item could not exist. Alas, the divinity in physical objects is encased in shells and mixed with dross. When it comes to foodstuffs, the recital of a benediction mystically extracts the divine from the physical item, separating it from the spiritual chaff. Manna, however, contained no spiritual dross; it was entirely divine. Consequently, manna needed no blessing! Shapira (1850) added a postscript:

> And I greatly enjoyed [the suggestion], for it appears to me that the words are close to the truth. Accordingly, I was surprised at the holy m[aster] R[abbi] M[enahem] A[zarya] who wrote that in the future we will have to recite a benediction over [manna] [*ma'amarei shabbatot*, para. 3:3].

Though the suggestion that manna needed no blessing was innovative, it was nonetheless legally problematic, as pointed out in a curious collection of responsa.

The collection—entitled *She'elot U-Teshuvot Torah Lishmah*, "Responsa of Law for Its Own Sake"—is presented as being the collated responsa of an unknown scholar identified as "Yehezkel Kahali." The collection was first published in Jerusalem in 1973, and the publisher announced that the manuscript was an autograph of the Baghdadi scholar Rabbi Yosef Hayim (1834–1909). In his introduction, the publisher—a grandson of Yosef Hayim—pointed out that the author had left a hint as to his identity in the *gematria* of the pseudo-author's name. *Gematria* is a numerological system that assigns value to each letter, and assumes a relationship between different words with identical numerical value. The *gematria* of the Hebrew name "Yehezkel" (156) is identical to that of "Yosef" (156), and the *gematria* of the surname "Kahali" (68) is identical to "Hayim" (68). Thus, argued the publisher, Yehezkel Kahali is none other than Yosef Hayim. Three years after the initial release of the work, a second edition appeared with a note from the publisher claiming that the identification of the author was not based solely on numerology. Recently further proof has been adduced to support the claim that the responsa are indeed the work of Yosef Hayim of Baghdad (Kahali, 1973, [p. 3]; 1976, [p. 3]; 2013, pp. 9–67).

While Yosef Hayim did not hold an official rabbinic position, he was a popular preacher and a recognized authority. In his sermons, Yosef Hayim skillfully wove together law and *aggada*, and his voluminous writings reflect this integrated approach. In addition, Yosef Hayim was well versed in the Jewish mystical tradition, and his legal rulings reflect his mystical sensitivities. It remains a mystery why Yosef Hayim penned this manuscript under a pseudonym. It is also ethically disconcerting that he claimed that the responsa were from the 17th century: while Jewish Law does not have a doctrine of binding precedent, there is still a notion of persuasive precedent and a two hundred year old responsum would presumably trump a contemporary ruling.

The questioner seemed to be familiar with Shapira's account: he opened by citing "a certain sage" who had suggested that the Israelites did not recite a blessing over manna since it was entirely divine with no spiritual dross.

The questioner noted that those present had argued with that sage. The questioner enquired: "Therefore we wanted to know—is the truth with those who say that they recited a blessing over it? Also, which blessing did they recite over it?" (Kahali, 1973, p. 59, para. 63).

The respondent opened by conceding some ground. From a mystical vantage the role of blessings is indeed to separate the holy from the unholy, and manna did not require this process. However, the recitation of a blessing is not just for mystical reasons; it is also a form of thanks for abundant goodness bestowed by God. Moreover, the Talmud says that when the manna descended, Moses instituted the first paragraph of Grace After Meals (*Babylonian Talmud*, *Berakhot* 48b). If Grace After Meals was said, surely a blessing before the meal was also recited! Indeed medieval sources stated that a blessing was recited over manna, though those sources did not record the wording of the benediction (*Zohar*, 2:62b).

Regarding the formulation of the blessing, the respondent referred to Menahem Azarya, but offered a slightly different wording: "Blessed are You, O Lord, king of the universe who *rains down* bread from the heaven." Indeed, manna descended from the heaven, and in two biblical passages the verb for raining is used (Exodus 16:4; Psalms 78:24). The respondent concluded his answer with the words: "And blessed is the one who knows," perhaps acknowledging that he had no way of proving his contention.

While Yosef Hayim was active in Baghdad, the blessing over manna was touched upon in Poland. Rabbi Meir Don Plotzki (1867–1928) was a successful rabbi, author, teacher, and political activist (*Encyclopaedia Judaica*, 2007, 16:241). Plotzki's fame spread over Poland in 1903 when he published the first part of his *Hemdat Yisra'el* (Delight of Israel). In the second volume of this work, Plotzki stated that the blessing over manna should be the same blessing that is recited over vegetables. Plotzki noted that the Bible describes the Israelites as going out to gather manna; indeed verb forms of "gather" appear an astounding nine times in the biblical account (Exodus 16:4–5, 16–18, 21–22, 26–27). Citing earlier sources, Plotzki explained that this verb is used when there is a link to the soil: the manna must have been nourished from the ground in some way. Hence the benediction: "Blessed are You, O Lord, king of the universe, who creates the fruit of the soil" (Plotzki, 1924, sec. 14, para. 2). It must be said that Plotzki was well aware of how surprising this approach was: it went against the grain of the biblical narrative and rabbinic tradition that saw manna as a metaphysical, mystical food; not something nourished from the soil.

Looking at the sweep of writings from Jewish jurists, we see how the rabbinic manna narrative precipitated a legal discussion, which was then creatively solved by drawing from the biblical manna narrative to formulate an appropriate benediction. The various proposals are interesting on a number of fronts. First, perhaps the most obvious answer was sidelined: That the blessing should conform to formulations canonized by the rabbis. Plotzki was a lone voice in suggesting a recognized formulation; but by his own admission his suggestion was questionable. This approach could take two forms—a staid version and a more adventurous proposition. In its staid version, this possibility might mean that the appropriate benediction was the catch-all formulation—the blessing to be recited over items that are not grown from the ground: "Blessed are You, O Lord, king of the universe, that everything came into being through His word." A more adventurous version of this approach might suggest that the blessing should use the formulation that is appropriate to the selected taste. Neither of these possibilities were raised. Apart from Plotzki, jurists preferred a creative route when grappling with the legal question and coined a new benediction formulation.

Second, the question was addressed by a broad spectrum: jurists of unequal standing, disparate genres of norm-generating writing, different cultural milieux, across centuries and across geographic regions. Despite the distances, at least two of the jurists were in conversation with a predecessor's proposal. This reminds us how Law in general, and Jewish Law in particular, is part of a multigenerational discourse that traverses geographic, temporal, and cultural boundaries. This is a salient point for the present study of magical phenomena in the eyes of the Law.

Third, for most of the jurists manna was a matter of past. When the Israelites reached the Promised Land they no longer enjoyed this magical food; only a solitary jar of manna was preserved for posterity (Exodus 16:33–35; Joshua 5:11–12). The jar was subsequently housed in the Ark of the Covenant which stood in the holiest precinct in the Temple. During the First Temple period, the Ark with its contents was hidden, and its whereabouts remains unknown (Maimonides, Laws of the Temple, 4:1). Thankfully, jurists did not discard the legal question to the dustbin of history, indicating how interest in Legal History is part of the Jewish legal tradition.

This leads to a fourth point: not only was the legal question concerning a bygone reality, it was largely anachronistic. Reciting benedictions over food was a practice instituted by the rabbis, centuries after the Israelites consumed manna. There is sound basis to simply say that no blessing was recited because blessings before food had yet to be legislated. Why were jurists concerned with an anachronistic question? Three possibilities present themselves. The jurists may not have considered the question anachronistic: There is a significant and intriguing rabbinic tradition that commandments, even patently rabbinic legislation, were observed by the forefathers long before they were legislated (see, for instance, *Mishna, Kiddushin* 4:14). If such assertions should be taken at face value, then the manna question may not be anachronistic. Alternatively—as was clear from Menahem Azarya's opinion—this may have been an exercise in legal imagination as jurists considered a future legal reality where manna would once again be consumed. Finally, this may have been an exercise in intellectual legal gymnastics and creativity. Much like hypothetical scenarios are standard fare in Law Schools, Jewish Law also has a penchant for analyzing liminal cases.

Taking these points together leads to a fifth aspect of note. The numerous answers to a legal question that has no immediate application indicate both uncertainty and care. It is as if the jurists were collectively saying: We may not know which blessing should be recited, but we are clear that this is a legal question that deserves consideration. The span of answers indicates that jurists were animated by the legal question, either as a question of historic Jewish Law, or as an intellectual challenge, or as a preparatory exploration for a long awaited eventuality which would entail new legal questions.

Ancient Magic, Ancient Law

Whether it is the ancient magic of love, or the love of an ancient legal system—I suggest that this study is significant for scholars of law on four interconnected levels. First, this exploration speaks to the possibility of cross-fertilization in Comparative Law. Second, the analysis presented here provides a window into the world of Jewish Law jurists. Third, the material discussed here contributes to our understanding of the reaches of the Jewish legal system. Fourth, the present discussion may be significant for the contemporary challenge of charting a course in legal education. I will conclude this essay with a few words about each of these implications.

Intellectual Cross-Fertilization

The three cases presented here demonstrate that aspects of the magical Hogwarts reality were considered by Jewish Law jurists. Thus the legal implications of Hogwarts may be of interest, *mutatis mutandis*, to scholars of Jewish Law. Conversely, legal scholars of the magical world may find fertile ground in Jewish Law for comparison and perhaps inspiration. Indeed, the enterprise of Comparative Law is inevitably enriching.

Moreover, this comparative analysis reminds us that legal opinions never really die. Even when not in use, Law merely hibernates, lying dormant, waiting for the sun to come out once again. While J. K. Rowling's achievements in depicting the world of wizardry are incontrovertible, the words of Ecclesiastes 1:9 ring true: "What has been will be again, what has been done will be done again; there is nothing new under the sun."

Judicial Biography

The cases discussed here may pique the interest of legal historians and judicial biographers who seek to unravel the complex world of the jurist.[19] Are the excurses on magical phenomena intellectual exercises much like the hypotheticals favored in socratic-style classrooms? Perhaps the discussions provide us with a window into the inner world of the jurists and the cultural environs in which they operated? Which texts were included in the jurist's legal library? As Justice Felix Frankfurter wrote: "Reading maketh a man only in part—yet how illuminating it would be to have a list of the books read by the justices" (Fairman, 1949, p. 368, citing a 1948 letter by Frankfurter).

Without a doubt—each era, each culture, each jurist, will provide a different set of answers to such questions. Raising the questions and discussing the possibilities is the first step towards a thick, nuanced account.

The Reaches of Law

What are the boundaries of Jewish Law's jurisdiction and what are the implications of those demarcations? Isaiah prophesied that the angels call to each other and declare: "Holy, holy, holy! The Lord of Hosts! His presence fills all the earth" (Isaiah 6:3). Aaron Barak, Chief Justice of the Israeli Supreme Court, ruled that everything was judicable; that is, the Supreme Court could hear and rule upon any case. This policy was summed up with a play on Isaiah's words: "*Law* fills all the earth" (Barak, 1993, pp. 485–487; Levitsky, 2001, pp. 227–243). Scholars have asked whether Jewish Law might stake a similar claim: "*Jewish Law* fills all the earth." In other words, is everything in this world judicable according to Jewish Law? This paper adds a fourth permutation to this discussion of the reach of law: Is Jewish Law also concerned with otherworldly phenomena? From the cases we have considered, it is apparent that Jewish Law does not see itself as confined to earthly matters; magical phenomena are also judicable.

The observations about intellectual cross-fertilization, the world of the jurist, and the reaches of law bring us to an additional point about jurisprudential boundaries: the nexus of *nomos* and narrative in Jewish Law. The cases discussed here reflect different interplays between the two realms. In these cases it is apparent that narrative has crossed into the realm of law, and law into the realm of narrative. While valiantly searching for a precedent for the notion that a lethal verbal attack is a guilty act, the jurist blurred the distinction between law and narrative; biblical and rabbinic narratives were conscripted to resolve a question in law. The entry of the bewitched quill into legal discourse is equally enchanting: rabbinic narratives about Moses' final day created a legal conundrum that was solved by reference to a magical narrative. The rabbinic manna narrative is full of flavor: the taste of manna precipitated a legal discussion, which was then resolved by returning to the biblical manna narrative or to narratives about the mystical valence of manna. Any claim for a law/narrative dichotomy is undermined by these cases. The complexity of the law and narrative relationship reminds us that the web of interfaces remains to be fully described.

Legal Education

The legal questions discussed in the parallels to Tom Riddle's Diary and Bertie Bott's Every Flavor Beans are specifically relevant to the world of Jewish law—a lawscape that prohibits writing on Sabbath and mandates blessings before eating. Modern law distinguishes between civil law and religious law; between secular interactions and religious rituals. As a legal system with ancient roots, Jewish Law predates this bifurcation. The same jurist who is called upon to adjudicate criminal culpability, might be called upon to answer questions of Sabbath observance or ritual recitation of benedictions before eating.

Alas, modern notions of law have largely removed much of Jewish law—and other legal systems defined as religious—from law schools. These rich legal systems have been consigned to history departments, religious and cultural studies, courses in literature, and the like. Law schools only entertain Jewish law when it addresses questions recognized by modern legal systems: evidence, tort, contracts, and so on. Setting aside significant swaths of Jewish law may be justified on functional or utilitarian grounds, but we would be remiss not to acknowledge the opportunity cost of such policies.

Cordoning off sections of Jewish law as *ex-territoria* impoverishes legal discourse and to an extent is mendacious. There is also an andragogical cost of lopping off sections of Jewish law; or worse yet—not considering Jewish law as a bona fide legal system because of modern demarcations of law. But let us approach the matter in positive terms: What are some of the advantages of expanding the parameters of legal education?

For the student of law, trained in addressing hypotheticals as a means of honing rigorous legal thinking, the magical world opens up new, challenging vistas. Contemporary legal education is not predicated on discussing real cases. Law professors notoriously do not allow students to dismiss hypotheticals with the argument that the scenario could never happen. The creative explorations discussed in this paper offer new ammunition for law professors.

There are also tangible benefits that should be considered: Criminal law classes will continue to teach about *mens rea* and *actus reus*. Students immersed in contemporary culture are likely to be animated by a discussion of the criminal elements of murder when they are refracted through the Hogwarts reality.

A final word: In addition to blessings before food, Jewish Law mandates the recital of blessings before the study of sacred texts; whether those texts are of a legal or a non-legal nature. While the text follows the standard benediction formulations, it includes additional wording:

> Now sweeten—O Lord our God—the words of Your Torah in our mouths and in the mouths of Your nation, the House of Israel. And may we—we, our descendants, and the descendants of Your nation, the House of Israel, all of us—be amongst those who know Your name and who engage with Your Torah [*Babylonian Talmud, Berakhot*, 11b].

The language of the blessing before study is unique. No other blessing in Jewish tradition includes a request that God "sweeten" the encounter, and no other blessing refers to bequeathing the experience to future generations (Cooper, 2012, pp. 98–103). This study suggest the possibility of exploring legal worlds that are beyond the boundaries of traditional curricula, offering an enjoyable, creative, and refreshing experience without sacrificing intellectual rigor. What could be sweeter than that?

Notes

1. This research was conducted while I had the privilege of being a postdoctoral fellow at the Buchmann Faculty of Law, Tel Aviv University. My thanks go to Mollie Feldman, Ariella Siegel, and Maya Zinkow of the Pardes Institute of Jewish Studies, Jerusalem, for their helpful comments.

2. For an overview of magic in Jewish tradition, see *Encyclopaedia Judaica*, 2007, 13:342–352.

3. For writing on Harry Potter from a Jewish perspective, see Krulwich, n.d., 2006. Krulwich's blog has posts from December 2006 through February 2013, and includes links to other online articles. The present study adopts a different methodological approach.

4. For an overview of Jewish criminal law, see Enker, 2014.

5. For Jewish sources of the magical word "Abracadabra," see Trachtenberg, 1939, pp. 80ff; 116ff.

6. Miller cited a later text, but this is the earlier source of the tradition.

7. On self-defense in Jewish law, see Enker, 2014, pp. 285–287.

8. The Hebrew word "*ba-rehitut*" could be translated as "with fluency," or it could refer to cursive script which is called "*ketav rahut*."

9. A play on the biblical verse "I sleep and my heart is awake" (Song of Songs 5:2).

10. Alas, Professor Meir Bar-Ilan who transcribed the formula could not recall its source. Underscored spaces appear in Bar-Ilan's transcription and indicate particular esoteric names of God. For a less poetic formula that is accompanied by a ceremony, see Scholem, 1978, pp. 91–92.

11. See, for instance, the account reproduced in Benayahu, 1959, pp. 563–568.

12. Rabbinic tradition calculated the date of his death as the 7th of the Hebrew month of Adar (*Babylonian Talmud, Kiddushin* 38a).

13. The verses are Psalms 36:7, 71:19, and 119:142.

14. Later rabbis added limitations which are not germane to our discussion; for instance, property may not perform work that creates unusual noise.

15. From Sofer's responsum it is apparent that Noah Gavriel offered an alternative explanation that used the notion of dual time—Sabbath in Heaven, Friday on Earth—to justify Moses' actions. Sofer roundly rejected this possibility. Noah Gavriel's second suggestion is unconnected to magic writing and hence beyond the current scope.

16. On manna in general, see Cheyne & Black, 1902; "*Man*," 1978.

17. On the different manuscripts and editions of *Sefer Hasidim*, see "Princeton University Sefer Hasidim Database (PUSHD)," n.d.

18. For more on manna as bread of heroes, see Shinan & Zakovitch, 2012, pp. 50–53.

19. On the enterprise of judicial biography, see Posner, 1995; Urofsky, 1998.

References

Amram bar Sheshna. (1971). *Seder Rav 'Amram Ga'on*. (D. Goldschmidt, Ed.). Jerusalem: Mossad Harav Kook.

Babylonian Talmud.

Barak, A. (1993). 'Al Hashkafat-'Olam Bi-Dvar Mishpat Ve-Shiput Ve-'Aktivizm Shiputi. *Iyunei Mishpat, 17*(3), 475–501.

Bar-Ilan, M. (2010). Hashba'at Ha-Kulmus. *Bar-Ilan University: Daf Shevu'i, 881*. Retrieved from http://www.biu.ac.il/JH/Parasha/simchat/mbip.pdf.

Benayahu, M. (1959). *Rabbi Hayim Yosef David Azulai*. Jerusalem: Mossad Harav Kook.

Bialik, H. N. (2000). Halachah and Aggadah. In *Revealment and concealment: Five essays* (pp. 45–87). Jerusalem: Ibis.

Brodt, E. (2014). New book announcement: Amudim be-Toldot ha-Sefer ha-Ivri (Volume Three). Retrieved from http://seforim.blogspot.co.il/2014/08/new-book-announcement-amudim-be-toldot.html.

Brodt, E. Y. (2010). *Likkutei Eli'ezer*. [Beitar Illit]: E. Brodt.

Ceccarelli Morolli, D. (2012). *A brief outline of Roman law*. Rome: Gangemi Editore.

Cheyne, T. K., & Black, J. S. (1902). Manna. In *Encyclopædia Biblica* (3:2929–2931). Adam and Charles Black.

Cooper, L. (2012). *Relics for the present: Contemporary reflections on the Talmud*. New Milford, CT: Maggid Books.

Cover, R. M. (1983). Nomos and narrative. *Harvard Law Review, 97*, 4–68.

Ehrenreich, H. L. (Ed.). (1924). *Sepher Ha-Pardes (Ha-Meyuhas Le-Rashi)*. Budapest: H. L. Ehrenreich.

Enker, A. (2014). Jewish Law. In M. D. Dubber & T. Hörnle (Eds.), *The Oxford handbook of criminal law* (pp. 269–294). Oxford: Oxford University Press.

Fairman, C. (1949). The writing of judicial biography—a symposium. *Indiana Law Journal 24*(2), 363–369.

Freehof, S. B. (1955). *The responsa literature*. Philadelphia: JPS.

Habba, Y. (1999). *Ha-Yesod Ha-Nafshi Ba-'Aveirat Retsah Be-Mishpat Ha-'Ivri (Mens rea in homicide according to Jewish law)*. Bar-Ilan University.

Hagiz, J. (1704). *Halakhot Ketanot*. Venice: A. Bragadin.

Hebrew Bible.

Jellinek, A. (Ed.). (1938). Midrash Petirat Moshe Rabbeinu. In *Beit Midrash* (pp. 115–129). Jerusalem. Retrieved from http://www.daat.ac.il/daat/tanach/tora/ptirat_moshe.pdf

Jerusalem Talmud.

Kahali, Y. [Yosef Hayim of Baghdad]. (1973). *She'elot U-Teshuvot Torah Lishmah*. Jerusalem.

Kahali, Y. [Yosef Hayim of Baghdad]. (1976). *She'elot U-Teshuvot Torah Lishmah*. Jerusalem.
Kahali, Y. [Yosef Hayim of Baghdad] (2013). *She'elot U-Teshuvot Torah Lishmah Ha-Shalem*. Jerusalem: Ahavat Shalom.
Kinstlikher, M. A. Z. (1993). *He-Hatam Sofer U-Venei Doro*. Bnei Braq: Makhon Le-Hotsa'at Sefarim Benei Moshe.
Krulwich, D. (n.d.). Harry Potter and Torah. Retrieved from http://harrypottertorah.blogspot.co.il.
Krulwich, D. (2006). *Harry Potter and Torah*.
Levitsky, N. (2001). *Kevodo: Aharon Barak Biyografiya*. Jerusalem: Keter.
Maimonides, M. *Mishne Torah*.
Man. (1978). In *Entsiklopediya Mikra'it* (2nd edition) (5:7–10). Bialik Institute.
Menahem Azarya da Fano. (1863). *Ma'amar Shabbtot Hashem*. Lemberg: Z. L. Flecker and Co.
Midrash Rabba. (1512). Constantinople: Samuel ibn Nahmias.
Midrash Tanhuma. (1522). Constantinople: Solomon ben Mazal Tov.
Miller, A. A. Y. (1991). *She'elot U-Teshuvot Hayei Asher*. Jerusalem.
Miller, P. (1984). *'Olamo Shel Aba*. Jerusalem: Hod.
Mishna.
MS Parma H 3280, *Sefer Hasidim*.
Palmer v. The Queen, AC 814, 832 [1971]
Plotzki, M. D. (1924). *Hemdat Yisra'el*. Piotrków: Sh. Belkhatovskii.
Posner, R. A. (1995). Judicial biography. *N.Y.U.L. Rev.*, *70*, 502–523.
Princeton University Sefer Hasidim Database (PUSHD). (n.d.). Retrieved from https://etc.princeton.edu/sefer_hasidim
R v. Lindsay, AER (D) 349 (2005)
Rashi.
Rosh.
Rowling, J. K. (2008). *The tales of Beedle the Bard*. New York: Children's High Level Group in association with Arthur A. Levine Books.
Runyan v. State, 57 Ind. 80, 20 Am. Rep. 52 (1877).
Scholem, G. (1978). Ha-Maggid Shel R. Yosef Taitazak Ve-Hagiluyim Ha-Meyuhasim Lo. *Sefunot*, *11*, 67–112.
Shapira, T. E. (1850). *Benei Yissaskhar*. Zolkiew: Saul Meyerhoffer.
Shinan, A., & Zakovitch, Y. (2012). *From Gods to Gods: How the Bible Debunked, Suppressed, or Changed Ancient Myths & Legends*. (V. Zakovitch, trans.). Lincoln: University of Nebraska Press.
Skolnik, F., et al. (Eds.). (2007). *Encyclopaedia Judaica* (2nd edition). Jerusalem: Keter.
Sofer, M. (1841). *She'elot U-Teshuvot Hatam Sofer*. Pressburg, Vienna, Munkacs: Y. Shlesinger.
Tishby, I. (1985). *Meshihiyut Be-Dor Geirushei Sefarad U-Fortugal*. Jerusalem: Shazar.
Trachtenberg, J. (1939). *Jewish Magic and Superstition: A Study in Folk Religion*. New York: Behrman's Jewish Book House.
Urofsky, M. I. (1998). Beyond the Bottom Line: The Value of Judicial Biography. *Journal of Supreme Court History*, *23*(2), 143–156.
Wisdom of Solomon.
Wistinetzki, J. (Ed.). (1891). *Sefer Hasidim*. Berlin: H. Itzkowski.
Yehuda ben Barzilai of Barcelona. (1903). *Sefer Ha-'Itim*. Krakow: Y. Fisher.
Zevin, S. Y. (1957). *Sippurei Hasidim: Mo'adim*. Tel Aviv: A. Zioni.
Zohar.

Building Harry Potter's Identity in Transmedia Contexts[1]

PILAR LACASA, SARA CORTÉS and RUT MARTÍNEZ-BORDA

The world of children and young people raises specific challenges when examining their relationship with new media. The goal of this essay is to analyze how children and young people build the character of Harry Potter, the hero of the series, by using multimodal discourses. The goal behind the study is to analyze how participants construct multiple representations of this hero mediated by contents appearing on different platforms, especially the video game *Harry Potter and the Order of the Phoenix (EA, 2007)*, the film, and oral and written narratives. Adolescents elaborate digital texts working with the teacher and the researcher at the school in a workshop integrated into language classes.

First, we introduce the theoretical model, supported by classical works and recent research, including three concepts: *transmedia representations* (Jenkins, 2006), *figured worlds* (Holland, Lachicotte, Skinner, & Cain, 1998), and Harry Potter as *the hero* (Bakhtin, 1990). Below we show the research context, developed from an ethnographic perspective and supported by action research. The data, as mentioned before, come from a workshop carried out in a public school where teenagers worked on a newspaper. Multimedia texts were finally published online after several revisions, and the results show how students built representations of Harry Potter which were closely related to the type of text they produced.

Building Imaginary Worlds in Transmedia Contexts

Some concepts help to understand how *adolescents* interpret Harry Potter in a multiplicity of texts, allowing us to speak of *intertextuality*. We under-

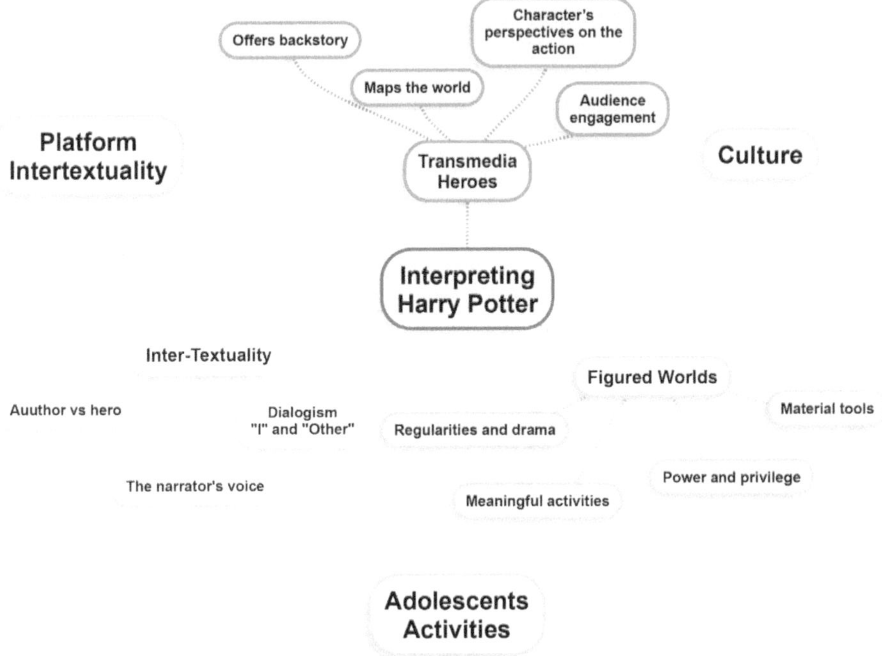

Figure 1. Interpreting Harry Potter

stand this interpretation as *social and cultural processes* that go beyond individuals, when they build world models and express them by elaborating narrative texts.

Our theoretical model, synthesized in Figure 1, is supported by three main concepts. The first one relates to the *transmedia representations* (Jenkins, 2007; 2011) that people elaborate including the information they receive from different communication channels. In the case of Harry Potter it's a hero who arises from J. K. Rowling's books and is also present in movies, video games and other cultural objects organized around its figure. These cultural conceptions are configured as maps of the world, providing backgrounds to the narrative constructions and contextualizing new media contents when people rebuild new information. The second concept backing our model is the notion of *figured worlds* (Holland et al., 1998). It focuses on the content of the representation rather than on the channel through which people receive media contents. They are also cultural constructions, including the rules that define a drama as context where the actions of the hero are significant. Finally, the third concept supporting the model is the notion of dialogue rooted in Bakhtin's works (e.g., 1990). We will examine how the dialogue between author, hero, and narrator, and even other characters, takes place.

Harry Potter: A Transmedia Phenomenon

Young people elaborate world interpretations combining what different media say about the same character or their adventures. At this moment, we are dealing with the transmedia concept. Let's see how Henry Jenkins defines it:

> A transmedia story unfolds across multiple media platforms, with each new text making a distinctive and valuable contribution to the whole. In the ideal form of transmedia storytelling, each medium does what it does best-so that a story might be introduced in film, expanded through game play or experienced as an amusement park attraction [Jenkins, 2006, p. 95–96].

We can think of the Harry Potter phenomenon as a transmedia experience when this character appears across multiple channels (video games, movies or books) and people represent him by developing the information displayed through all of them. In this research, young people approached Harry Potter when the video game, *Harry Potter and the Order of the Phoenix (EA, 2007)* was introduced in the classroom. The students produced a newspaper dedicated to this digital hero. We are talking about a phenomenon that involves the construction of the character from a multiplicity of perspectives. There is not a single episode, we speak of transmedia navigation as a literacy ability that allows following the flow of different stories on different texts and expressive modes. The stories move around, and audiences engage with content across multiple forms of expression. Functions attributed to the concept of transmedia (Jenkins, 2011) support the way in which we can interpret the students' texts. According to this author, most transmedia content serves one or more of the following functions:

First, transmedia universes *offer a backstory*. Different elements, scattered across multiple texts, are integrated to create a coordinated representation. The experience implies intertextuality, supporting continuity against multiplicity in the sense that the texts complement each other.

Second, transmedia phenomena *map the world*. It goes beyond the fact that a content is present on multiple platforms. It is inseparable from the representation people build from particular contents. Different types of practices configure the world, associated with the environment, where other characters interact with the main hero.

Third, the transmedia experience offers *other character's perspectives on the action*. Each one of the texts contains and includes different types of actions, attributed to characters, and contextualized in certain times and spaces. In addition to this, these actions are supported by different goals, and each of them has a specific meaning.

Fourth, the transmedia experience *deepens audience engagement*. The goals of those who live there are associated with a commitment to the contents, leading to particular interpretations. Even they are hybrid phenomena, where the elements of a space involve those coming from others. Different people produce something to build something new, and each one has a different commitment with his/her production.

In short, the first axis of the proposed model focuses on the functions attributed to the concept of transmedia. The phenomena depend on the students' activities when they produce multiple texts, introducing different perspectives from which to approach Harry Potter's character.

Figured Worlds as Reconstruction of the Content

As previously presented, the *transmedia* concept refers to representations that people build as a media universe. Focusing on the hero, the phenomena *can also be understood in relation to the concept of figured worlds*, introduced by Holland et al. (1998) and adopted by other authors (Daniels, 2007; Long & Moore, 2012). Here is a definition:

> By "figured world," then, we mean to socially and culturally constructed realm of interpretation in which particular characters and actors are recognized, significance is assigned to certain acts, and particular outcomes are valued over others. Each is a simplified world populated by a set of agents (in the world of romance: attractive women, lovers, boyfriends and fiancés) who engage in a limited range of meaningful acts or changes of state (flirting with, falling in love with, dumping, having sex with) as moved by a specific set of forces (attractiveness, love, lust) [Holland et al., 1998, p. 52].

Holland and his co-authors described *figured* worlds as historical and social phenomena closely linked to what people do. This can be summarized considering the following aspects:

- They are *a culturally organized world*. It involves both abstractions of significant regularities from everyday life. It is an abstraction related to "narrativized" and "dramatized" universes.
- *Agents engage in meaningful acts*, apart from purely imaginary. All this attracts people and wraps them in what we might call immersion processes.
- Other people value both activities and their results. In this context, *power and privilege* appear. These particular relationships between participants contribute to set up interpretations of their activity.
- People's activities rely in building imaginary worlds on *material artifacts*. Tools always mediate human relationships.

Summing up, Holland and his co-authors (1998) put forward an analysis in which they adopt a bidirectional model that redefines the relationships between the person and society.

Intertextuality and Dialogism

The concept of transmedia is still insufficient to understand how people face the hero. Bakhtin's works expand the framework to interpret our data (Holquist, 1990; Brandist, 2015; Morson & Emerson, 1990; Vice, 1997). In this framework, the notion of intertextuality, even though this term does not appear in the writings of Bakhtin, can synthesize his approach (Kristeva, 1980; Perlina, 2014; Harder, 2006). It allows us to understand the relationship between different textual supports from a double perspective. On the one hand, to explore the meanings created around the hero's activities, taking into account the relations between parts of the same text. On the other hand, it refers to the relations between multiple texts produced in specific contexts.

Deepening the concept of intertextuality (Brandist, 2015), and focusing on the Bakhtinian tradition, three issues relevant to the model build from these pages. The first involves the relationship between *Author and Hero in Aesthetic Activity* (1924–7), a study included in *Art and Answerability* (Bakhtin, 1990). The second relates to the *narrator's voice*, which the author addresses in *Problems of Dostoevsky Poetics* (Bakhtin, 1929/1999). Third, we are interested in the *concept of meaning*, which allows us to enter into dialogical universes, both dynamic and unfinished. The topic is explored in *Marxism and the Philosophy of Language* (Voloshinov, Matejka, & Titunik, 1929/1973).

The Author and the Hero

The relationship between the author and his hero are at the core of the creative process in transmedia contexts. Digital media have transformed teenagers' communications environments, who now live in a global world. This is where Harry Potter appears. Bakhtin (1990) contributes to understanding this relationship from a dual perspective: first, by looking at the hero as a totality. The author approaches him as a human being by assembling all the cognitive-ethical determinations that make him a unique figure, a whole, a unit of meaning. Second, in order to make this possible, the author goes out of his/her inner self: "He must become another in relation to himself, must look at himself through the eyes of another." (pos.,1154, Kindle Ed.). If this relationship does not occur in particular events, other less fruitful and creative interactions appear. The following are mentioned by Bakhtin:

- The hero takes possession of the author, and he cannot see the world of objects through any other eyes but those of the hero. The hero's activities are defined by him and not by the author.

- The author takes possession of the hero, somehow overrides him, his voice and his autonomy.
- Finally, the hero himself is the author, and he interprets himself, he plays the role he chooses to play.

Bakhtin considers the creation of the hero as an aesthetic process based on the dialogue that he has built from the notion of totality and exteriority. These situations, as described in the former paragraphs, inhibit the aesthetic experience.

The Narrator's Voice

Dialogue, however, does not take place between the author and the hero only, the voice of the narrator may also be present in the text. Bakhtin explores dialogue in his book *Problems of Dostoevsky's Poetics* (Bakhtin & Emerson, 1984). According to him, novels can be narrated by the author, the narrator or the characters. Dostoevsky constructs external portraits of the characters directly from the author or the narrator. These stories do not create fixed and static images, but dynamic and open worlds.

The narrator could be an identifiable voice, no longer equivalent to the author. It is another sound that shapes the characters and dialogues with all of them, even with that author. The narrator gives privileged information, while the characters narrate to themselves. Each one of them has limits; they are multiple voices that coexist in polyphonic texts.

According to Bakhtin (1999), a narrator's narration may be developed in the form of literary discourse or oral speech. The narrator is an organizer whose task is to assemble the story materials. This is the most important component, since information is filtered through it. From here, we can even classify narrator types: objective, subjective, direct or indirect eyewitness of the facts, which depends on their capacity and the way new informative data are introduced. The narrator introduces a certain perspective of reality that depends on the point of view chosen to convey it.

Dialogism: The Self and the Other

The relationships between the Self and the Other allow us to interpret how teenagers reconstruct the figure of Harry Potter (Holquist, 1990). Reality is experienced, not only perceived, and in this sense dialogism implies a multiplicity of human perceptions. The self (author) is defined from a relationship that allows for the construction of meanings related to specific times and spaces. The concepts of simultaneous and relative contribute to its definition. Meaning is relative because it is the relationship between two people who simultaneously occupy different spaces. From this perspective, Bakhtin concerns himself with the presence of the "other" to generate a creative understanding of the self:

> Creative understanding does not renounce itself, its own place in time, its own culture; and it forgets nothing. In order to understand, it is immensely important for the person who understands to be located outside the object of his or her creative understanding—in time, in space, in culture. For one cannot even really see one's own exterior and comprehend it as a whole, and no mirrors or photographs can help; our real exterior can be seen and understood only by other people, because they are located outside us in space ad because they are others [Bakhtin, Holquist, and Emerson, 1986, p. 7].

Dialogism assumes that the world perception is related to life experiences and perspectives. Space and time limit the "I" in front of the others and nothing is perceived as independent from his/her context. That is why the world is a set of meanings, hence the concept of heteroglossia (Voloshinov et al., 1973). Bakhtin (1981) referred to this idea in a later work, *Discourse in the Novel (1934–35)*. Language, culture, and art are made of non-systematic alterations to transform meanings. Even cultural tools are never something closed. *Heteroglossia* is a way of conceiving the world in relation to multiple languages, each of which has distinct properties. These are never purely formal, each of them has a set of distinctive values and presuppositions associated. "Heteroglossia governs the operation of meaning in the kind of utterance we call a literary text, as it does in any utterance" (Holquist, 1990, pos. 1370, Kindle ed.).

We must bear in mind that language is not a unitary system, but a cultural phenomenon that continuously auto recreates and completes. It is a task and a never-finished project. Language is the main tool in daily life, which acquires more complexity when it becomes a creative experience in art or literature. Each of these languages reflects its historical quota and the conditions that have made it possible. This is the world in which the characters of Harry Potter are recreated. Moving through other works by Bakhtin (1965 / 1984) we found the idea of *carnivalization*, introduced in *Rabelais and his world* (1939–41); it extends and deepens the processes by which the "I" is recreated in interaction with the "Others."

In sum, Bakhtin's works provide the basis from which to interpret how adolescents build the character of Harry Potter through their texts. In these, as we will see below, the interaction of both author and hero is presented by dynamic and complementary relationships in both the real and the figurative world.

Research Background

Our methodological approach is based on *case study* techniques, combined with the use of some *practices of ethnography* and an *ecological approach*

(Lacasa, Martínez-Borda, & Méndez, 2013). The objective value of their contributions is not based on the frequency with which a phenomenon occurs. Rather, their validity is based on a detailed description of the cases in which we can explain how people make sense of their activities in defined sociocultural contexts. The focus is on ethnography because we see people's activities in specifics contexts, namely, a series of workshops addressed to adolescent students.

The data collected and analyzed for this research were gathered at a public secondary school in the Madrid region. Students were aged 12–13 years old, and they worked with video games, more specifically with *Harry Potter and the Order of the Phoenix* (2007, EA) on a *Nintendo Wii* game console. The workshop took place during school hours and regular lessons of a Spanish language class. What is different from regular activity is the methodology, not the content. At that time, video games were one more element of a wide transmedia context (Jenkins, 2006). For example, besides game consoles and computer games, books, notebooks and the Internet were also present in the classroom. Moreover, participants combined the use of a number of technologies: cameras, mobile phones and any other tools that may be deemed necessary. The teacher was highly experienced, very education-minded and innovative. He had already participated in a previous workshop with another game and another group of Year 7 students. This made me aware of how important it is to play the video game in advance and, in fact, he had already completed 100 percent of the game levels by the time the workshop came to an end. The work sessions took place for a month in the last part of the school year.

This was one of the teacher's objectives: working with issues related to literary creations, narrative texts, and the comparison of different media telling stories, etc., by using Harry Potter. Later on, we discovered that, on top of the objective of working on literary texts, there were many other topics researchers and teachers had to deal with, such as the fact that an adventure game became a task resolution game.

The Workshop

The sessions mainly focused on cooperative teamwork (in both small and large teams) based on dialogue and reflection on the activities carried out by the students. Those activities, created by adults, promoted debate and the possibility to take on new challenges or think about what the students discovered. Describing or explaining it, either orally or in writing, helped them become aware of what they had learned.

Figure 2 (above and right). The secondary school classroom and the tools.

Table 1: Learning Narratives with Harry Potter

Activities	*Session*	*Description*
Playing–Becoming experienced players	1, 2, 4, 9	This took place in the computer room (also known as "video games room." During this time, the students entered the dynamics of the game and discovered the goals set by the teacher and their evolution in a real situation. The students had to become both explorers and observers, taking note of everything that happened for their final project. Teachers and researchers became aware of the video game's main feature: problem solving.
Reflection and curricular activities	3, 5, 6, 7, 8, 10, 11, 12	Sessions held by the teacher during a regular class with a more "curricular" attitude. We refer to those moments in which the teacher taught the material in the language book from a different perspective, since the video game became a work and reflection tool. We can thus talk about applying knowledge after the workshop.
Creating and publishing Harry Potter narratives	13, 14	It focuses on the creation of final products: 36 texts included in Manuel de Falla's *"The Prophet"* newspaper. The teacher proposed the creation of several documents ("articles") to be gathered in the newspaper. These documents went through three phases: a first phase of creation in paper, its Word digitalization with images and writing and, finally, posting on the blog.

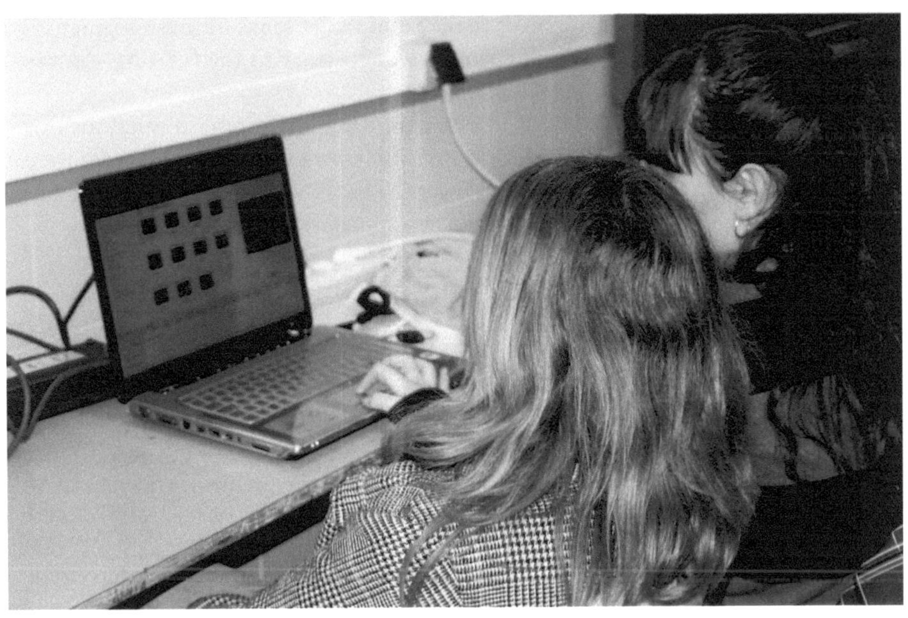

The Analytical Process

Our units of analysis are not individually isolated elements, but activities organized by cultural principles in which participants look for specific goals to make sense of these activities within the social and cultural processes in which they take place (Lacasa et al., 2013). We consider two main units of analysis for exploring the data presented in this paper, the first one being all the papers produced in different formats (paper, pdf, and Internet publications), and the second one being each of the texts created by the students and included in these newspapers.

Phases of Analysis

NVivo 10 (software for qualitative analysis) was used. The analytical process was divided into three phases, combining macro and micro perspectives for the research process:

- **First phase.** The software allowed us to combine *projects and documents*. The projects created in *NVivo* worked as a "container" of all the documents that the researcher created for the study of the research topic, that is, data, ideas and the connections between both.
- **Second phase.** This was *oriented to systematize and code*. In this context, we decided to establish relations between each text considered as a whole, and specific fragments included in each of them. The software allowed us to contextualize and make sense of these segmentations while going back as much as necessary to the full text. At this stage, text types were defined.
- **Third phase:** Its goal is to compare texts and establish relationships among them by considering specific fragments. *Branched nodes were defined*, which were created from the three central cores we will detail in the next paragraph: categories of analysis.

Categories of Analysis

Table 2. Types of text considering their function and content

Text type	*Definition*
Approach to the learning contexts	They focus on the specific context of the workshop, the classroom and the school. They bring perspective in a learning environment as they experience it, considering both positive and negative aspects. They even propose other types of workshops.
Informative dossier on Harry Potter	They mention a set of websites where they found information about Harry Potter

Text type	*Definition*
Interviews with Harry Potter	Students become interviewers of Harry Potter, with whom they have a conversation, by asking for his opinion on the experiences they live in a fantasy world.
Stories about Harry Potter's universe	These may be recreations of scenes occurring during the game, the movie or imagined by the authors.

The categories proposed above emerged inductively from the data, bearing in mind the proposed theoretical model. We defined two category systems: First, categories that allow classifying the type of text as related to its expressive function. This arises from the authors' intentions and interests in the context of the workshop. The students were free to choose the type of production, and each full text was classified. The categories allow us to organize each text considered as a whole.

Also, we defined a second level of categories aimed to deepen the dimensions from which the figure of Harry Potter is constructed. This will allow us to compare how the former dimensions were present in different types of text.

Table 3. Dimensions in the Construction of Harry Potter

Conceptual core	*Dimension*	*Definition*
Transmedia	Codes	Use of images and texts in a complementary manner to approach the hero
	Platforms	Connections between different media in which the world of Harry Potter is developed: video games, film and books.
Figurative world	Spatial context	Elements of the text related to the spatial description. They refer to the figurative world or the real world. Sometimes, there are also connections between both of them.
	Temporal succession	The text includes mentions to a succession of events, actions, problem-solving, and game mechanics. Sometimes, there are connections between the temporal dimension in the game and the real world.
Dialogism	Identification with the character	The use of the first person when authors identify themselves with Harry Potter.
	Role of the Narrator	We have considered two types: a) The use of the first person when the author situates himself within the narrated text; and b) The author uses the third person, being outside the text.
	Harry Potter as "the other"	References to the character from physical elements, qualities, and actions that characterize him.

Harry Potter in Manuel de Falla's "The Prophet" Newspaper

After having played and thought about the character of Harry Potter during the workshop sessions, students were faced with the task of producing a text. The teacher suggested discussing the experiences of the workshop in very general terms, focusing on the hero. He was considering this idea from the first moment, according to what appears in the research summary after a preparatory meeting.

> *Fragment 1, prepared for the edition of the newspaper*
> *Session 1. 2009-05-05. Research Summary.*
>
> *I had a conversation with Javier, the teacher, about the workshop. He told me that his idea was to prepare a digital newspaper as a final product (like a blog or a website). He will be working with the two groups. Something like a newspaper special edition for the Harry Potter saga ("the Prophet"). Through the newspaper articles, they will explain the game, the workshop and the characters. His idea is to connect this with the language (curriculum) contents in this last quarter. They must go through several types of texts and also discuss media discourses. It is very interesting that he has raised it as well. Let's see how it goes.*

The task was carried out once the workshop sessions were completed. Then, it was time for the students to develop a text about their experiences with Harry Potter. They reconstructed the figure of Harry Potter through different texts. We will see how this situation defined by the teacher and shared by the students can be understood from the theoretical model proposed in the previous pages (summarized in Figure 1). Firstly, a *transmedia world* is present (Jenkins, 2007; 2011), populated with representations built from the image of Harry Potter and provided by different platforms. The world map places the activity of the characters, also providing the background for the story. Each author will build his/her perspective from a commitment with specific contexts. Second, a *figurative world* (Holland et al., 1998) is the general frame for the hero and his companions' activities. It combines drama and unexpected excitement with laws and regularities from which elements acquire meaning as a whole. The hero emerges as a figure situated in the center, and around him there are other people defining power and privilege relationships. Finally, such relationships are best understood from the concept of *dialogue between author and hero* (Bakhtin, 1990). In order to have a real dialogue, both the author and the hero must be placed outside themselves to mutually understand their own perspectives. Only thus, watching each other from the outside, can they become autonomous.

In sum, each student will prepare a text related to the workshop introducing the Harry Potter character. The authors may transmit their messages, texts and images, based on their experience with the game.

The Figure of Harry Potter in Different Types of Texts

We will now focus on the types of texts produced and published in the digital newspaper (which can be viewed at http://bit.ly/1L8Jxy0). It is a summary of 31 documents, and it will be useful to examine how students represented the character of Harry Potter. The texts were analyzed inductively, as noted above, and the result was the definition of a set of categories (see Table 3). Through a qualitative analysis, we will explore the relationships between the different types of texts and the figure of Harry Potter present in them. It is about finding regularities that allow for comparison. As indicated above, exploring the presence or absence of the categories of analysis in the texts and graphing them allows us to establish relationships between them.

We examine what's in each text and focus on the presence or absence of categories in each of the four types previously defined. We start by *the texts related to the learning contexts* (13 texts, 42 percent). They refer to the real world and describe the workshop. We observe that the categories, which are most frequently used, relate to the learning process and the spatial context that, in this case, is the classroom environment. The game is a material and cultural tool that could open the door to transmedia experiences (Holland et al., 1998). It appears as a learning instrument, isolated from other mass media. In addition to this, the texts are generated from the immediate context. Only four of the thirteen texts (22/30, 22/31, 24/32 and 30/6) transcend into the figurative world of Hogwarts, to draw a comparison between the school and the world of fiction. Considering the dialogic dimension of these texts, it shows that the author has been imposed on the hero and has even cancelled his voice. In this case, Harry Potter is a fictional character, a living being which becomes a starting point for the curriculum contents.

We will now focus on the documents relating to *the search for information about Harry Potter* (Information Pack-3 texts, 10 percent). The texts are distributed in two dimensions, the presence of references related to transmedia environment and the dialogic processes.

In this case, the students present Harry Potter in different platforms, for example, the video game and the film. On the other hand, placing the texts in a dialogical context we observe that the figure of Harry Potter set him as "the other." Harry Potter is outside the author, imposed on him, and that eliminates the author's creativity.

The third type of text we discussed relates to *the interviews with Harry Potter* (7 texts, 23 percent). The interview presents a space shared by students and characters alike. The adolescents who feel part of the figured world were able to interact with the hero (Holland et al., 1998). Spatial and temporal dimensions are present in the setting. Real and imaginary universes interact. The real world generated the interaction format between the author and the hero, in a transmedia environment (Jenkins, 2006). For example, most of the texts are television or radio interviews. At the same time, the contents and the topics of the interview situate both the author and the hero in a figurative world. Also, the dialogic dimension (Bakhtin, 1999) appears in almost 100 percent of the documents, considering the information related to the main character. Harry Potter is presented as a hero admired by many fans. Author and hero will talk as equals, neither outperforms the other.

Finally, considering the *stories* about the Harry Potter universe (8 texts, 26 percent) we observe that students define special and temporarily figurative worlds. In addition to this, the events occur in a certain order, and from there particular meanings arise. It should be noted that this dimension is more present in stories that in interviews. We explain this fact because students could describe the context in which Harry Potter appears in more detail. Also, the figure of a narrator introduced in the stories was less frequent in interviews and the presence of Harry as a hero is clear.

Interviews and stories seem to be the most complex texts, and there are differences between them if we look at the dimensions related to the figurative worlds and dialog. We will explore them in depth in the next paragraphs.

Interviews and Stories in a Magical Universe

As indicated, the interviews and stories are the most interesting texts to explore in depth how students construct the figure of Harry Potter. Figure 3 shows how the three conceptual nuclei defined in our theoretical model are present in each of the texts. Looking at these data, the differences between the two types of texts focused on transmedia and dialogism dimensions, but are lower when they mention figurative worlds.

These data can be explained because interviewing the hero situates him in a transmedia context (Jenkins, 2007). Mass media provide a particular map of the world, a background to build the narrative, a perspective that places the hero's activities and a commitment of the author to his audience. More difficult to explain is why the dialogic dimension appears more often in the stories than in the interviews (Bakhtin, 1981; 1990; 1999). Figure 4 helps to delve into these data. There are interesting differences between the two types of texts, considering the categories previously defined to understand how students characterize Harry Potter.

Categories related to *transmedia representations* are most evident in the interviews. As mentioned above, real radio or television platforms have moved into fiction and contribute to generate a map of the world, a back-

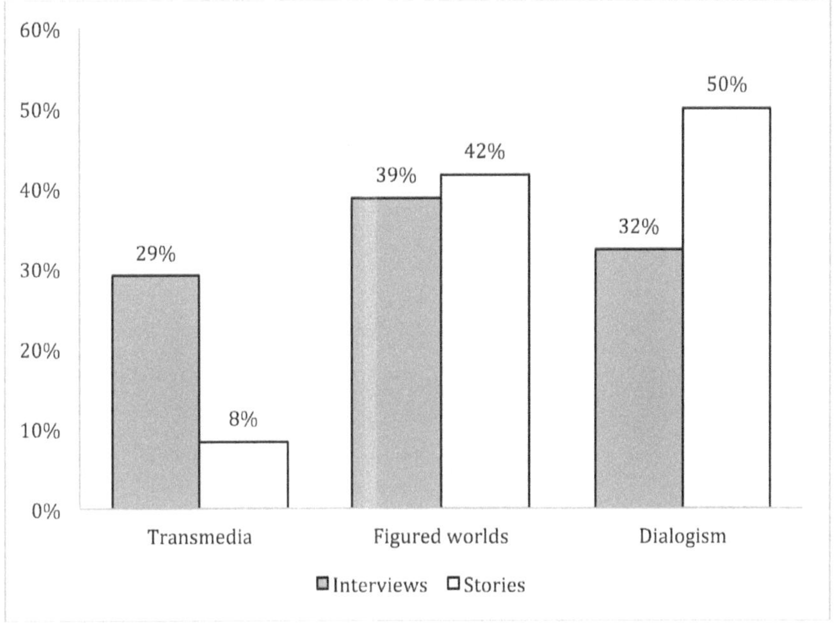

	Transmedia	Figured worlds	Dialogism	Total
Interviews	9	12	10	31
Stories	4	19	24	47

Figure 3. Conceptual dimensions in the interviews and stories

ground that gives meaning to the story. On the other hand, the presence of different expressive codes in interviews refers to the fact that students often include text images of the character as a way of presenting the hero.

Considering the figurative worlds, differences between the two types of texts appear. Consequently, references to the spatial context appear most often in interviews, while temporal succession relates to the construction of stories. Spatial and temporal contexts provide a framework to generate the meaning of the story. In addition to this, these meanings relate to the presence of the drama and the laws that regulate it.

Referring to the *dialogic dimension*, we notice references to the hero in both types of texts. He is more present in stories than in interviews. The identification between the hero and the author is low, almost non-existent; it does not appear in the interviews and only once in the stories. We explain this fact because both of them observed themselves from outside, thus preventing identification. On the other hand, the presence of a narrator in the stories is easily explainable. Bakhtin (1984) defined this figure as a text

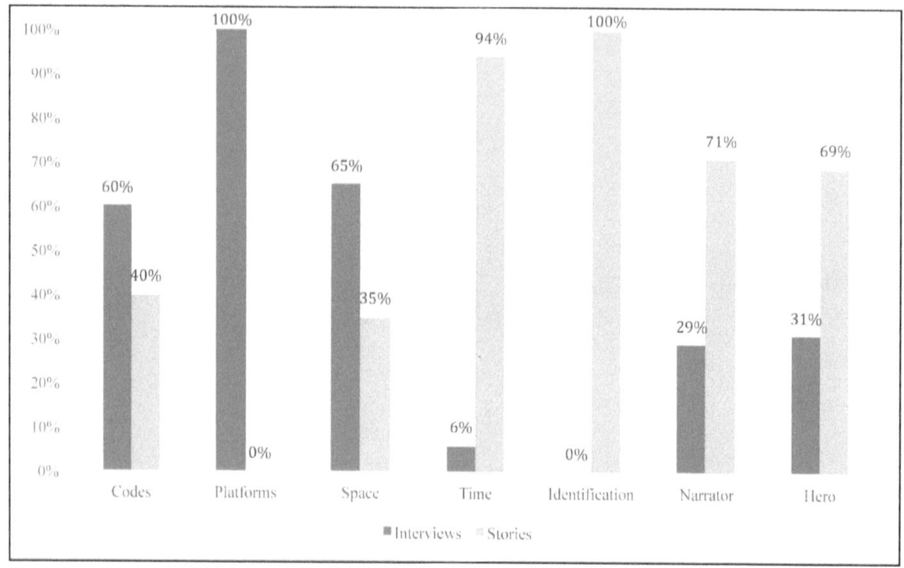

	Codes	Platforms	Space	Time	Identification	Narrator	Hero	Total
Interviews	6	3	11	1		2	8	31
Stories	4		6	14	1	5	18	48
Total	10	3	17	15	1	7	26	79

Figure 4. Conceptual dimensions and categories in the interviews and stories

organizer, useful to unify elements that would otherwise be scattered without his voice. Something similar occurs with the figure of the hero as such, whose direct reference in the text is more present in stories that in interviews. When the hero is physically present in a real or figured world, people don't need to refer to him because he speaks for himself.

Finally, we will focus on two complete texts produced by the students: interviews and stories. They are examples of how they build Harry Potter's figure.

Dialogue with Harry Potter

We begin by analyzing how Pablo, one of the students, interviewed Harry Potter.[2] The text includes a dialogue between two people who pretend to be real, but they are situated in a fictional world.

Fragment 2. Interviewing Harry Potter, by Pablo Cánovas (IES Manuel de Falla, 2009)

1. *Hello everyone, we have a very special guest today. It is someone who is succeeding among teenage crowds because of his books and films. Without further ado, here is Harry Potter. Hello, Harry!*

2. *Hi, Pablo, I am delighted to be here with you.*

3. *As you know, you are having a lot of success all around the world because of the books and movies narrating your adventures. How do you find this luxurious life?*

4. *Well, not everything is luxuries and a good life. People think it is very easy to do this, but it is not so. I get up at 6:30 in the morning every day. At Hogwarts, not everything is adventures and holidays, there are also other things like at regular schools, there are millions of exams and homework. Well, I will not say anything else, I'm going off-topic here....*

5. *Feel free to comment whatever you like, Harry, make yourself at home. But we can talk about something else, if you like....*

6. *Yes, I would prefer that, Pablo.*

7. *OK, then. Could you tell us how it was to say goodbye to your aunt and uncle?*

8. *A complete chaos since my family are ridiculous. I think they are not actual people, they are more like animals.*

9. *And what can you tell us about your stay at the headquarters of the Order of the Phoenix?*

10. *That was one of the moments I enjoyed the most; I could see all my friends working together with a common goal, the destruction of Voldemort.*

11. *Well, I see what you said in the beginning is not entirely true because all you've told me so far is very interesting.*

12. *I know, Pablo, but that's because you are not asking anything boring since you are interested in all the adventures I've lived.*

13. *Well, looks like you are insisting I make you one of those boring questions like teachers do!*

14. *No, no, I didn't want to say that, only that I'm not speaking about failings, since you only ask me things that I can't answer with other words.*

15. *OK, the misunderstanding is now over, but also the time for the interview. So I must say goodbye. See you soon, Harry, we hope you continue like this. Goodbye!*

16. *Thank you for everything, Pablo, I hope that's the case! Goodbye and thank you for the interview, I was delighted.*

We look at the text as a whole, an example to explore how this student elaborates the figure of Harry Potter. To do this, we will focus on the categories that we presented as the analytical framework, organized around three main dimensions.

The text starts in the framework of a *transmedia narrative* (paragraphs 1–3), including references to multiple media. On the other hand, the student uses two codes, text and image, to represent the figure of Harry Potter. The first idea transmitted by this text is that the interview takes place at a show (a television or a radio setting). This context provides a background for understanding the phenomenon. Additionally, this is a map of the world, and both the interviewer and the interviewee assume a commitment to their activities and their audiences (Jenkins, 2007; 2011). Focusing on the content of the interview, we observe that Harry has become a winner among teenagers.

For this reason, adolescents are placed in a transmedia universe. Their stories unfold across multiple platforms (novels and books), and each text makes a specific and valuable contribution to all of the adventures that make him a renowned and popular hero.

We immediately enter into a figurative world (paragraph 4) which arises by presenting a description, extended with personal considerations about life in Hogwarts. In this context, aspects of real life and the figurative world are continuously intertwined. The real author is Pablo, a secondary school student, present in a fictional world to become an interviewer, talking with his favorite hero. Thus, both worlds are present: the character through the figurative world and the real world that represents the student. There are also references to personal assessments (paragraphs 11 to 14) and interactions. In that sense, it's important to notice the introduction of the names of the interviewer and the interviewee (paragraphs 5, 6, 15, 16). Also, there are direct references to the author and the hero through personal pronouns that are increasingly frequent (7, 8, 9, 13). The meaning arises from personal interactions marked by symmetry, in what refers to the relations of power between the author and his hero (Holland et al., 1998). Also, the regularity of the figurative world arises from questions and answers that occur in the usual order that takes place in an interview.

We will now focus on the dialogic model that organizes the relations between the author and his hero, considering the text as whole, and also specific categories for exploring its contents. First of all, it draws our attention to how the author of the text has a conversation with the hero. Pablo, the interviewer, stood out of himself when he reconstructed his role at that time, and also dialogued with the audience of the show. The initial paragraph is what we have interpreted as the voice of a narrator (Bakhtin, 1984). On the other hand, all of the text is a sample of how the author speaks with "the other," which has been characterized by specific traits (1990). The topic of conversation refers to various activities and forms of life. For example, the hero is famous, he has a family, he has feelings, and he gives reasons when he expresses his views. It also highlights how the hero's feelings are present in the texts, for example, when mentioning friendship at the time he is talking about the Order of the Phoenix: he was happy meeting all his friends and having a common goal. In the end, Harry Potter almost becomes a real person.

The Harry Potter Universe

It is time to examine the text defined as a narrative. The authors are two students, and they discuss their experiences interacting with the video game in the workshop. Although the authors wrote the text in a single paragraph, we have differentiated three parts to facilitate its analysis. The text content defines its structure, at least to some extent.

As we can see, the first part is an environment description, emphasizing spaces. It refers to corridors, stairs and also a more specific decoration, with reference to specific objects. The second part includes a brief reference to the people who live there and includes temporal references. The last part includes a set of actions and activities, also described through a temporal sequence.

Fragment 3. What is Hogwarts like and what we did there, by Veronica Gil and Cristina Green[3]

1. Hogwarts was an old medieval castle in which we are now studying magic. There are secret corridors at Hogwarts; the stairs move as they want, the pictures speak and the doors have painted guardians to control who comes and who leaves. It is forbidden to access some areas, such as the left third floor or the dark forest.

2. The first day we arrived at Hogwarts: Hermione, Ron, our colleagues and I, Harry Potter.

3. We carried out these activities during the year: we went to the shed to find Lee Jordan, Fred and George Weasley. We helped them to put some boxes in a few boats. We had to uncover the boats, put the boxes inside and cover them again. We also fed the seagulls. Then, we made a box explode and there were fireworks. Later on we went to the front yard and had to sweep the corners until a symbol appeared. We had to make a few logs levitate to be able to light some torches. We walked the side aisles used the spell "incendio" in the mounds of stone and arranged the central statues. Then we went to the stone bridge on the first floor, where we had to light the torches that are next to the doors. To be able to ward off bats, we had to climb down a pipe and scare them away. Then we went to the third-floor bridge and we had to turn on other torches, shy all the crows and fix the pipe that was next to the torch.

There is no explicit reference to the transmedia universe. It is difficult to tell that the author has gone beyond the video game to tell his story. What the author is presenting in the third paragraph is a description of his activities during the game. In addition to this, space and time are present in the text; these are the main dimensions related to figurative worlds. Space references appear when they describe the castle of Hogwarts. Mentions to the idea of time emerge from a double perspective: first, the reference to the day the characters arrived in Hogwarts and, second, the succession of actions presented in the third paragraph. Both the presentation of the space and the time generate a regularity and contribute to understanding the story. We speak of a figurative world culturally delimited (Holland et al., 1998), defined by a particular space, linked to a succession of events, actions, problem-solving and game-mechanics descriptions. Emerging stories, experienced by the author and the hero, emerge in a magical world.

In relation to the dialogic dimension of the text, we can say that the narrator's perspective appears when the author speaks using the third person when he describes the castle of Hogwarts (Bakhtin, 1984). He moves out of the text, situating himself in an outsider perspective. On the contrary, in paragraphs 2 and 3, the identification between the author and the hero appears. The author speaks in the first person, as a result of his identification with Harry Potter (Bakhtin, 1990). In this case, the author and the character are the same, assuming, for this reason, the characteristics that define it and performing the hero's activities during the game.

In short, we have two texts about how adolescents present the figure of Harry Potter. We will note that they were those who chose the format and rebuilt both the character and its universe.

Conclusions

The main goal of this essay was to examine how young people build the figure of Harry Potter through different texts published in a digital newspaper. They participated in a workshop playing, discussing and reflecting on the video game *Harry Potter and the Order of the Phoenix* (EA, 2007). The game was a tool for learning in the language classroom.

This essay provides a theoretical model from which to interpret the texts written by the teenagers. The first approach to the data allowed us to inductively define various types of texts. First, we examined 31 texts produced by students, considering their functional character. From this perspective, texts differ among themselves in the way in which the author expressed his perspective on the experience. This approach is what we consider to be the function of the text. We carried out a second revision of the data, on the basis of the conceptual nuclei present in our theoretical model in interaction with an inductive approach to the texts. All this allowed us to define different categories of analysis that have served as a starting point to define the way in which students construct the figure of Harry Potter.

As a result of the relationship between these two levels of analysis, *we delimited four Harry Potter figures in the texts.* Each one of them may be associated with a type of text, related to the perspective from which the students seem to build real and figurative worlds.

The first type of texts relates to learning contexts. All of them draw a very specific figure of Harry Potter. At that time, the hero is an instrument present in the game and, above all, a mediator in the learning process. He is someone we know at the school, the hero of the video game. This result leads us to question the role of objects designed for entertainment when inserted in the school (Lacasa et al., 2013). In the case of students who built this type of text, the hero was annulled as such and rebuilt in a new environment, away from the fantasy and figurative worlds that often characterize Harry Potter in entertainment contexts.

A second category of texts was defined as a result of *a search* around different websites while looking *for information about Harry Potter*. The author becomes a simple compiler that just associated the character with the information found. This type of texts is typical of the school context. The hero in this case is assembled from the sum of a set of characteristics that do not define a whole (Bakhtin, 1990). Moreover, the hero has been overridden by the amount of information conveyed. We can even say that the character disappears, he no longer exists.

There are also other types of text where the character is built in a much more creative way, becoming someone who can establish a dialog with his author. There, students have become interviewers of the hero, building the world and the universe of fiction appearing in the game, movies or novels (Jenkins, 2007; 2011). In addition to this, if we interpret these texts from Bakhtin's ideas (1990), we will say that both the author and the hero can take an external perspective to themselves. They relate to one another as creators in a dialog.

Finally, there is one last type of texts in which the authors builds a narrative that involves, in most cases, identification with the character. They are *stories about the Harry Potter universe*, with which the author identifies himself. Other characters are interpreted in the context of human relationships. They appear as they are usually presented in the real world, but now they live in a magical world built from fantasy. In this case, the author disappears to make way for the hero. It is the hero who takes more strength and even overrides the author.

To sum up, our general conclusion is that texts generated in a temporary space, in this case the school context, bring very different visions of the world with different degrees of development. Each of these visions is associated with a perspective from which to reconstruct the world and the hero of the text, in this case Harry Potter. We personally prefer to build texts that lead us to figurative and transmedia worlds, where the dialog between the author and the hero is possible.

Notes

1. This research was carried out with funding from the Spanish Ministry of Industry, Energy and Tourism and Electronic Arts Spain.
2. http://bit.ly/1uBw9k6. Paragraphs are numbered to facilitate the discussion.
3. http://bit.ly/1CWRNOK.

References

Bakhtin, M. M. (1929/1999). *Problems of Dostoevsky's Poetics* (C. Emerson, Trans.). Minnesota: University of Minnesota Press.

Bakhtin, M. M. (1965/1984). *Rabelais and his world.* (Hélène Iswolsky, Trans.) Bloomington: Indiana University Press.

Bakhtin, M. M. (1981). Discourse in the novel. In M. Holquist (Ed.), *The dialogic imagination* (pp. 259–422). Austin: University of Texas Press.

Bakhtin, M. M. (1990). *Art and answerability. Early philosophical essays.* (Michael Holquist and Vadim Liapunov, Eds.) Austin: University of Texas Press.

Bakhtin, M. M., & Emerson, C. (1984). *Problems of Dostoevsky poetics.* Minneapolis: University of Minnesota Press.

Brandist, C. (2015). The Bakhtin circle. *The Internet encyclopedia of philosophy. A peer-reviewed academic resource.* http://www.iep.utm.edu/bakhtin/. Accessed 2015-01-21.

Bruner, J. (2002). *Making stories. Law, literature, life.* Cambridge: Harvard University Press.

Daniels, H. (2007). Discourse and identity in cultural-historical activity theory: A response. *International Journal of Educational Research, 46*(1–2), 94–99. Doi: http://dx.doi.org/10.1016/j.ijer.2007.07.009

Harder, H. (2006). A few introductory remarks on Bakhtin and Intertextuality. http://www.scm.uni-halle.de/reporting_list/study_days/sektion1/2303855_2303900/?lang=en. Accessed 2015-01-21.

Holland, D., Lachicotte, W., Skinner, D., & Cain, C. (1998). *Identity and agency in cultural worlds.* Cambridge: Harvard University Press.

Holquist, M. (1990). *Dialogism: Bakhtin and his world.* New York: Routledge.

Jenkins, H. (2006). *Convergence culture where old and new media collide.* New York: New York University Press.

Jenkins, H. (2007). Transmedia storytelling 101. *Confessions of an aca-fan: The official blog of Henry Jenkins.* http://henryjenkins.org/2007/03/transmedia_storytelling_101.html.

Jenkins, H. (2011). TransMedia 202: Further reflections. http://henryjenkins.org/2011/08/defining_transmedia_further_re.html. *Confessions of an aca-fan: The official blog of Henry Jenkins.*

Kristeva, J. (1980). *Desire in language: A semiotic approach to literature and art.* New York: Columbia University Press.

Lacasa, P., Martínez-Borda, R., & Méndez, L. (2013). Half as practice: Narrative and conceptual approach for qualitative data analysis. *Studies in Media and Communication, 1*(1), 132–149. http://redfame.com/journal/index.php/smc/article/view/231/233.

Long, N. J., & Moore, H. L. (2012). *Sociality: New directions.* New York: Berghahn Books.

Morson, G. S., & Emerson, C. (1990). *Mikhail Bakhtin: Creation of Prosaics.* Stanford: Stanford University Press.

Perlina, N. (2014). Dostoevsky in Bakhtin's Collected Works. *Russian Studies in Literature, 50*(4), 16–27. Doi: 10.2753/RSL1061-1975500403.

Vice, S. (1997). *Introducing Bakhtin.* Manchester: Manchester University Press.

Voloshinov, V. N., Matejka, L., & Titunik, I. R. (1929 / 1973). *Marxism and the philosophy of language.* New York: Seminar Press.

Creating Equality Through Quidditch: A Rhetorical Analysis of Quidditch Blogs

Ryan S. Rigda

In their 2013 book, Anthony Gierzynski and Kathryn Eddy claim the *Harry Potter* series gave rise to the Harry Potter generation: a group of readers who grew up with the characters and thus influenced the political views of the Millennial Generation. Gierzynski and Eddy described how members of this generation waited patiently for their own Hogwart's acceptance letter, dressed up for every midnight book release and movie premier, cried when their favorite characters met an untimely death, and even hoped for their own broomstick. J. K. Rowling created such an elaborate and inviting world that many readers, children and adults alike, dreamed of being there. In an effort to make this dream more tangible, Universal Studios partnered with Warner Bros. to create two sections of their theme parks modeled after the Wizarding World. However, the translation from fantasy world to real life did not stop there, as fans started clubs and organizations that allowed them to bring their fantasies out of the fictional world. One of the most popular fandom translations of the *Harry Potter* franchise is none other than the magical sport of Quidditch.

Traditionally, Quidditch is played in the air with magical broomsticks, but to the dismay of many *Harry Potter* fans, magical broomsticks do not exist. Despite this tradition, fandom athletes have managed to adapt the sport to be played without magic and thus without flying. Even with this major difference, modern Quidditch maintains the standard set by J. K. Rowling. Similar to the muggle sport of soccer, the goal is to pass the ball down the field to score through one of three hoops. For those who are not familiar with *Harry Potter*, the sport would seem quite strange; however, the sport has become so popular that the International Quidditch Association (IQA) was developed to regulate the thousands of college and university teams around the world. In response to this popularity, an exhibition match between five countries was held during the 2012 Summer Olympics to showcase national talents (Dockterman, 2012). This sudden popularity may be fueled by the unique make-up of the players and fans. Even though Quidditch has become more than a fan-fiction sport, it still maintains the co-ed team structure that J. K. Rowling wrote into the *Harry Potter* series. Knowing that gender is not binary, the IQA organizers, as well as players across the nation, work to include people of all genders and identities into their league. Therefore, because of this sudden popularity and unique team structure, it is important to examine to what extent the sport was translated into a real-life game.

Many scholars argue that J. K. Rowling conforms to traditional gender roles through her narration of the *Harry Potter* series. Pugh and Wallace (2006) argue that even though the books seemed to be oozing support for those that are different, there are many instances where gender stereotypes are perpetuated. Ruthann Mayes-Elma (2006) found that throughout the book, the female characters were given strict gender boundaries and labeled as the "other." Additionally, she claimed that these characters were only allowed to triumph when it benefited a male character. Heilman and Donaldson (2009) argued that females were subjected to the same forms of rhetoric when J. K. Rowling described Quidditch. She stated that female players experienced traditional male-dominated sport inequality because they were only allowed to score when it would not change the outcome of the game. For example, in *OotP*, Lee Jordan quickly turns his commentary on Angelina Johnson's goal into a rant about her not agreeing to go out with him. While Jordan acknowledges the mid-game goal, Johnson has no real impact on the outcome of the game, because Harry would go on to win this game by catching the golden snitch, thus alluding that Johnson was only there to make the scene interesting and dramatic.

While many literary scholars suggest that all aspects of J. K. Rowling's text represent women in a subordinate position (Mayel-Elma, 2006; Heilman & Donaldson, 2009; etc.), I argue that through the translation of Quidditch to a muggle sport, J. K. Rowling's concept of Quidditch breaks traditional gender roles and stereotypes in modern sport. Through the use of a four maximum gender rule, the IQA creates a sport culture where men and women are meant to be equal, unlike traditional sports that separate men and women into different leagues. Additionally, the rule recognizes the differences between sex and gender, something traditional sports cultures do not. Thus, I argue that the sport of Quidditch and the female characters many authors are critiquing are a misrepresentation of modern Quidditch. Because muggle Quidditch mirrors the wizarding sport, and threatens to change the traditional culture of sport, I propose the following research questions:

> Research Question 1: Does Quidditch create a space in the sport culture where hegemonic masculinity is negated?
> Research Question 2: How do females use agency in Quidditch blogs to create their identity within the sport?

The Nature of Quidditch

While Quidditch is rapidly growing in popularity and participation, it is still considered an alternative sport (Cohen, Brown & Welty Peachey, 2012). According to the International Quidditch Association website, Quidditch was started in 2005 at Middlebury College as an attempt to recreate the fictional sport portrayed in Harry Potter. The modern version of the sport combines aspects of dodge ball, rugby, tag, and capture-the-flag. A team is made up of seven players, who carry brooms between their legs in order to simulate the original flying version, each with a different role. Three chasers on each team try to throw the quaffle (a volleyball) into one of three hoops. In an effort to stop them, two beaters from the opposing team throw bludgers (dodge balls) at opponents that halt the movement of the quaffle. Meanwhile, a seeker from each team is attempting to capture the elusive golden snitch. In this version, the snitch is an impartial player who dresses in yellow and has a flag attached to his or her waist. The capturing of the snitch successfully ends the game. Due to the variety of positions on a team, the sport of Quidditch attracts athletes of all kinds. Additionally, because the sport is based in the realm of fan-fiction, it attracts non-traditional athletes. Thus, the nature of Quidditch creates a unique niche for athletes who share five common traits: identification with Harry Potter, camaraderie and friendship, desire to have fun, desire to try something new, and a desire to get in shape (Cohen et al., 2012).

In accordance with the fictional game of Quidditch, modern Quidditch is mandated as coed by the IQA. The International Quidditch Association website prides itself on being one of the only true coed sports (IQA, n.d.). Their current rulebook features a "four maximum rule." It states, "A Quidditch game allows each team have a maximum of four players, not including the seeker, who identify as the same gender in active play on the field at the same time" (IQA Rulebook, 8th Ed., p. 18). The IQA realizes that there is a distinction between sex and gender, a construct that most sports organizations fail to recognize. Additionally, the organization created Title 9¾, modeled after the current Title IX legislation, in order to promote gender equality and inclusivity within the sport. While many sports alter rules when females play, Quidditch does not. Every athlete is held to the same standards, just as J. K. Rowling portrayed it in her series. Cohen, Melton, and Welty Peachey (2013) found that the co-ed aspect leads to a positive experience for men and women on the field. Additionally, they noted that both genders reported stereotype reduction due to participation in the sport. This notion challenges the traditional view of hegemonic masculinity. As such, Edwards (2006) suggests that hegemonic masculinity is actually a fragile construct that is in danger of being overturned. Therefore, Quidditch could be the spark needed for social change within the organization of sport. However, despite these findings, they noticed that there was still an underlying prejudice towards female athletes. Thus, they ask whether or not this prejudice will increase as the sport becomes more popular.

Masculinity in Sport

The original function of organized sport was for middle-class white males to display their superiority over women and over race-and-class subordinated groups of men (Kimmel, 1990; McKay, 1991; Messner, 1988; Whitson, 1990). The nature of Quidditch, however, challenges the traditional culture of sport. As Cohen et al. (2013) found, men and women experienced a desire for inclusivity and equality, thus posing a challenge to traditional male-only sports. Unfortunately, due to cultural norms and reified behavior, sport is inherently masculine (Butterworth, 2008). As athletes conform to the accepted norms, the notion of hegemonic masculinity is both perpetuated and reinforced in the culture (Connell, 1995; Sartore & Cunningham, 2009). Gramsci (1971) coined the term hegemony to explain the process in which the one group is coerced into thinking subordination is the norm. Cohen et al., (2013) questions whether Quidditch can maintain the inclusivity of having men and women on the same team. The professional sports culture, which shapes the general idea of sports, portrays the image that in order to be accepted as an athlete, you have to embody masculinity. Papa et al. (2008) explains that in an organization, "members create and recreate the system that becomes their social context" (p. 128). Miller (2005) advances the notion of duality of structure when using Giddens to state, "Structures are the rules, norms, and beliefs that characterize the social world. Agency is the behavior and interaction of humans within that world (p. 71)." As humans, we are the agents that produce these structures, but these structures are the same medium in which agency operates. Over time, our interactions with the world of sport have created a set of norms that we feel obligated to follow.

The important question is whether or not the culture of sport can accept a coed team. Butterworth (2008) examined the story of Katie Hnida, a kicker at Colorado University, and her allegations of rape and harassment while on the team. This study reaffirmed male superiority in a male-dominated space, thus allowing Hnida to be classified as an intruder and marginalized as a player. This intruder effect demonstrates how stubborn and rigid conceptions of gender are today, especially in sports. Comments reduced her to "a girl" and a "distraction" thus undermining any sense of equality. In their study, Cohen et al. (2013) noted that despite their acceptance of female Quidditch players, men did claim that females made the game slower, less physical, and often less competitive. Thus, to truly see equality and acceptance, both by the individual and the culture, the language of gender and sex must be challenged.

Dunning (1986) explains that the prevalence of the male advantage in sport is due to hegemonic masculinity. Borisoff and Victor (1998) explain the hegemonic ideology of what men and women should and should not do. Men are masculine and women are feminine. Due to the belief in traditional gender roles, women are defined by the portrayal of women's sports. Traditionally, women were encouraged to participate in feminine sports such as gymnastics, swimming, and diving (Bernstein, 2002). Additionally, in order to accentuate the differences between men and women, golf courses were shortened, basketballs were smaller, and women were discouraged from participating in sports such as football. Women were perceived as less than men and were supposed to stay that way by participating in sports deemed less masculine. Messner (1988) supports this notion, stating that the current portrayal of sport makes it seem natural to view those who appear most masculine or most competitive to be superior athletes. Thus, sports were segregated based on the strict definitions of sex and gender. Booth (2011), however, used an episode of *Queer Eye for the Straight Guy* featuring a bisexual transsexual man to demonstrate how hegemony can be disrupted by the introduction of liminality through sexual orientation. As Tuner (1969) demonstrates, the attributes of liminal *personae* are meant to be ambiguous and different from typical social structure. Thus when an individual does not fit the hegemonic culture, their presence may elicit discomfort in others, such as in the case of the bisexual transsexual man on *Queer Eye for the Straight Guy* that did not fit typical identity constructs. Dunning (1986) goes on to argue that when the sexes desegregate, the male advantage erodes. Whitson (1990) agrees with these statements and claims that men become threatened by these changes in gender relations, which is why we see an increase in support for men's only institutions and the importance of confrontation among male athletes. In this case, by allowing men and women to participate on the same team, it creates tension between the athletes as they try to fill gender roles. As previously noted, Quidditch does not alter the rules for female athletes. Therefore, both men and women experience the physical aspects of the game. Players are allowed to tackle one another in order to stop progress of the quaffle or to prevent another player from handling the quaffle. This creates a physical atmosphere and reifies a masculine environment; a belief has been created and recreated in our society. Therefore, the contested meanings of sex and gender function as a source of conflict in communication when we break culturally acceptable boundaries. Quidditch challenges these assumptions as men and women are placed into the same arena and are subject to the same level of physicality.

The Sport Blogosphere

The prevalence of social media has created space where participants can go to engage in discourse that is typically ignored by mainstream culture and media. As a result, blogs are host to a collection of individuals who freely post about a given topic. The space where individuals come to engage in this social space is known as the blogosphere, and Park and Jeong (2011) defined the blogger public as "a group of bloggers who face a problem, recognize a problem, and engage in blogging about how to proceed or organize to take action" (p. 390). *Sports Illustrated* author Chris Ballard asserted that sports blogs are a place of empowerment for the sports fan (Ballard, 2006). The question is whether or not this holds true for every blog. Clavio and Eagleman (2011) found that men are portrayed physically in blogs more frequently than women, and when women are portrayed it is usually in a sexual manner. Antunovic and Hardin (2013), on the other hand, argue that sports blogs can both hinder and help the female voice in sports. While there are some sport blogs that conform to the male ideal of sport, others are addressed from a female perspective and rejects sport as a masculine domain. Gurak and Antonijevic (2008) claim that individuals create an online identity through the narratives posted on blogs. Thus Quidditch blogs would function to help create the identity of a female Quidditch player. This is further supported by findings that women are more likely to create blogs (Jones, Johnson-Yale, Willermeier & Perez, 2009) and maintain them (Henning, 2003) than are their male counterparts.

It is important to determine whether or not the images created by female Quidditch blogs are indicative of traditional hegemonic masculinity, or if they actually empower female athletes. Stavrositu and Sundar (2012) found that there is a relationship between women who blog and a psychological sense of empowerment. Since the game of Quidditch has been translated outside of the book to mirror the wizarding game, women Quidditch players have the potential to break traditional hegemonic masculinity ideals that are represented in the sport culture. By blogging about their experiences, they offer insight to their perspective of how the culture of the sport functions.

Quidditch blogs

The popularity of the sport around the nation, and even the world, has given rise to numerous blog sites that allow commentary on the games, teams, and even athletes the world has come to love. Based on its rising popularity, numerous Quidditch blogs have been added to the blogosphere. Blogs such as *Life After Quidditch, Fuck Yes Quidditch,* and even a Quidditch forum on the social media site Reddit.com have been created to chat about various aspects of the game. Topics such as "Teams to watch" and "The hottest snitches" create outlets for athletes and spectators to critique the game. Therefore, the popularity and controversy surrounding the topic of gender within the *Harry Potter* series makes Quidditch blogs an ideal text to analyze from a rhetorical standpoint. For purposes of this study, four Quidditch blogs will be examined. The blogs can be found at lifeafterquidditch.tumblr.com, fuckyesquidditch.tumblr.com, buttsandbrooms.tumblr.com, and reddit.com/r/Quidditch. All four of these blog sites are part of larger social media websites that attract millions of users per day. The tumblr.com blogs were obtained from the website quiddichblogsasemble.tumblr.com, a blog post devoted to compiling a list of Quidditch blogs for players and fans to follow. While only one individual (or a restricted group of individuals) is in control of tumblr.com blog, you can tell a post's popularity by the number of times it was reblogged to other sites. The reddit.com blog on the other hand is a social media site that allows any user to post content. I have chosen to select two different blog versions to gain perspective of more than one voice from the Quidditch world. Additionally, these blogs were chosen for their popularity, continuous maintenance, and their place in the Quidditch community. In order to limit the amount of blog posts that need to be analyzed, I will be focusing on posts that occurred during the 2013-2014 and 2014-2015 Quidditch season.

Theoretical Framework

Thus far, I have argued that Quidditch creates a unique atmosphere for athletes to participate in a nontraditional sport. However, since the culture of sport is inherently masculine, the culture of inclusion and equality established by the IQA is threatened as hegemonic masculinity has the potential to take over. As such, it is important to study the culture of Quidditch by examining Quidditch blogs to determine if it is indeed equal for all players. Because Quidditch is not limited to a single gender, men and women are required to play on the same team with the same set of rules. This allows every player to experience the same level of physicality, making Quidditch an ideal site for studying hegemonic masculinity. Using the framework proposed by Ruthann Mayes-Elma (2006) in her examination of the female characters in the *Sorcerer's Stone*, it is possible to identify sites of feminist agency in Quidditch. Mayes-Elma argued that to successfully analyze all aspects of J. K. Rowling's text, the methodology must combine critical theory, feminist theory, and agency. I argue that same methodology applies to the female voice in Quidditch blogs because of their unique place within a male-dominated environment. Therefore, the combination of these three theories allows for an interpretation of not only the meaning behind the text and the idea of gender, but also how we socially construct gender.

Critical theory

Critical theory is interested with power relations, as they exist in relation to race, class, gender, and sexuality (Mayes-Elma, 2006). Mayes-Elma utilizes Lather's (1994) definition of critical theory by stating that critical theory takes "into account how our lives are mediated by systems of inequality such as classism, racism, sexism, and heterosexism" and the need to challenge these systems (p. 140). According to Miller (2004), within the study of critical-cultural theory, a dominant minority has the ability to shape cultural practices through economic and political control. This means that as members become active participants in the control process a hegemonic culture is produced. When it comes to text, critical theorists look for the underlying meaning. They ascertain that there is no one truth, but rather the truth is subjective and has many interpretations. Mayes-Elma (2006) suggests that critical theory is appropriate to use because it looks to find the voice of those that are marginalized or silenced by the majority. In terms of *Harry Potter*, Mayes-Elma found that J. K. Rowling only portrayed female characters as background information or male enablers.

Outside of the literary examination of Quidditch, critical theory becomes even more important for identifying the female perspective in Quidditch. Within the field of critical theory, cultural studies becomes a tool for examining the connections among media, politics, economy, and the practices of individuals in a cultural system (Miller, 2005). Burgess (2006) notes that

> the task for cultural studies is not to speak heroically on *behalf* of ordinary voices but to find ways to understand and practically engage with the full diversity of existing and emerging media contexts in which they are, or are not, being heard [p. 212].

From the critical perspective, culture is not a unitary thing, but rather shaped by the experiences of the individuals within that culture (Warren & Vavrus, 2002). Sport is an ideal place to study critical theory because of the power struggles within the culture that are represented by hegemony (Hargreaves, 1994). Furthermore, Quidditch represents a unique culture that has yet to be examined with this lens.

Feminist theory

Next, feminist rhetorical theory can be used to examine the female's perspective of Quidditch. When developing this methodology, Mayes-Elma (2006) notes that definitions of what feminist theory actually means are highly debated. Delmar (1994) stated that feminist theory is, "an active desire to change women's position in society" (p. 9). The methodology used by Mayes-Elma (2006) follows five tenets of feminism (Osmond & Thorne, 1993). Traditionally, women have been ignored and devalued by male voices. Therefore, the first tenet focuses on centrality and value of women's experiences. By giving the women of Quidditch a voice, it will also give them authority. Second, the use of methodologies that are value committed and social change oriented seeks to promote gender equality and the well being of women. The third tenet, rejection of a unitary notion of the family, shows how gender roles are constructed and reinforced in how we portray a family. Next, an analysis of gender within specific sociocultural and historical contexts explains how we perpetuate gender stereotypes in society. The authors explain that gender is a historical construct that is reified over time. Finally, the last feminist tenet states that gender is socially constructed. Gender relations are found in almost every context and constantly constructed over and over again through our social relationships. This final tenet will be the most important in terms of this research. Since gender is socially constructed and is historically bound, the concept of Quidditch creates an arena where gender roles can be reconstructed.

However, from a feminist standpoint, it is important to point out that J. K. Rowling's text is considered to perpetuate traditional gender roles (Heilman & Donaldson, 2009; Mayes-Elma, 2006). During her research, Mayes-Elma (2006) noticed that five themes emerged from her analysis of *Harry Potter and the Sorcerers Stone*. These themes are rule following and breaking, intelligence, validating/enabling, mothering, and bounded resistance. These themes showed that women in the first book of the series only existed as background characters or enablers of the male characters. Therefore, it is important to see how this portrayal of female characters affects the female players of Quidditch. If the original portrayal of Quidditch portrayed women in a subordinate way, will the modern version create the same form of hegemonic masculinity?

Agency

Finally, Mayes-Elma defines agency as actively participating in the construction of identity and resisting oppression. This means that we are active participants in how we create our individual selves. The two dimensions of agency that Mayes-Elma uses are identity and resistance. She defines identity as " becoming aware of oneself as a person, expressing one's uniqueness, and expressing one's commonalities" (p. 56). In a patriarchal society, women are often labeled as the other and choose language that portrays them opposite of men. Resistance, on the other hand, is "confronting an oppressive force in the hopes of enacting change" (p. 57). This can be both internal and external. However, an individual must believe in resistance and the possibility of change for any change to actually occur. Mayes-Elma found five themes within *Harry Potter* female characters used to demonstrate agency. They are: rule following and breaking, intelligence, validating/enabling, mothering, and bounded resistance. The presence of these themes in *SS* suggests that J. K. Rowling conformed to the normal discourse on gender. Quidditch, however, offers a unique ability for agency because the women participating in the sport have a unique identity and an external path to resistance. The coed nature of Quidditch offers them the possibility to believe that change can occur. As a result, they are not bound by the same oppressive structures that J. K. Rowling placed on her characters.

Therefore, through the use of critical theory, feminist theory, and agency, the conversations developed by Mayes-Elma (2006) and Cohen et al. (2013) can be continued. While Mayes-Elma argues that J. K. Rowling's text is oppressive to women, Cohen et al. found that the sport of Quidditch reinforces positive attitudes about sex and gender within sport. Since Quidditch was translated into a coed sport, it becomes a unique tool for social change if participants choose to work to create a culture that is inclusive and equal.

Feminist Agency in Quidditch

Blogging has become a place of female empowerment (Stavrositu & Sundar, 2012), which is often lacking in the male-dominated world of sport. The nature and structure of Quidditch, therefore, offers a way for the female voice to be heard. Those voices are rhetorically created through blogs about Quidditch. The following section draws from those rhetorical constructions of the female voice to demonstrate feminist agency in Quidditch.

Throughout the analysis of the chosen Quidditch blogs several themes emerged. Those themes included game statistics, experiences with Quidditch, player profiles, gender debates, and player gear. Because of relevance to the topic, the discussion on game statistics and player gear (sometimes expressed as fashion) will be ignored. By game statistics, I mean game and tournament results, as well as current rankings in each league. However, the other themes present in these blogs helped to rhetorically define the Quidditch culture that is discussed by the players. While player and game statistics are generally straightforward, they do offer insight into how players are talked about. Because of the enforced gender rule, statistics featured both male and female players. The same thing can be said for player profiles, which alternated between female and male profiles. All of the blogs examined had multiple references to the gender rule and usually lead to a discussion of what that rule means for the sport. Finally, the individuality of the blogs allowed for posts that demonstrated experiences that were had during Quidditch. These posts were most interesting because of the insight they gave into the nature of Quidditch.

The Quidditch Experience

The most important theme to the discussion of agency falls under the category of the Quidditch Experience. All of the blogs contained posts that reflected experiences both on and off the pitch. These narratives work to establish identity and share perspective about the sport. As a result, these experiences are the best sources to look for identity and resistance within the sport of Quidditch. These ideas are best represented in an article titled "Redefining the Standard" in which Mollie Lensing describes her experience with Quidditch (14 December 2012). She states,

> [T]he most unique aspect of quidditch is that it is a coed, full-contact, team sport. Sure, college intramural sports and adult sports leagues are proponents of coed teams, but they often handicap with rules such as women's goals counting for double, while quidditch has everyone play on an even playing field.

Mollie's description of the Quidditch experience highlights the resistance players feel by participating in an unaltered co-ed sport. The narratives found in the chose blogs echo these sentiments and help to reinforce the gender equality established by the IQA.

In accordance with Mayes-Elma's facets of agency, the posts about the Quidditch experience help to establish identity. One post featured a set of stories from the website Quidd.co/stories which told of the positive effect Quidditch had on its players lives. One story read,

> Quidditch helped me come to terms with my sexuality which had previously been an issue that created a lot of frustration and unhappiness. My Quidditch friends would remind me that everything is ok and that I am loved and accepted for who I am [Fuck Yes Quidditch, 7 Sept., 2013].

Another story reads, "Quidditch gave me a confidence in my life that would not be there otherwise, and for that, I will be forever grateful" (Fuck Yes Quidditch, 7 Sept., 2013). Stories like these show the ways in which Quidditch helps to create a positive self-identity for its participants. As a result, the these narratives resists traditional structures of male sport that encourage individuals to hide qualities that may be unmasculine.

Player Profiles

Many of the blogs that were examined in this study featured player profiles. These profiles ranged from simple biographies of important players or discussions of who was the best in each position at a given time period. However, some of these posts objectified both men and women. In one post, "Butts and Brooms Presents: The Attractive All-Americans (Female Edition)," featured females were chosen based on a combination of skill and "hotness." The post reads, "This team is comprised of female players who embody the greatest combination of skill and hotness" (12 June 2013). Unfortunately, posts like this objectify the female body by subjecting them to the male gaze, something that is nearly impossible to escape in sports.

Gender Debates

Each blog examined had at least one reference to the gender rule that was established by the IQA. Additionally, each blog featured some sort of discussion or analysis of this gender rule and its impact on Quidditch. Most of these discussions praised the minimum gender rule and wrote of the positive way it influences all players. For instance the writer of *Fuck Yes Quidditch* posted a picture of the old "two-minimum" gender rule that existed in the IQA. Other blogs featured similar pictures or segments from the rulebook. A few posts on reddit.com were dedicated to increasing gender equality in the sport to make it more inclusive. Because of posts like this, there is no clear evidence of one gender dominating the other by means of content. This suggests that Quidditch is a sport where men and women can coexist and have the same experience.

However, there were also sentiments that the gender minimum causes frustration among the players. One blogger on *Life After Quidditch* had this to say,

> Focusing back in on quidditch and the gender rule, the biggest frustration for most people is that in many cases this forces teams to play not so good players over their better players, which absolutely sucks and I hate that to be honest. I do love the coed aspect of quidditch and many female players can bring a lot of unique aspects to the game (I wrote an article on that for T8M awhile back), but the reality is that what seeks to promote equality actually diminishes the fairness

> in determining who is most worthy of playing and who isn't. The best deserve to play no matter what, no matter the gender. That is what is fair [*Life After Quidditch*, 31 May 2013].

This post was noted to be the sixth or seventh version of the same debate. Clearly players are struggling with overcoming traditional gender roles and the physical differences between the male and female body. The post goes on to argue that the best players should play, no matter their gender, and the team should not be limited by a gender rule. The author does note that there are plenty of talented female Quidditch players and that they should ignore this post completely. For instance,

> We have gotten to a point to where the best female players in the game are widely recognized as such and would not be denied a roster spot on many teams even if there wasn't a mandated gender ratio. I will say that thanks to the gender rule many female players with the potential to do great have succeeded thus far and have shown that it isn't impossible to compete alongside the boys. The unfortunate truth however is that there aren't a ton and many of these players might not end up being starters because as great as they are, there are many male players that are still better [*Life After Quidditch*, 31 May 2013].

Unfortunately, debates such as this are often geared at females, labeling them as the weaker players. As a result, the gender debate reverts back to preconceived gender notions and takes agency away from female athletes.

Conclusion

While it started out as a simple fan fiction game, Quidditch is now a competitive collegiate sport. Due the unique nature of the sport, it has the potential to alter our current cultural expectations of sport and how we view gender within the sports culture. Unfortunately, the current communication literature on the fandom sport of Quidditch and the resulting interpretation of gender roles is lacking. Few, if any, studies have attempted to explore how the nature of Quidditch will threaten the mainstream masculine sport culture as men and women co-create the team and sport culture. While some studies have determined the marketable niche of Quidditch (Cohen et al., 2012) and its effects on participants (Cohen et al., 2013), this is the first study on how the co-ed nature empowers female athletes and presents an outlet for social change. The sport of Quidditch is rapidly gaining popularity around the world and is therefore a potential source of agency for female athletes. The efforts by the IQA to create an inclusive sport for both men and women has been successful thus far. Although the rhetoric used in the blogosphere still shows signs of hegemonic masculinity, which are reflected in that of a traditional male sports blog, there does seem to be mutual ground for all players to share.

This study does not come without its limitations. Because of the nature of blogs and the bias of the bloggers, the perspectives about the nature of Quidditch are limited. If a wider range of blogs were analyzed, a clearer picture would be revealed about the impact of the minimum gender rule. Additionally, because blogs are managed on an individual basis, it is impossible to account for post frequency and upkeep of each blog. This may have skewed results and allowed for more data to be pulled from one blog over the other. Future work on the topic of female agency would benefit from a more traditional qualitative study that focuses on individual experiences in the sport.

Despite the inclusive nature of Quidditch, it is far from completely changing the world of sport. Some argue that the use of brooms takes away from the seriousness of the sport and locks it within the realm of fandom rather than labeling it as a real sport. However, when Quidditch is taken more seriously, it does have the ability to impact our view of gender in sports. If children were taught at a younger age that it is acceptable for men and women to compete on the same level, it could have tremendous affects on how we talk about the body in relation to sport. If Quidditch is any indication, men and women are capable of competing together. However, because of our strict gender binaries, even Quidditch is susceptible to hegemonic masculinity.

The purpose of this study is to question whether or not Quidditch is truly inclusive or if it reifies hegemonic masculinity, but to examine site of feminist agency within a sports context. Using a combination of critical theory, feminist rhetoric, and agency, I argue that Quidditch is empowering for female athletes. While *Harry Potter* and the sport of Quidditch may seem like a fan craze, it is becoming a prominent and respected sport. Anthony Gierzynski and Kathryn Eddy (2013) argue that the *Boy Who Lived* has become a prominent figure with the Millennial Generation, and J. K. Rowling's writings have greatly influenced their lives. Consequently, Quidditch is influencing the way some athletes view gender in sports.

References

Ballard, C. (2006). Writing up a storm. *Sports Illustrated, 104*(13). Retrieved from http://si.com/vault/article/magazine/MAG1110302/index.htm.

Bernstein, A. (2002). Is it time for victory lap? Changes in the media coverage of women in sport. *International Review for the Sociology of Sport, 37*(3–4): 415–428.

Butts and Brooms. Retrieved from http://buttsandbrooms.tumblr.com/post/52824428050/butts-and-brooms-presents-the-attractive.

Clavio, G., & Eagleman, A. (2011). Gender and sexually suggestive images in sports blogs. *Journal of Sport Management, 7*, 295–304.

Cohen, A., Brown, B., & Welty Peachey, J., (2012). The intersection of pop culture and nontraditional sports: A segmentation analysis of Quidditch players. *International Journal of Sport Management and Marketing, 12*(3/4), 180–197.

Cohen, A., Melton, E. N., & Welty Peachey, J. (2014). Investigating a co-ed sport's ability to encourage inclusion and equality. *Journal of Sport Management, 28,* 220–235.

Connell, R. W. (1995). *Masculinities.* Berkeley: University of California Press.

Delmar, R. (1994). What is feminism? In A. C. Herrmann & A. J. Stewart (Eds.), *Reading de Man reading* (pp. 25–65). Minneapolis: University of Minnesota Press.

Dockterman, E. (2012, July 16). Quidditch players have become wizards. Now they want to be Olympians too. *Time.* Retrieved from http://newsfeed.time.com/2012/07/16/watch-should-quidditch-be-an-olympic-sport/.

Fuck Yes Quidditch. Retrieved from http://fuckyesquidditch.tumblr.com.

Gierzynski, A., & Eddy, K. (2013). *Harry Potter and the millennials: Research methods and the politics of the muggle generation.* Baltimore: John Hopkins University Press.

Gramsci, A. (1971). *Selections from the prison notebooks* (Q. Hoare & G. Nowell Smith, Trans.) New York: International.

Gurak, L. J., & Antonijevic, S. (2008). The psychology of blogging: You, me, and everyone in between. *American Behavioral Scientist, 52,* 60–68.

Hargreaves, J. (1994). *Sporting females: Critical issues in the history and sociology of women's sport.* London: Routledge.

Heilman, E. E., & Donaldson, T. (2009). From sexist to (sort-of) feminist: Representations of gender in the Harry Potter series. In E. E. Heilman (Ed.), *Critical perspectives on Harry Potter* (2nd edition) (pp. 139–161). New York: Routledge.

Henning, J. (2003). The blogging iceberg- of 4.12 million hosted weblogs, most little seen, quickly abandoned. *Perseus Development Corp. White Papers.* Retrieved from http://www. Perseus.com/blogsurvey/thebloggingiceberg.html.

Jones, S., Johnson-Yale, C., Millermaier, S., & Perez, F. S. (2009). U.S. college students' internet use: Race, gender and digital divides. *Journal of Computer-Mediated Communication, 14,* 244–264.

Kimmel, M. S. (1990). Baseball and the reconstruction of American masculinity, 1880–1920. In M. A. Messner and D. F. Sabo (Eds.), *Sport, Men, and the Gender Order* (pp. 55–66). Champaign, IL: Human Kinetics.

Lather, P. (1994). Critical inquiry in qualitative research: Feminist and poststructural perspectives: Science "after truth." In B. Crabtree (Ed.), *Exploring collaborative research in primary care* (pp. 140–155). London: Sage.

Lensing, Mollie. (2012, December 14). Redefining the standard. *Eighth Man.* Retrieved from http://www.eighthman.com/2012/12/14/redefining-the-standard/.

Life After Quidditch. Retrieved from http://lifeafterquidditch.tumblr.com.

Mayes-Elma, R. (2006). *Females in Harry Potter: Not all that empowering.* Lanham, MD: Rowman and Littlefield.

McKay, J. (1991). *No pain, no gain? Sport and Australian culture.* Englewood Cliffs, NJ: Prentice Hall.

Messner, M. A. (1988). Sports and male domination: The female athlete as contested ideological terrain. *Sociology of Sport Journal, 5,* 151–170.

Miller, K. (2005). *Communication theories: Perspectives, processes, and contexts* (2nd edition). Boston: McGraw-Hill

Osmond, M. W., & Thorne, B. (1993). Feminist theories: The social construction of gender in families and society. In P. G. Boss, W. J. Doherty, R. LaRossa, W. R. Schumm, & S. K. Steinmetz (eds.), *Sourcebook of family theories and methods: A contextual approach* (pp. 591–623). New York: Plenum Press.

Park, N., & Jeong, J. (2011). Findings publics within the blogosphere: The blogger public segmentation model. *Asian Journal of Communication, 21*(4): 389–408.

Pugh, T., & Wallace, D. L. (2006). Heternormative heroism and queering the school story in J. K. Rowling's Harry Potter series. *Children's Literature Association Quarterly, 31*(3): 260–281.

Rowling, J. K. (2003). *Harry Potter and the Order of the Phoenix.* New York: Scholastic.

Sartore, M. L., & Cunningham, G. B. (2009). Gender, sexual prejudice, and sport participation: Implications for sexual minorities. *Sex Roles, 60,* 100–113.

Stavrositu, C., & Sundar, S. S. (2012). Does blogging empower women? Exploring the role of agency and community. *Journal of Computer-Mediated Communication, 17,* 369–386.

Turner, V. (1969). *The ritual process: Structure and anti-structure.* Ithaca: Cornell University Press.

Whitson, D. (1990). Sport in the social construction of masculinity. In M. A. Messner and D. F. Sabo (Eds.), *Sport, Men, and the Gender Order* (pp. 19–30). Champaign, IL: Human Kinetics.

About the Contributors

Dr. Christopher E. **Bell** is an assistant professor of media studies at the University of Colorado–Colorado Springs. He is also the director of graduate studies for the Department of Communication. He specializes in the study of popular culture, focusing on the ways in which race, class and gender intersect in different forms of media.

Jelena **Borojević** is a Ph.D. student in the Department of English Language and Literature, University of Novi Sad, Serbia. Her thesis is concerned with mythopoetics in the works of J.R.R. Tolkien, Philip Pullman and J.K. Rowling. She is also interested in fan studies, popular culture, and the modern representation of fairy tales.

Lauren R. **Camacci** is a Ph.D. candidate in the Department of Communication Arts and Sciences at Pennsylvania State University, where she also earned her M.A. Her research interests include rhetorical criticism, masculinities and popular culture, all which will feature in her upcoming dissertation work.

Dr. Kristen L. **Cole** is a visiting assistant professor in communication at Denison University. Her research is on interpersonal and intercultural communication in mediated contexts, with an interest in the ways gender and sexuality, race and ethnicity, citizenship and immigration, conflict and community, and science and technology influence persons within marginalized communities.

Dr. Levi **Cooper** is a postdoctoral fellow in Tel-Aviv University's Faculty of Law. He teaches at the Pardes Institute of Jewish Studies in Jerusalem. His research focuses on legal history in the late modern period, law and literature, and the interplays between Jewish legal writing and broader legal, intellectual, and cultural contexts. He is particularly interested in the interplay of law and other cultural creations.

Dr. Sara **Cortés-Gómez** is an assistant professor in audiovisual communication at the University of Alcalá, Spain. She is interested the role of new technologies and video games as cultural tools aimed to develop new literacies in a global world. She has been a visiting scholar at LCMI (University of Luxembourg) and GLS at the University of Madison.

Brendan G. A. **Hughes** is a doctoral student in communication studies and an Inclusive Excellence Fellow at the University of Denver. His field of study sits at the intersection of rhetorical and critical/cultural studies with a strong emphasis in rhetorical criticism. His research interests focus on rhetorical intersections of stigma, GLBTQ studies, HIV, and monstrosity within (popular) American culture.

Dr. Hillary A. **Jones** is an assistant professor in the Department of Communication at California State University–Fresno. Her areas of interest are rhetorical theory and criticism, studies of popular media and visual culture, and radical politics (particularly anarchism and feminism) in speculative fiction. Her research is on the ways that radical politics are depicted in narrative texts across media.

Dr. Pilar **Lacasa** is a professor of audiovisual communication and researcher on the faculty of humanities at the University of Alcalá, Spain. Her research work has been developed from a socio-cultural approach. She has been a visiting researcher at the University of Utah, at the Comparative Media Studies program at M.I.T.. and at the University of Southern California–Annenberg Innovation Lab.

Dr. Rut **Martínez-Borda** is an associate professor of audiovisual communication and a research fellow at the University of Alcalá, Spain. Her research interests include video games, new technologies and audiovisual narratives. She has been a visiting scholar at the Institute of Education (University of London), University of Westminster in London, and the University of Delaware in Philadelphia.

Ryan S. **Rigda** is a doctoral student at Texas A&M University. His is interested in the intersection of rhetoric, sports communication and gender studies. Previous work has examined the coming out speeches of professional athletes Jason Collins and Michael Sam and the impact of gay athletes on the sport community.

Dr. Raymond I. **Schuck** is an assistant professor of communication at Bowling Green State University–Firelands. His research has focused on critical and rhetorical analysis of popular culture in various forms. In addition to a number of journal articles and book chapters, he is co-editor, with his father, of the book *Do You Believe in Rock and Roll? Essays on Don McLean's "American Pie"* (McFarland, 2012).

Dr. Shira **Wolosky** teaches at Hebrew University. She had published books on Emily Dickinson, poetry, poetry and public discourse and feminist theory. Her awards include a Guggenheim Fellowship, a fellowship at the Princeton Institute for Advanced Studies, the Drue Heinz Visiting Professorship at Oxford, and a Tikvah Fellowship at NYU Law School.

Index

www.ingramcontent.com/pod-product-compliance
Ingram Content Group UK Ltd.
Pitfield, Milton Keynes, MK11 3LW, UK
UKHW011959300626
13473UKWH00003B/367

9 780786 499304